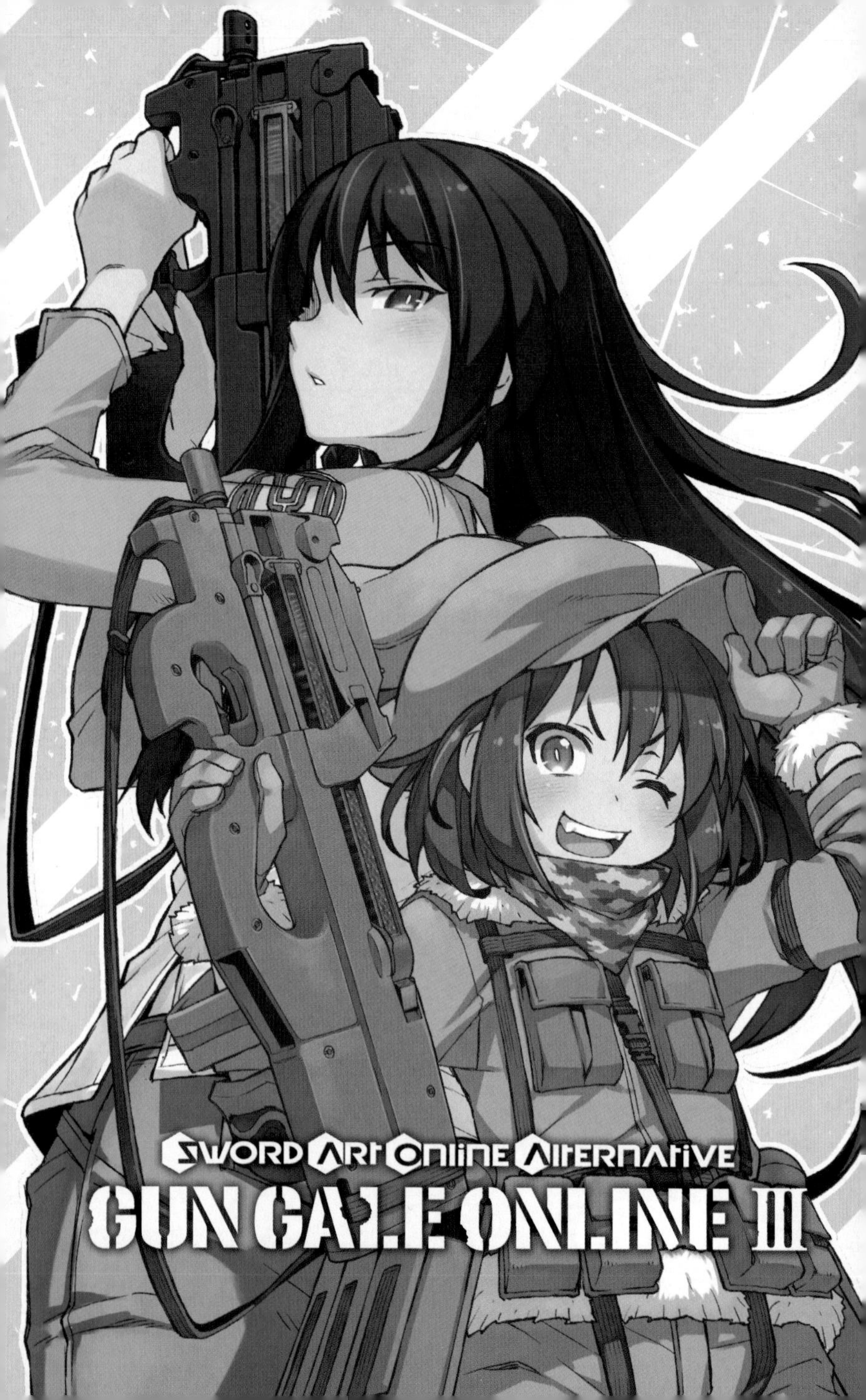
SWORD ART ONLINE ALTERNATIVE
GUN GALE ONLINE III

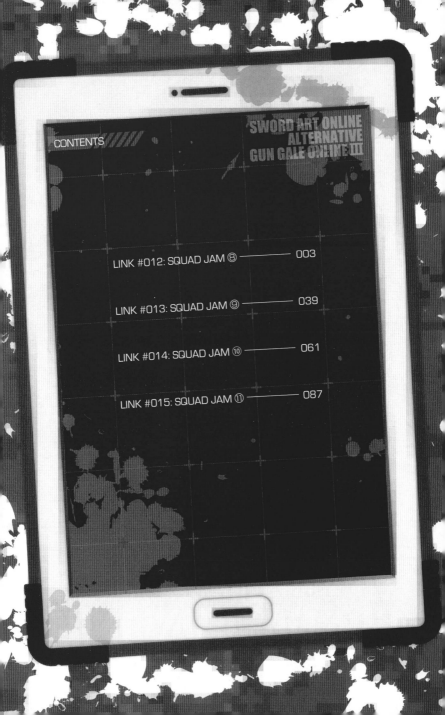

CONTENTS

SWORD ART ONLINE
ALTERNATIVE
GUN GALE ONLINE III

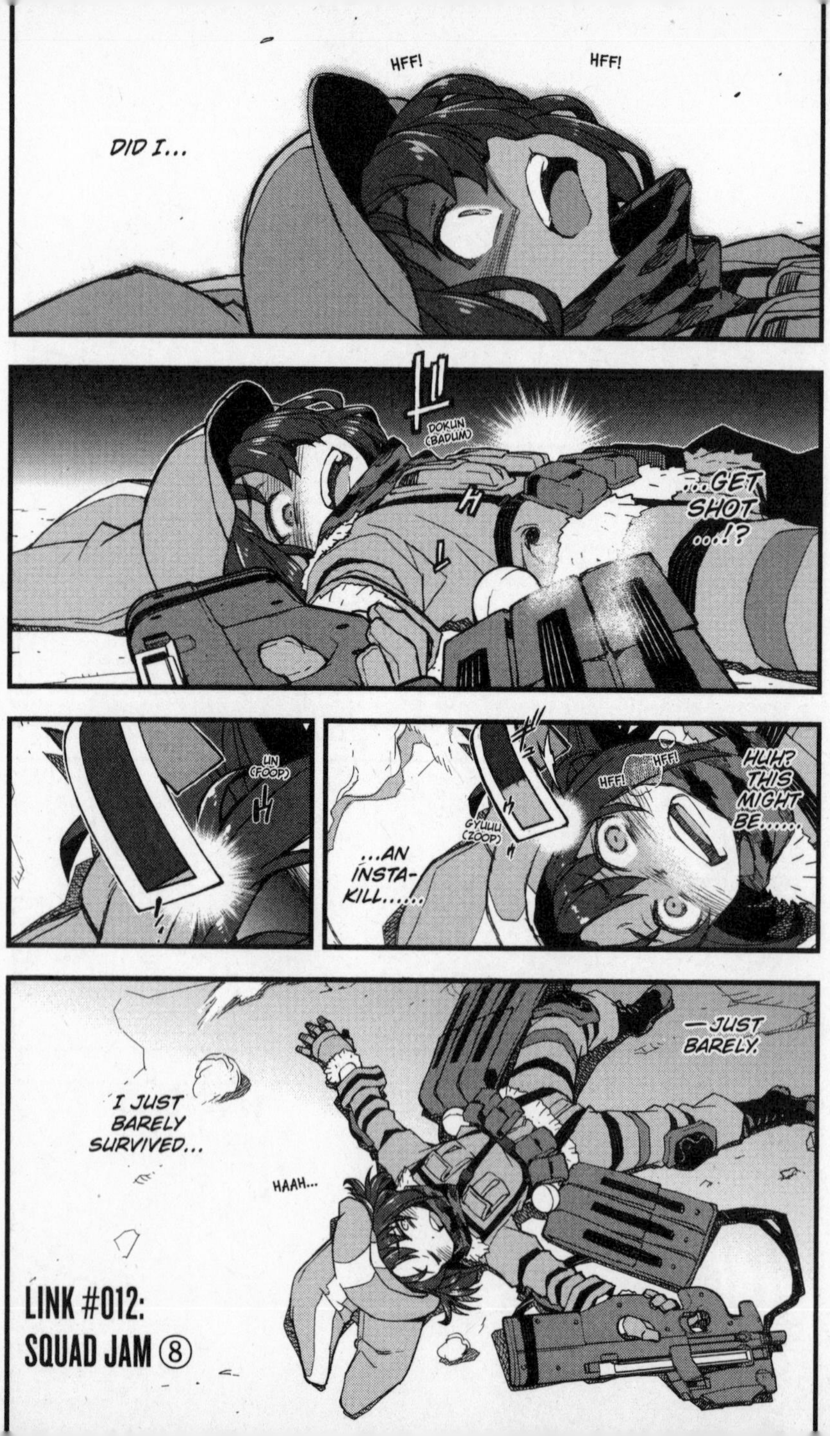
HFF!
HFF!
DID I...
...GET SHOT ...!?
DOKUN (BADUM)
HUH? THIS MIGHT BE......
HFF! HFF!
GYUUU (ZOOP)
...AN INSTA-KILL......
UN (FOOP)
—JUST BARELY.
I JUST BARELY SURVIVED...
HAAH...
LINK #012: SQUAD JAM ⑧

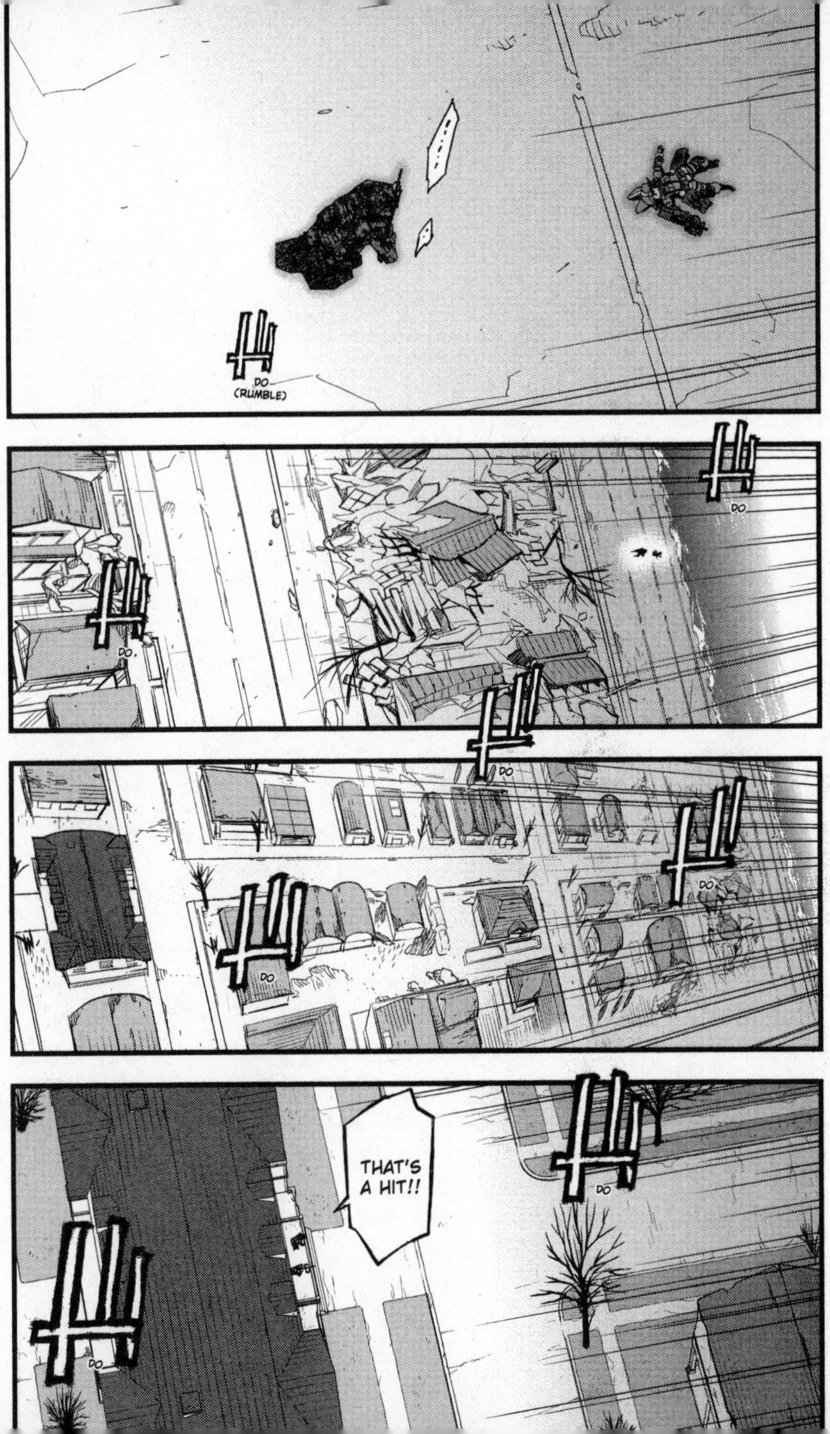
...
DO (RUMBLE)
DO
DO
DO
DO
DO
DO
THAT'S A HIT!!
DO

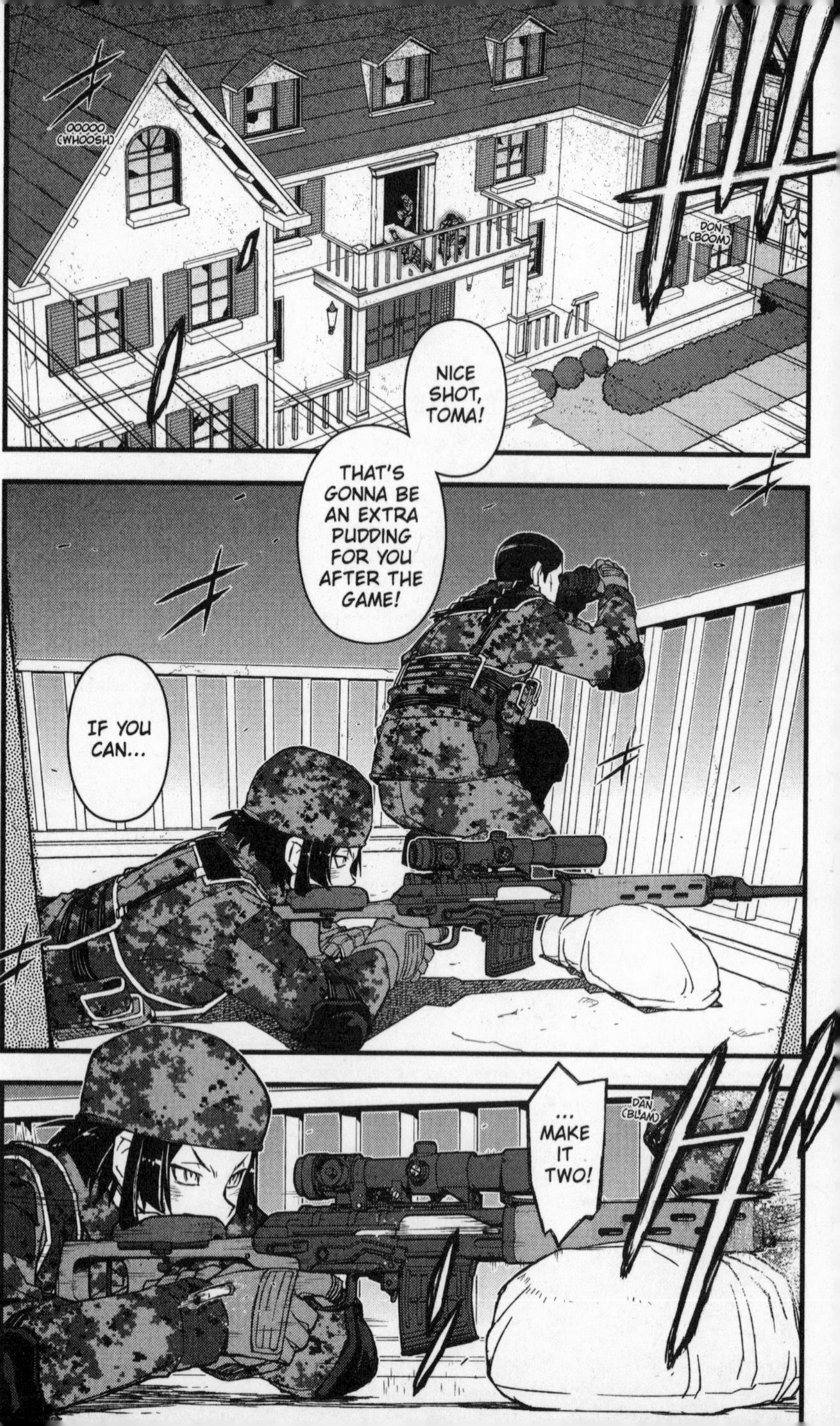
DON (BOOM)
OOOOO (WHOOSH)
NICE SHOT, TOMA!
THAT'S GONNA BE AN EXTRA PUDDING FOR YOU AFTER THE GAME!
IF YOU CAN...
DAN (BLAM)
... MAKE IT TWO!

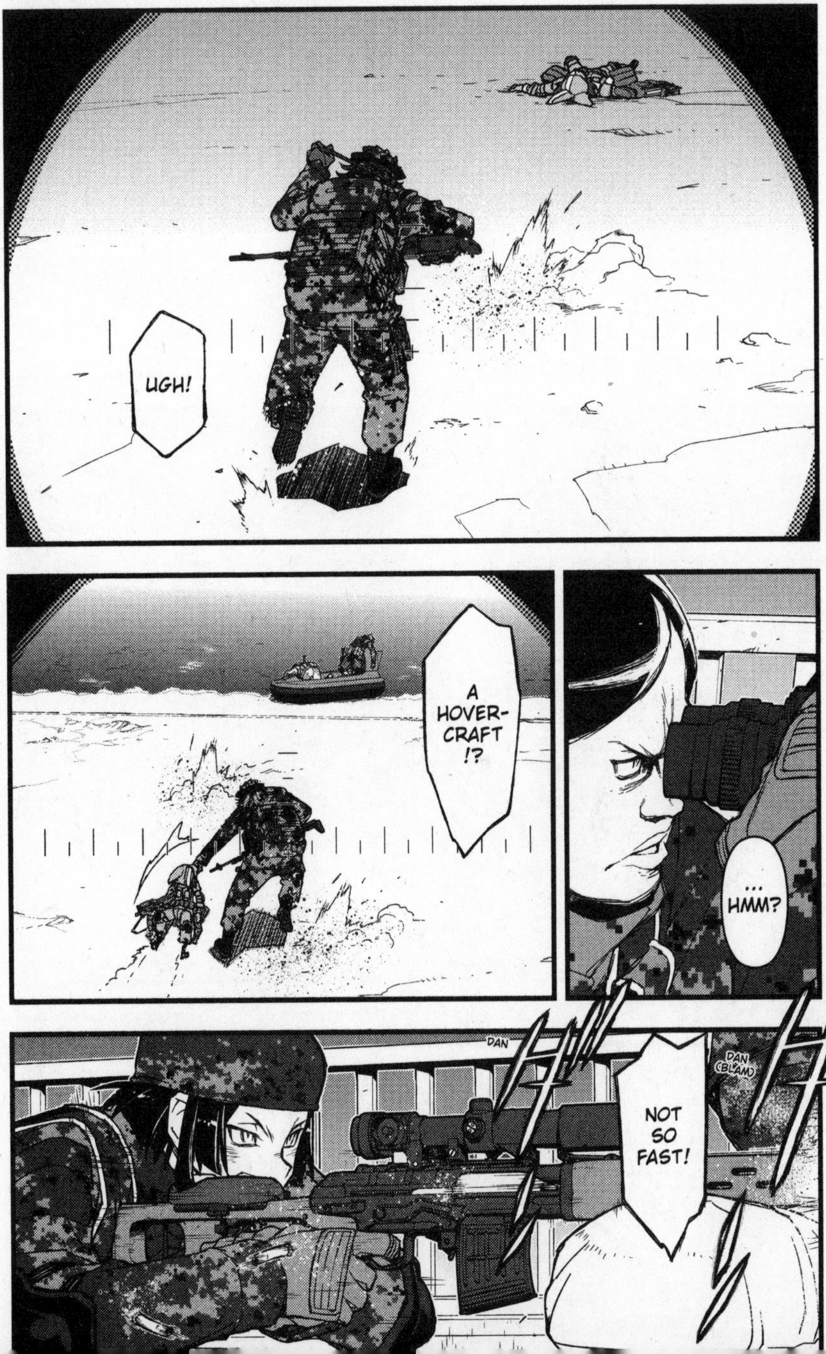
UGH!
... HMM?
A HOVER-CRAFT !?
DAN (BLAM)
NOT SO FAST!
DAN

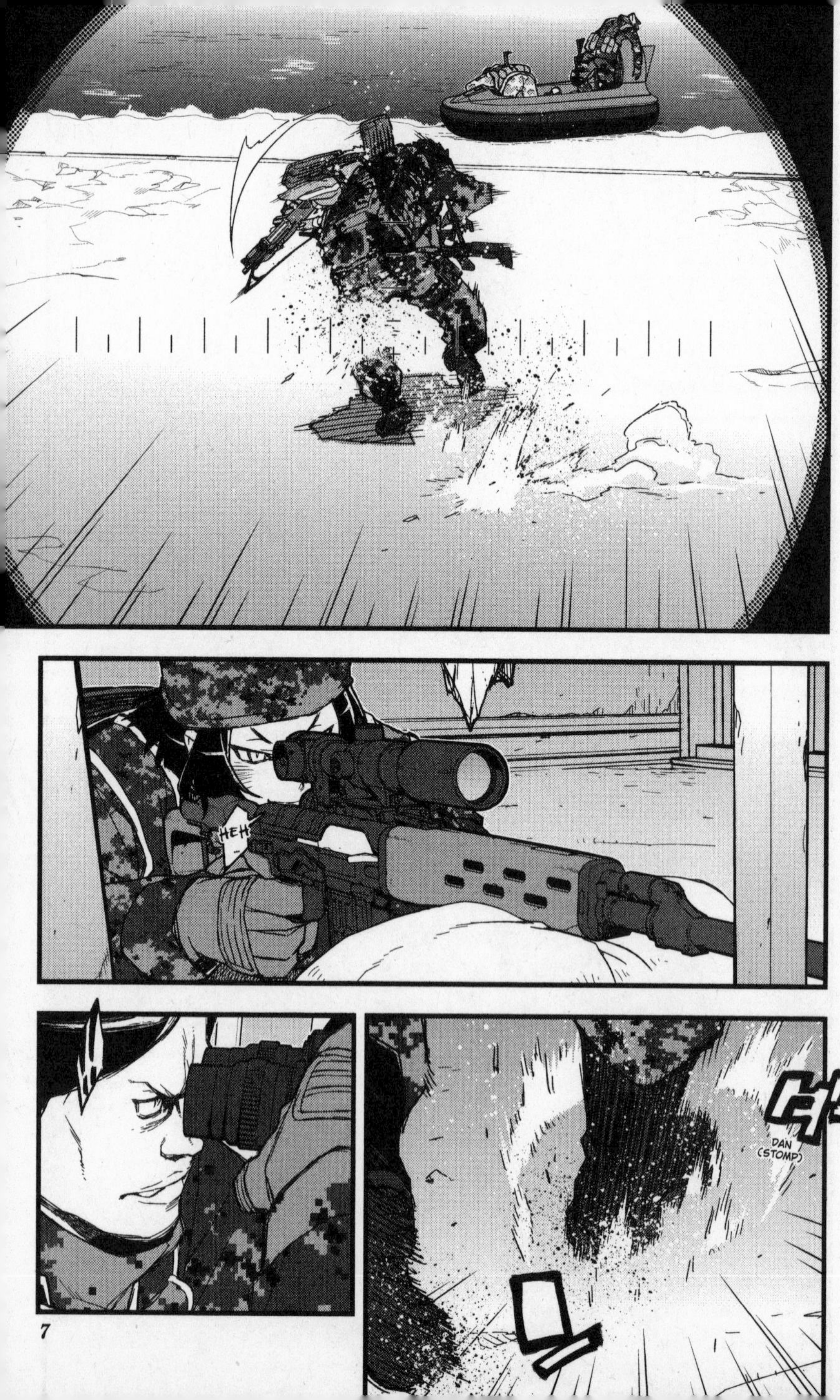
HEH...
DAN
(STOMP)

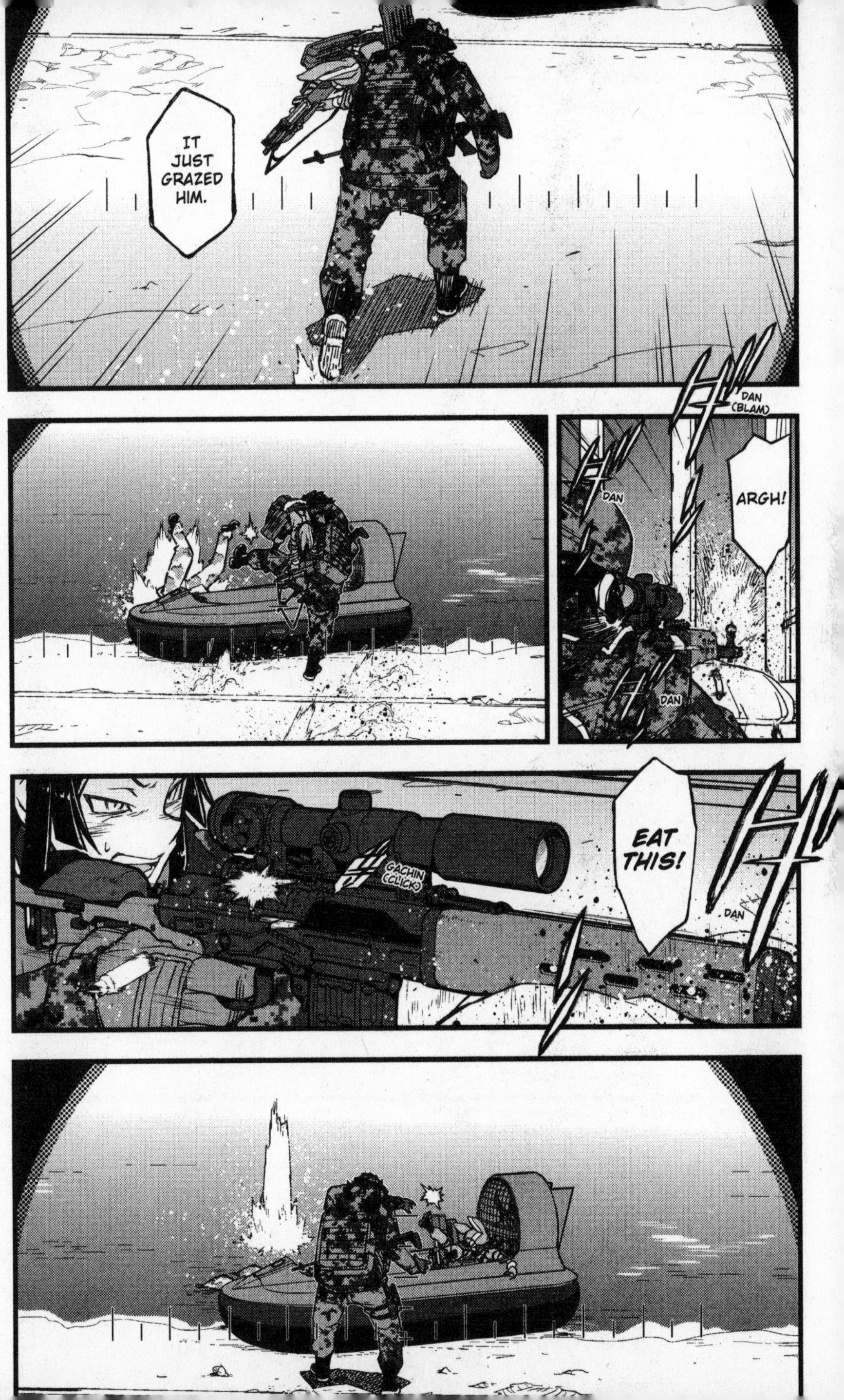
IT JUST GRAZED HIM.
DAN (BLAM)
ARGH!
DAN
DAN
EAT THIS!
DAN
GACHIN (CLICK)

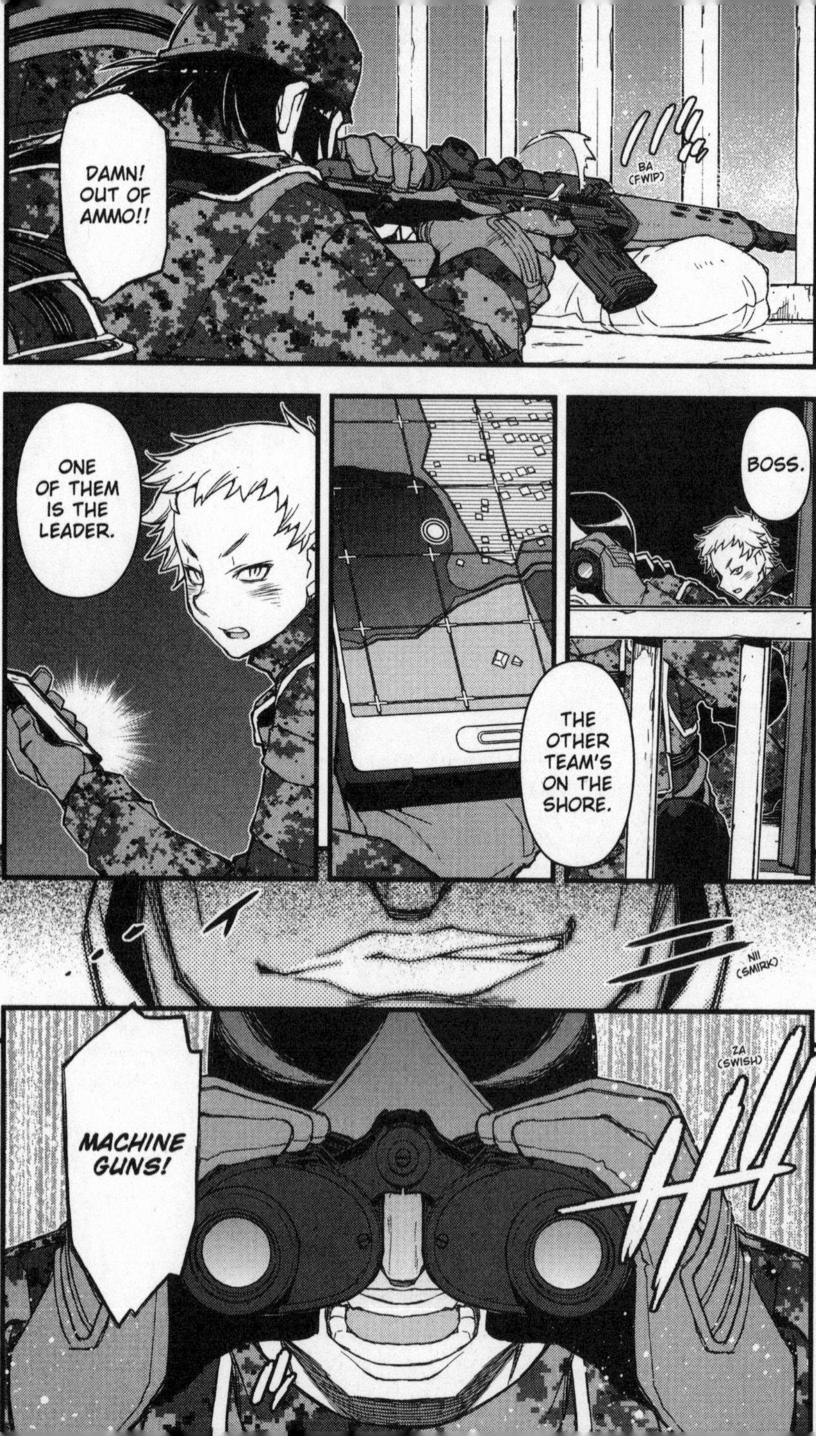
BA (FWIP)
DAMN! OUT OF AMMO!!
BOSS.
THE OTHER TEAM'S ON THE SHORE.
ONE OF THEM IS THE LEADER.
NII (SMIRK)
ZA (SWISH)
MACHINE GUNS!

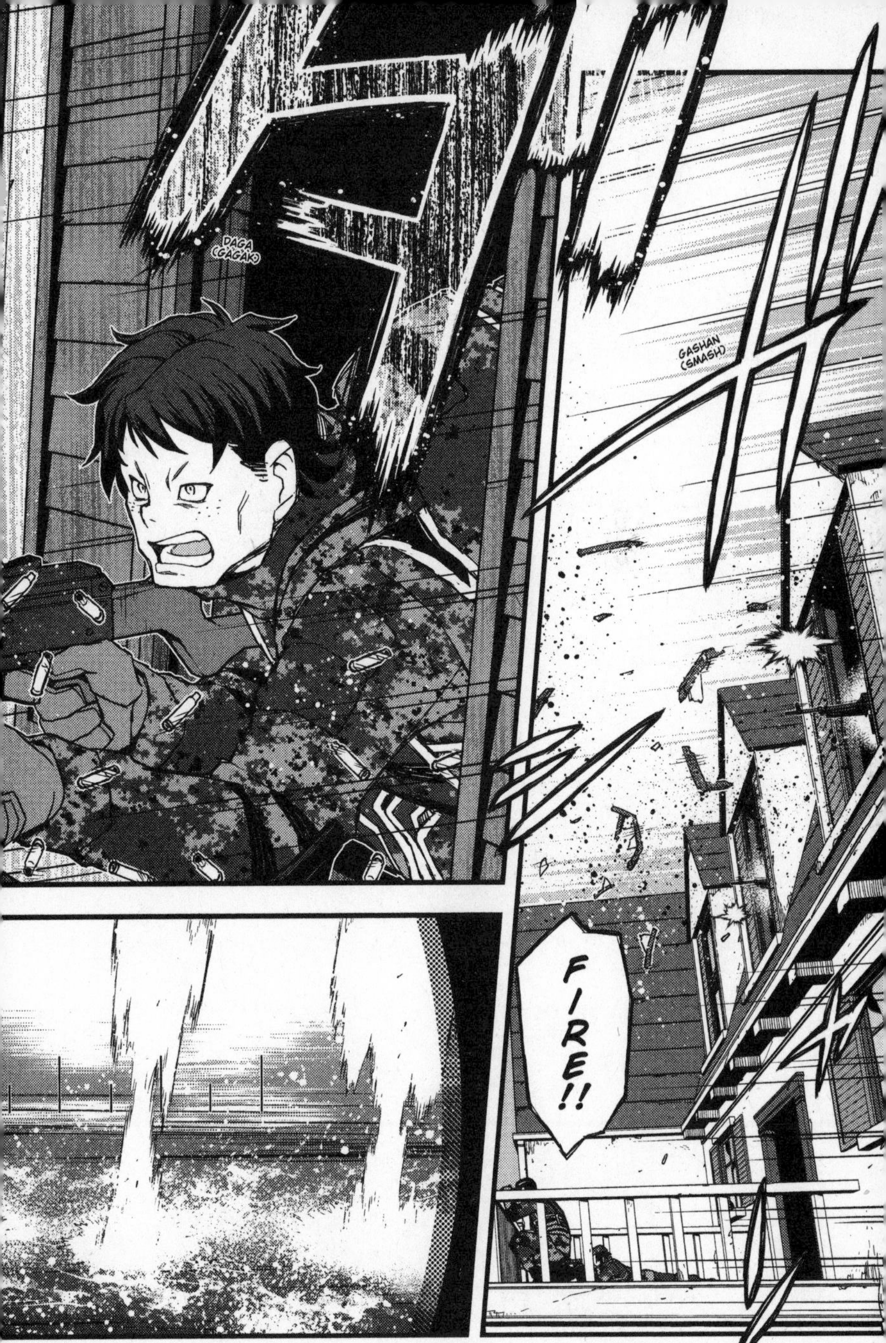
GASHAN (SMASH)
FIRE!!
DAGA (GAGAK)

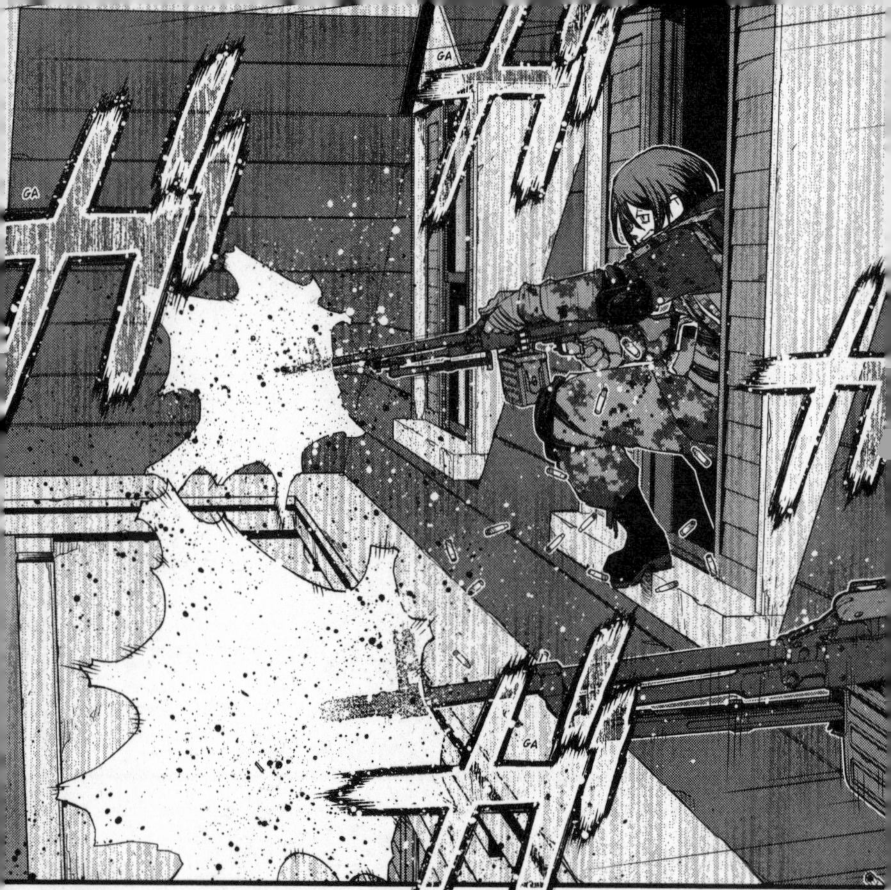
GA
GA
GA

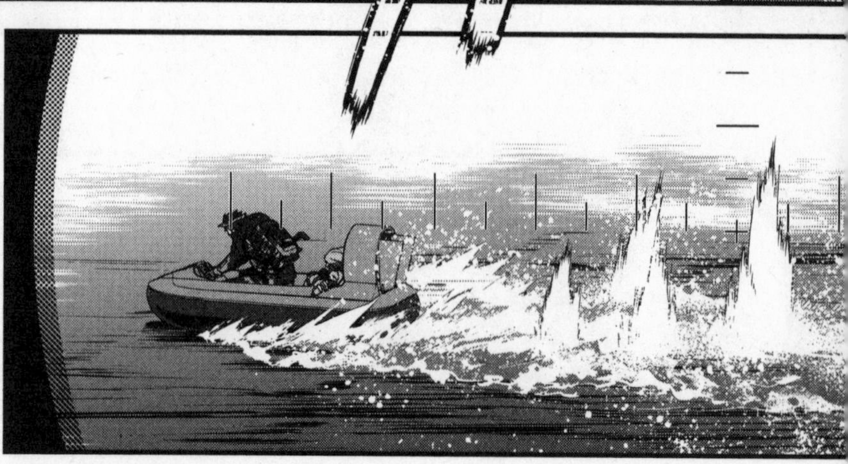

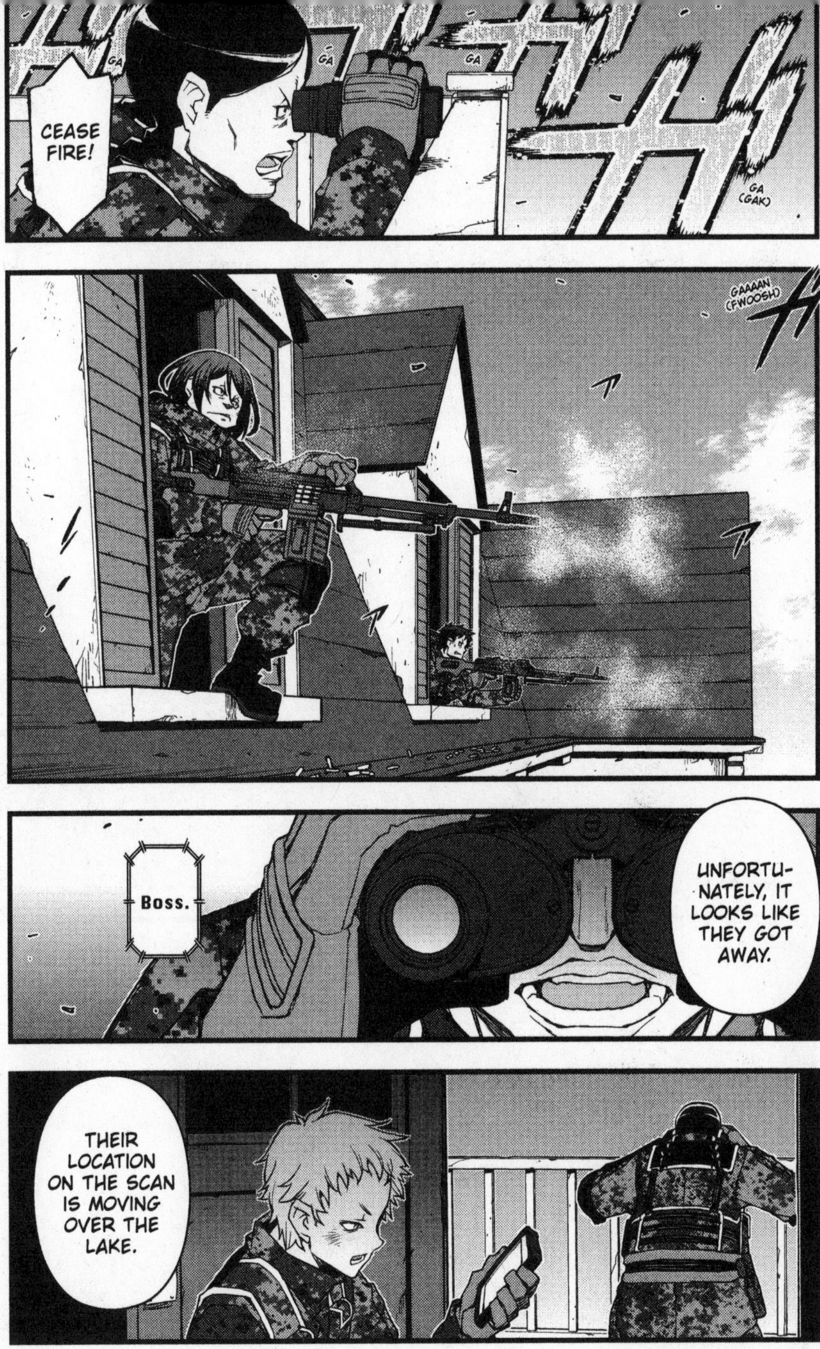
GA
GA
GA
CEASE FIRE!
GA (GAK)
GAAAAN (FWOOSH)
UNFORTU-NATELY, IT LOOKS LIKE THEY GOT AWAY.
Boss.
THEIR LOCATION ON THE SCAN IS MOVING OVER THE LAKE.

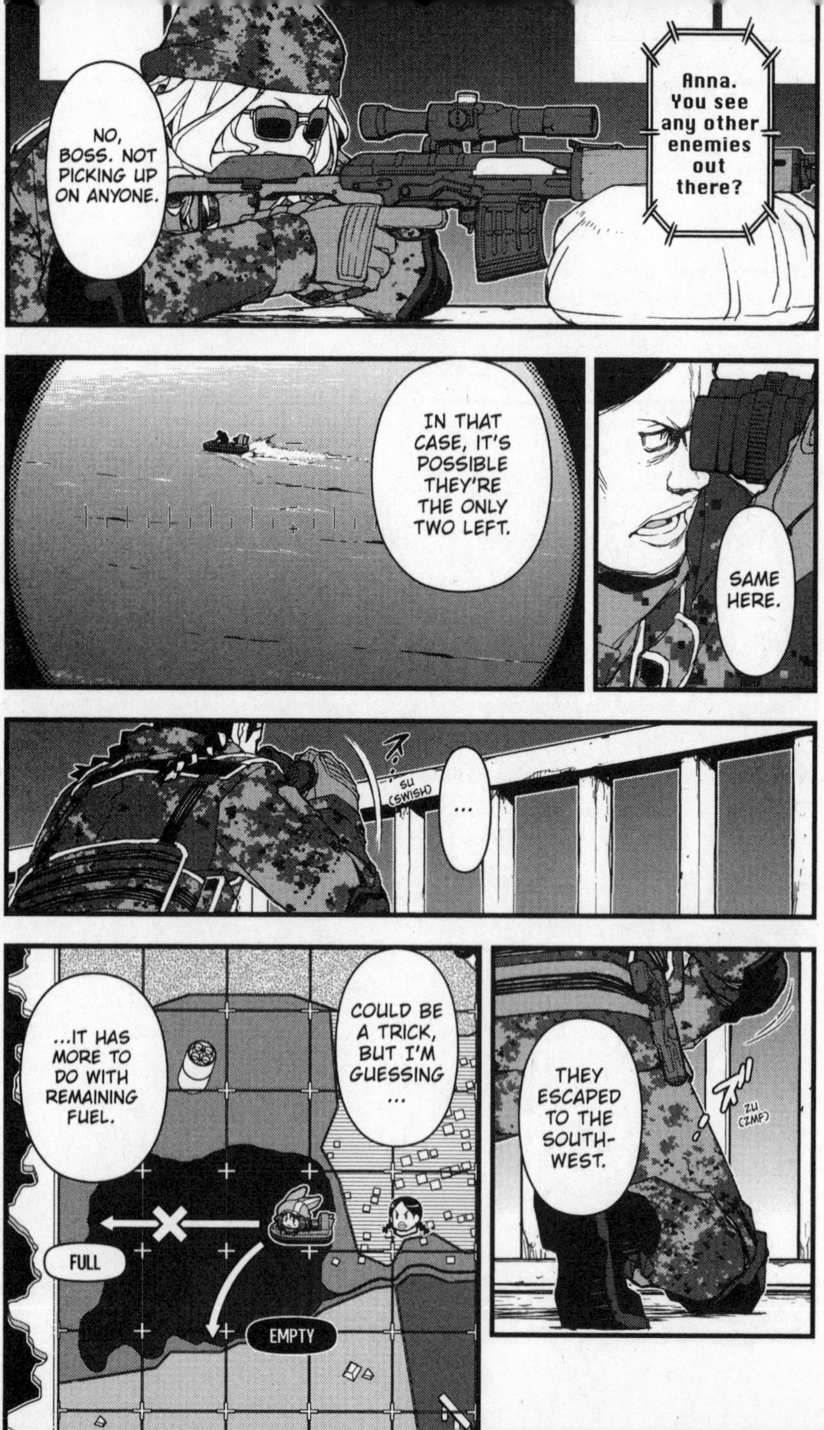
Anna. You see any other enemies out there?
NO, BOSS. NOT PICKING UP ON ANYONE.
SAME HERE.
IN THAT CASE, IT'S POSSIBLE THEY'RE THE ONLY TWO LEFT.
...
SU (SWISH)
ZU (ZMF)
THEY ESCAPED TO THE SOUTH-WEST.
COULD BE A TRICK, BUT I'M GUESSING...
...IT HAS MORE TO DO WITH REMAINING FUEL.
FULL
EMPTY

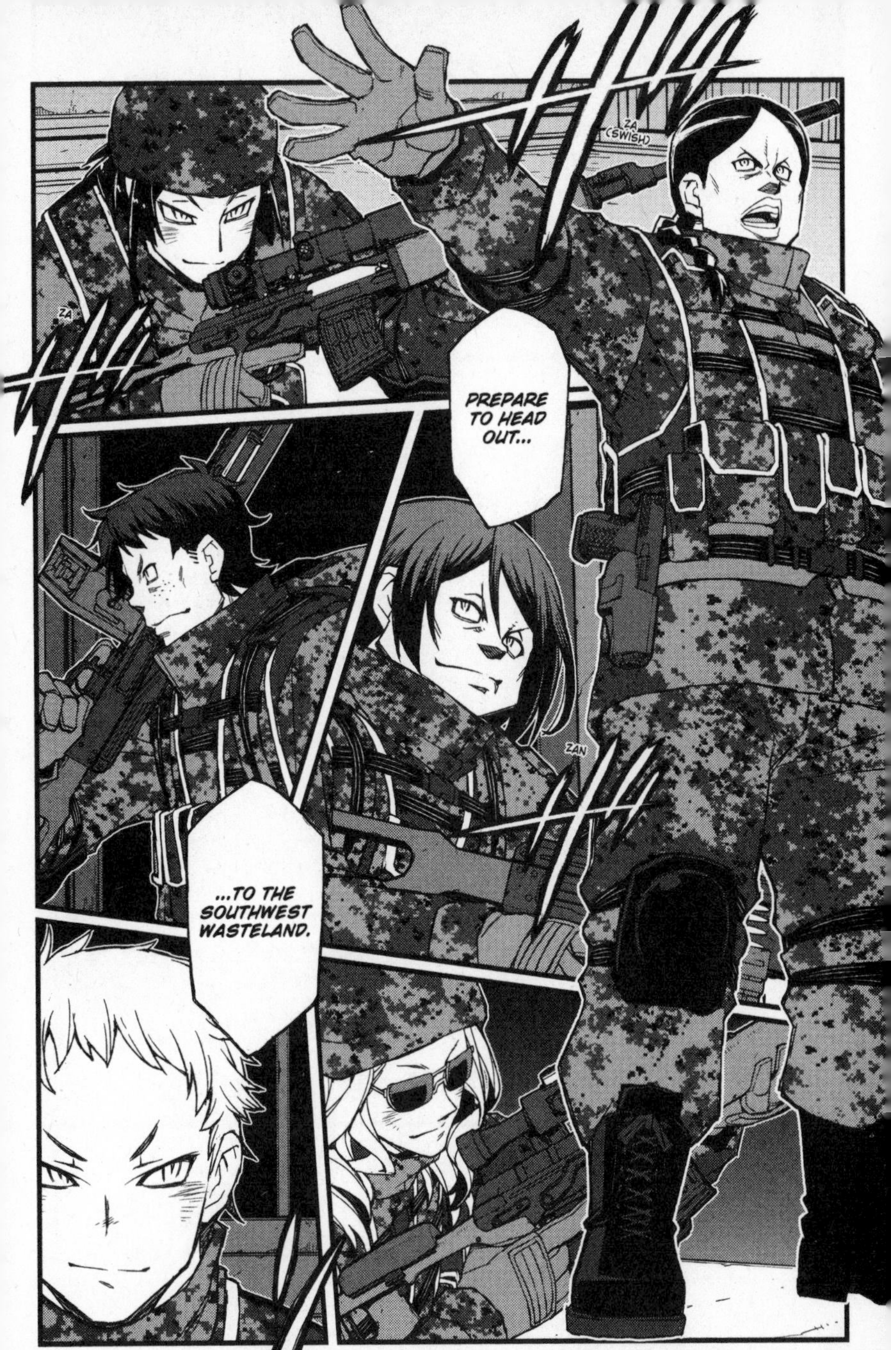
ZA (SWISH)
ZA
PREPARE TO HEAD OUT...
ZAN
...TO THE SOUTHWEST WASTELAND.

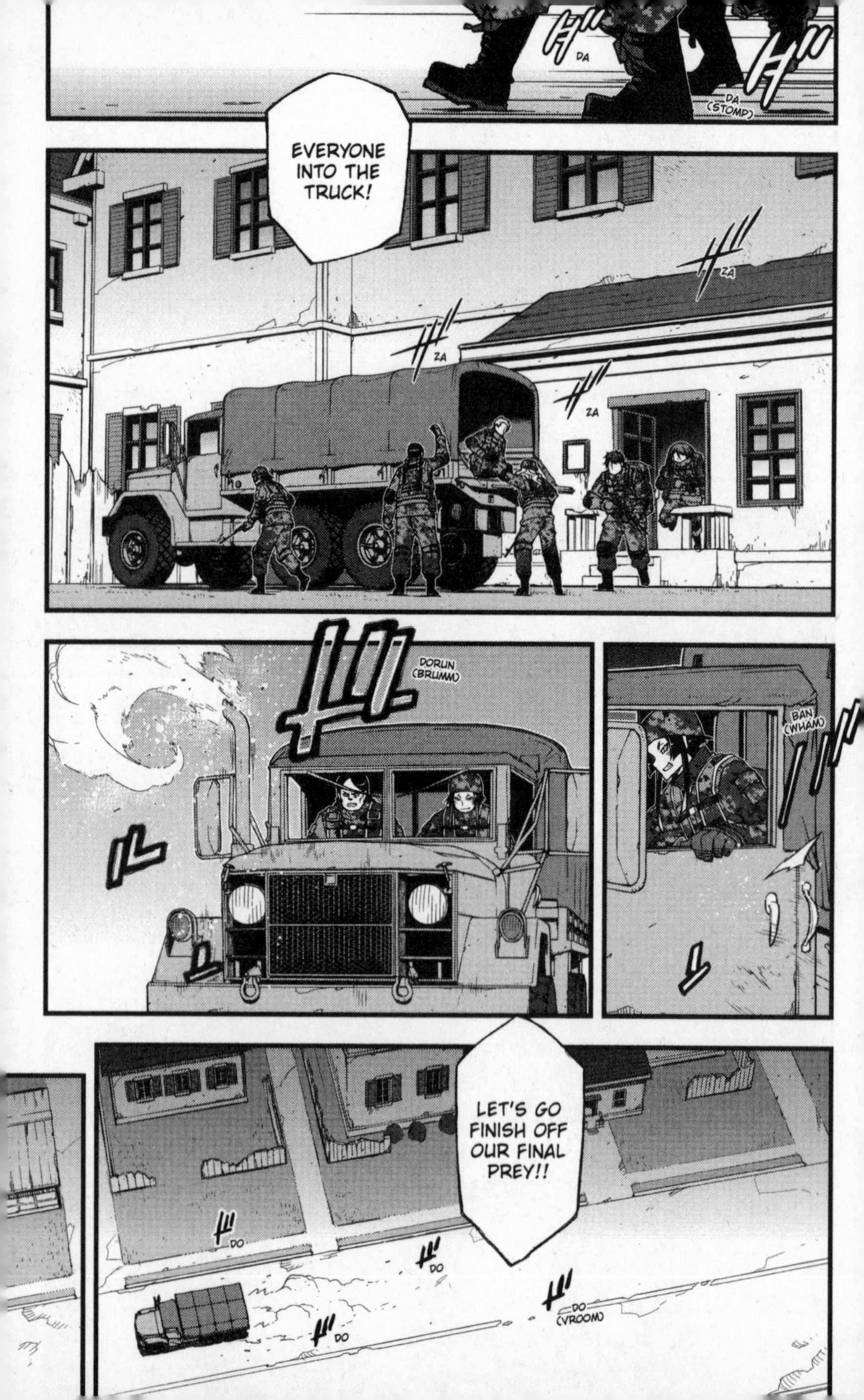

DA
DA (STOMP)
EVERYONE INTO THE TRUCK!
ZA
ZA
ZA
BAN (WHAM)
DORUN (BRUMM)
LET'S GO FINISH OFF OUR FINAL PREY!!
DO
DO
DO (VROOM)
DO

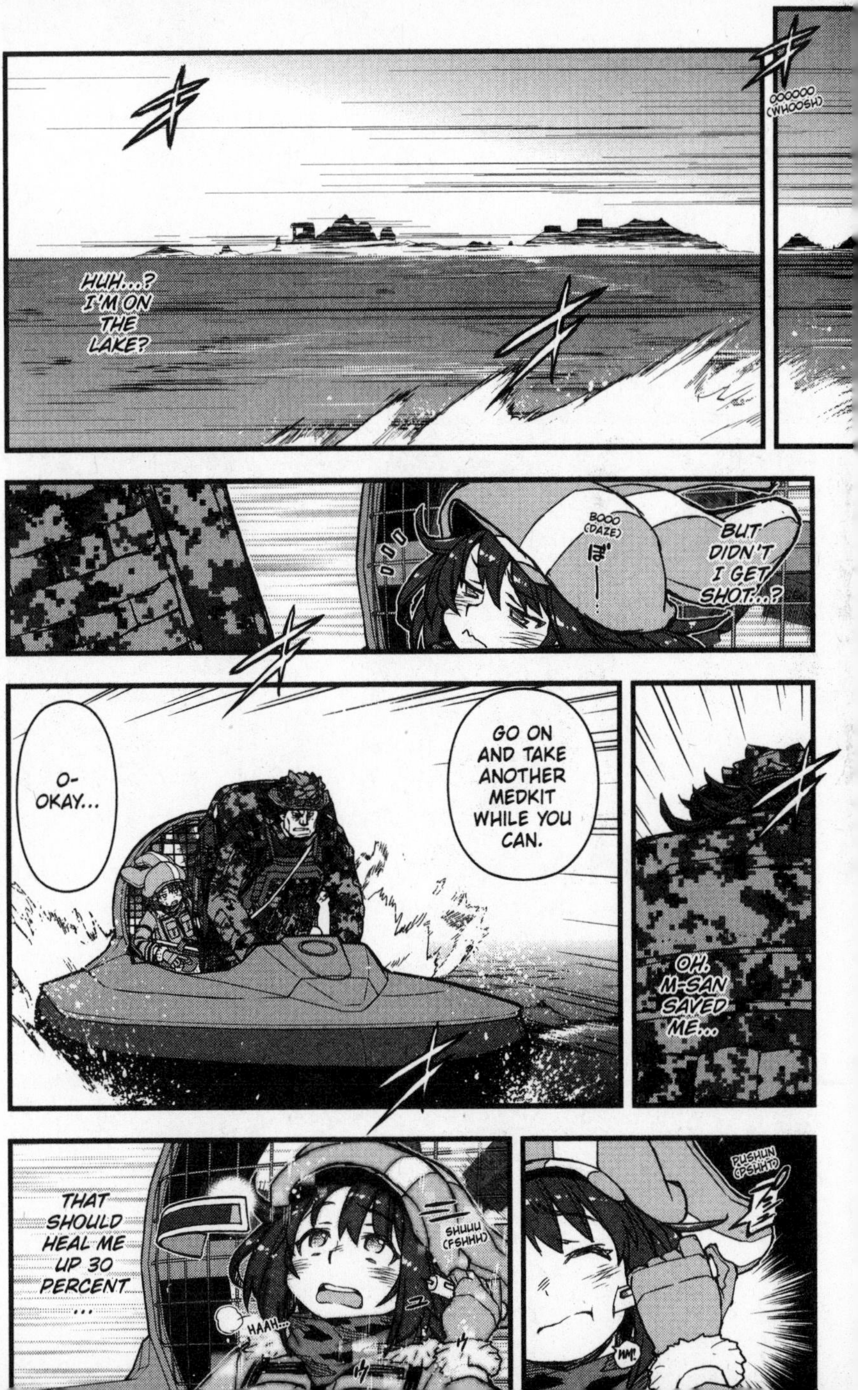
OOOOOO (WHOOSH)
HUH...? I'M ON THE LAKE?
BUT DIDN'T I GET SHOT...?
BOOO (DAZE)
OH. M-SAN SAVED ME...
GO ON AND TAKE ANOTHER MEDKIT WHILE YOU CAN.
O-OKAY...
PUSHUN (PSHHT)
NM!
THAT SHOULD HEAL ME UP 30 PERCENT...
SHUUU (FSHHH)
HAAH...

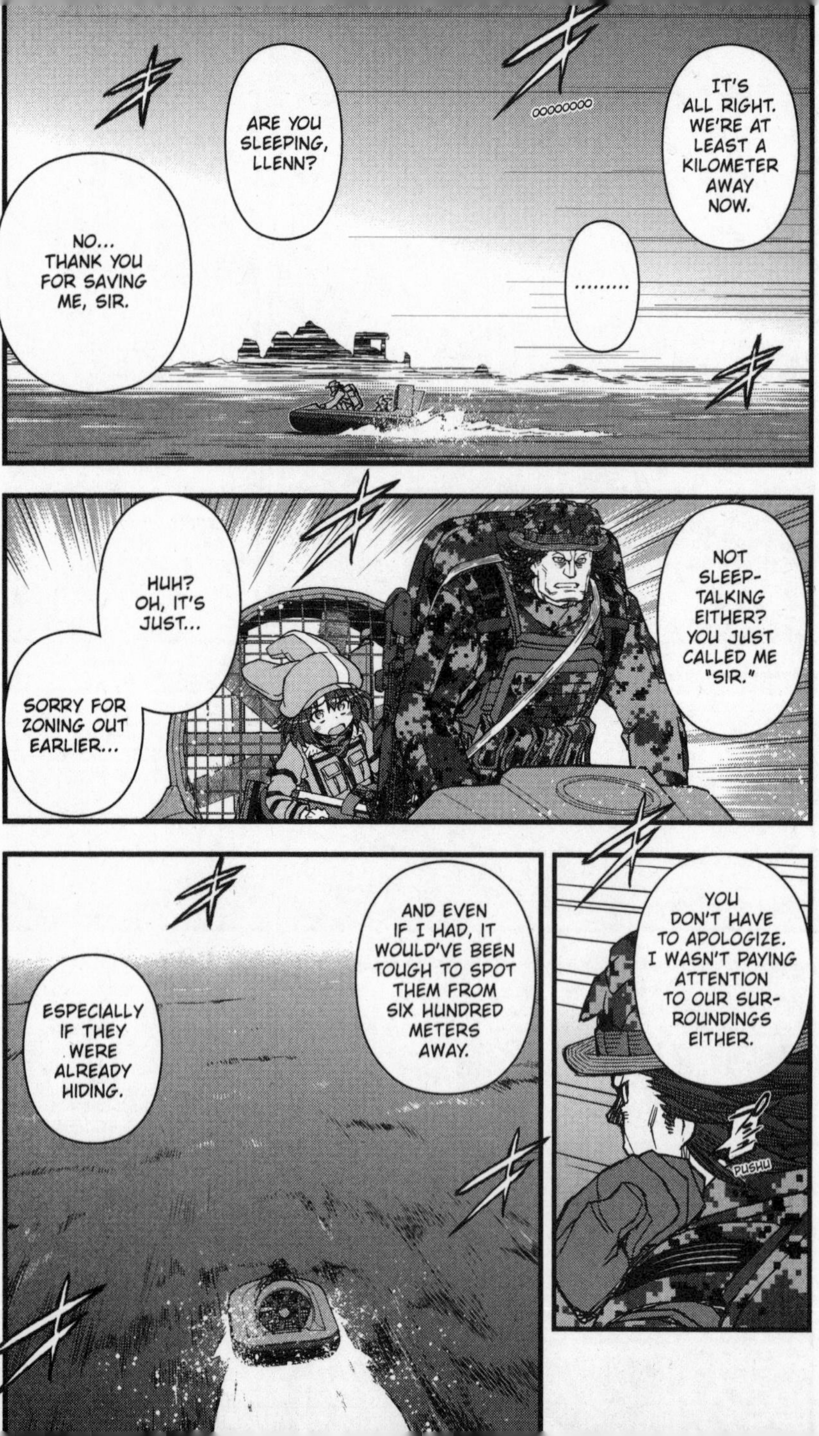
IT'S ALL RIGHT. WE'RE AT LEAST A KILOMETER AWAY NOW.
OOOOOOOO
....
ARE YOU SLEEPING, LLENN?
NO... THANK YOU FOR SAVING ME, SIR.
NOT SLEEP-TALKING EITHER? YOU JUST CALLED ME "SIR."
HUH? OH, IT'S JUST...
SORRY FOR ZONING OUT EARLIER...
YOU DON'T HAVE TO APOLOGIZE. I WASN'T PAYING ATTENTION TO OUR SUR-ROUNDINGS EITHER.
PUSHU
AND EVEN IF I HAD, IT WOULD'VE BEEN TOUGH TO SPOT THEM FROM SIX HUNDRED METERS AWAY.
ESPECIALLY IF THEY WERE ALREADY HIDING.

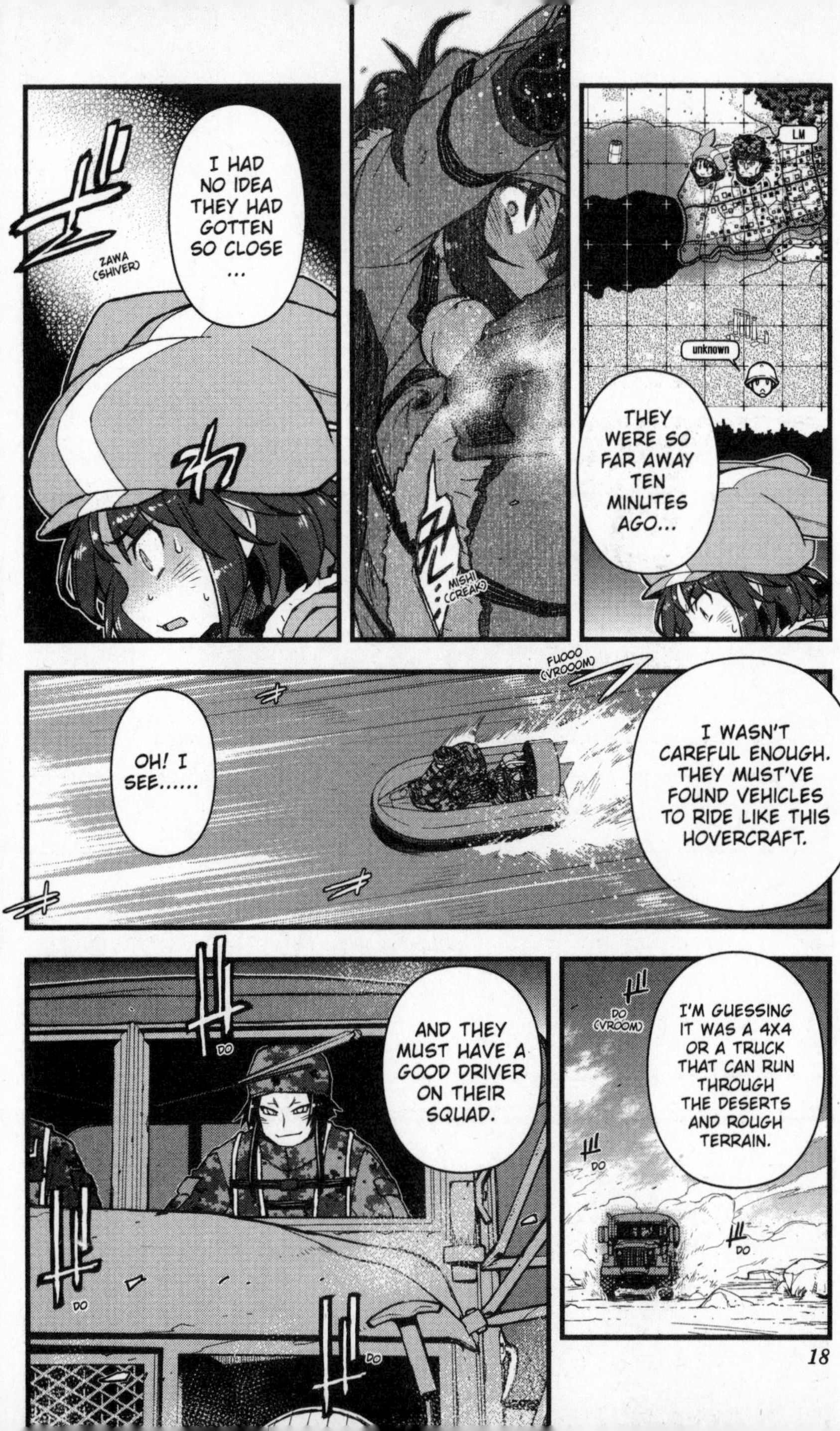

LM
unknown
THEY WERE SO FAR AWAY TEN MINUTES AGO...
MISHI (CREAK)
I HAD NO IDEA THEY HAD GOTTEN SO CLOSE ...
ZAWA (SHIVER)
FUOOO (VROOOM)
I WASN'T CAREFUL ENOUGH. THEY MUST'VE FOUND VEHICLES TO RIDE LIKE THIS HOVERCRAFT.
OH! I SEE......
DO (VROOM)
I'M GUESSING IT WAS A 4X4 OR A TRUCK THAT CAN RUN THROUGH THE DESERTS AND ROUGH TERRAIN.
DO
DO
AND THEY MUST HAVE A GOOD DRIVER ON THEIR SQUAD.
DO
DO
DO

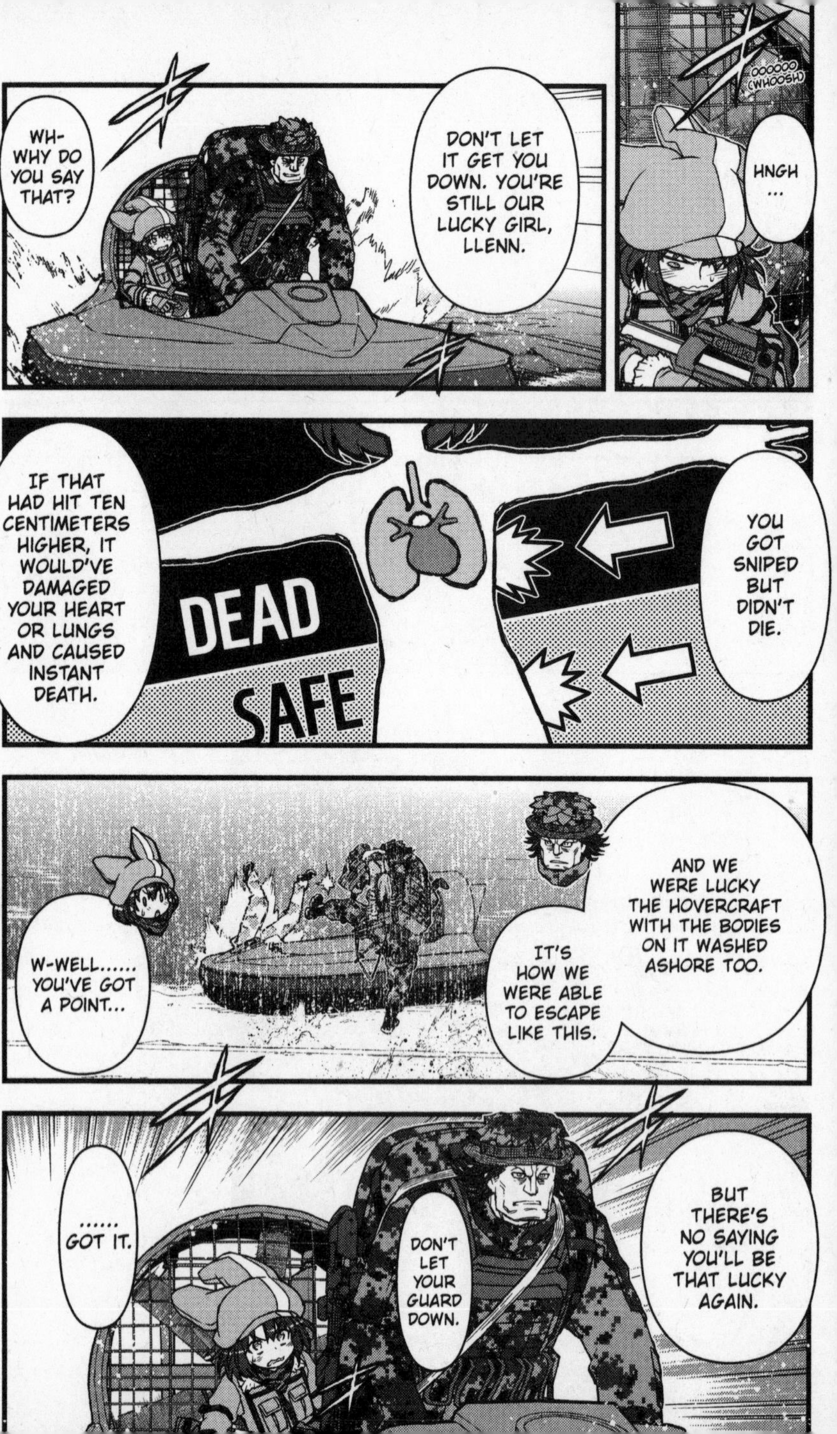
OOOOOO (WHOOSH)
HNGH ...
DON'T LET IT GET YOU DOWN. YOU'RE STILL OUR LUCKY GIRL, LLENN.
WH- WHY DO YOU SAY THAT?
YOU GOT SNIPED BUT DIDN'T DIE.
DEAD
SAFE
IF THAT HAD HIT TEN CENTIMETERS HIGHER, IT WOULD'VE DAMAGED YOUR HEART OR LUNGS AND CAUSED INSTANT DEATH.
AND WE WERE LUCKY THE HOVERCRAFT WITH THE BODIES ON IT WASHED ASHORE TOO.
IT'S HOW WE WERE ABLE TO ESCAPE LIKE THIS.
W-WELL...... YOU'VE GOT A POINT...
BUT THERE'S NO SAYING YOU'LL BE THAT LUCKY AGAIN.
DON'T LET YOUR GUARD DOWN.
...... GOT IT.

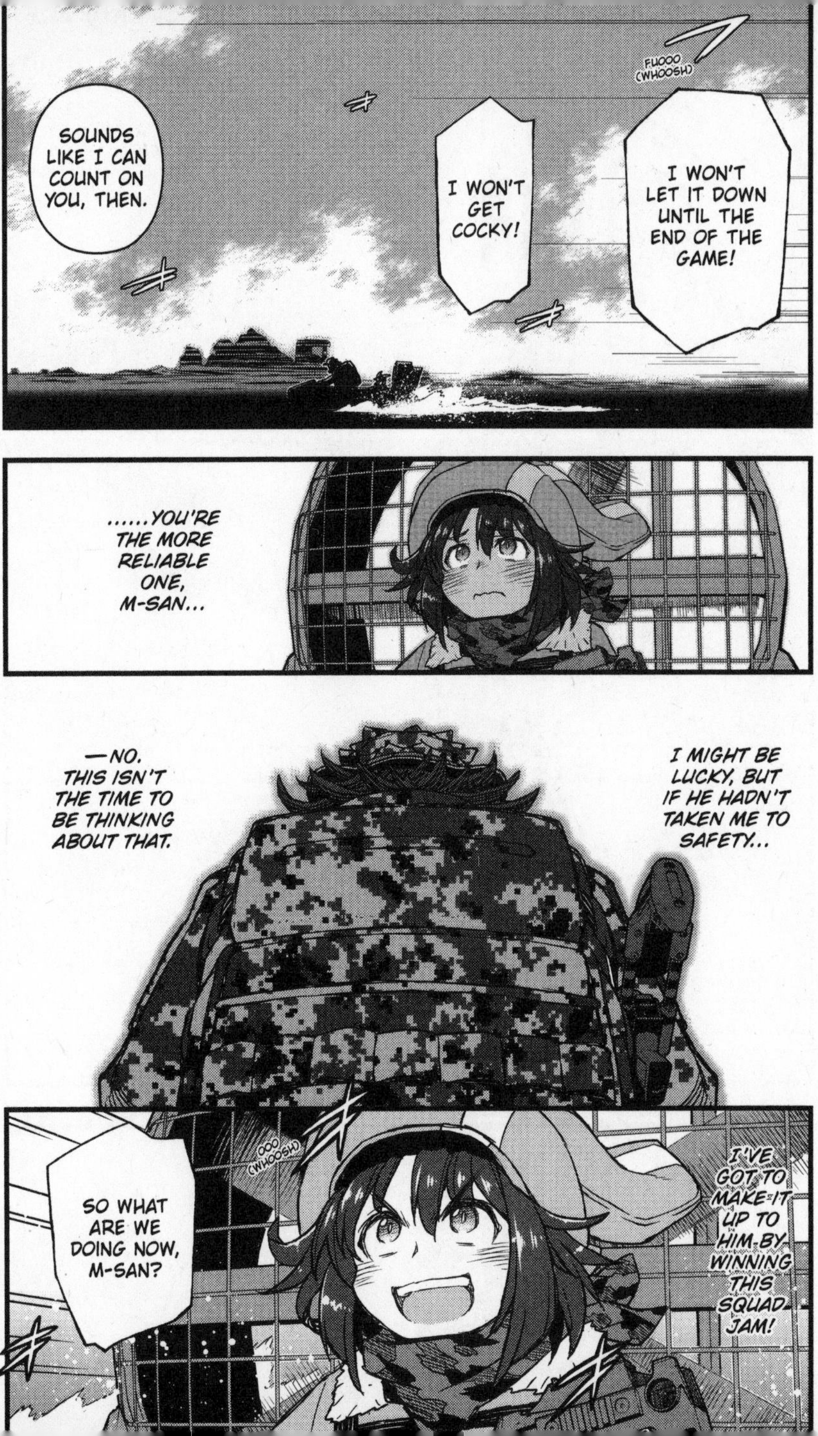
FUOOO (WHOOSH)
I WON'T LET IT DOWN UNTIL THE END OF THE GAME!
I WON'T GET COCKY!
SOUNDS LIKE I CAN COUNT ON YOU, THEN.
......YOU'RE THE MORE RELIABLE ONE, M-SAN...
I MIGHT BE LUCKY, BUT IF HE HADN'T TAKEN ME TO SAFETY...
—NO. THIS ISN'T THE TIME TO BE THINKING ABOUT THAT.
I'VE GOT TO MAKE IT UP TO HIM BY WINNING THIS SQUAD JAM!
OOO (WHOOSH)
SO WHAT ARE WE DOING NOW, M-SAN?

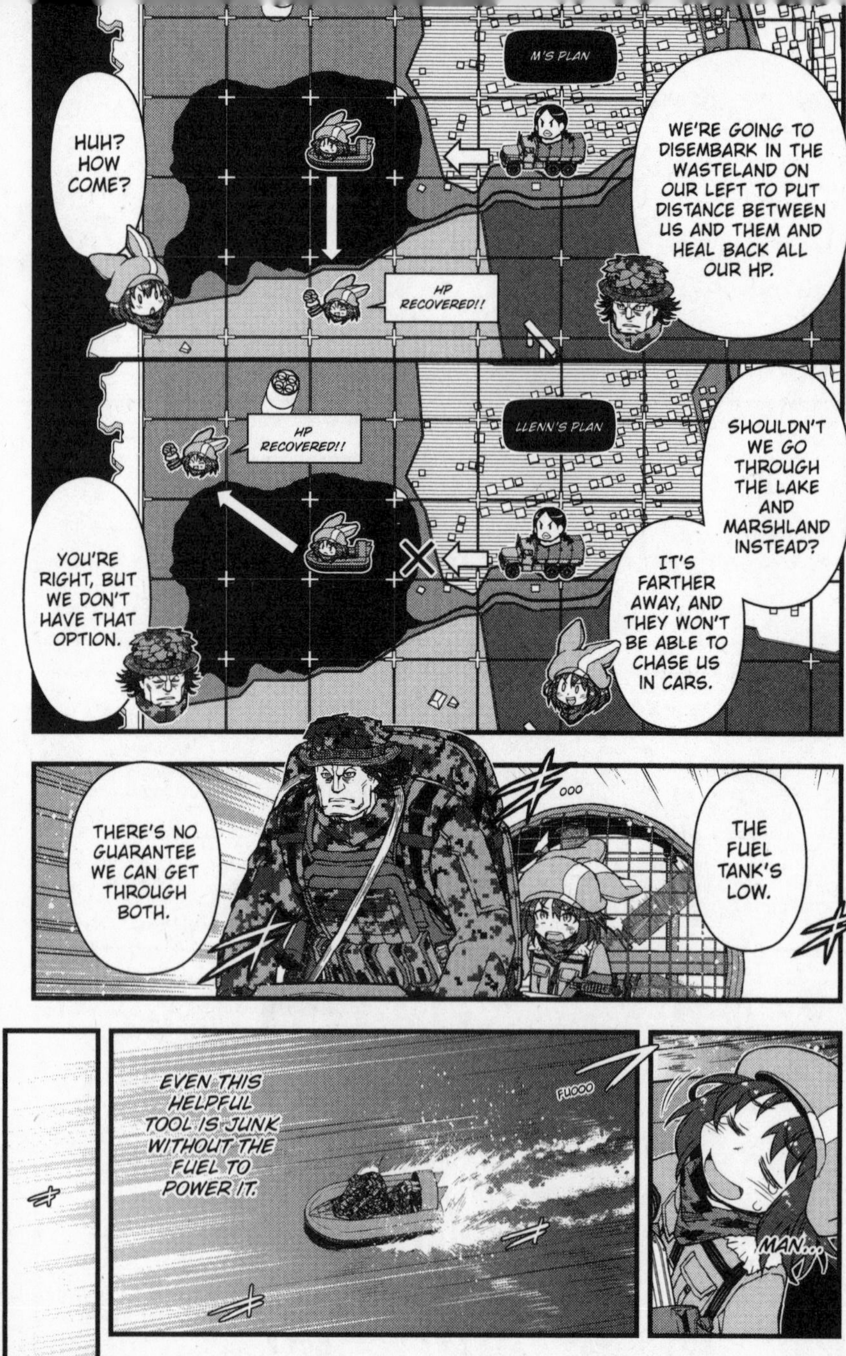
M'S PLAN
WE'RE GOING TO DISEMBARK IN THE WASTELAND ON OUR LEFT TO PUT DISTANCE BETWEEN US AND THEM AND HEAL BACK ALL OUR HP.
HP RECOVERED!!
HUH? HOW COME?
LLENN'S PLAN
SHOULDN'T WE GO THROUGH THE LAKE AND MARSHLAND INSTEAD?
IT'S FARTHER AWAY, AND THEY WON'T BE ABLE TO CHASE US IN CARS.
HP RECOVERED!!
YOU'RE RIGHT, BUT WE DON'T HAVE THAT OPTION.
THE FUEL TANK'S LOW.
OOO
THERE'S NO GUARANTEE WE CAN GET THROUGH BOTH.
MANooo
FUOOO
EVEN THIS HELPFUL TOOL IS JUNK WITHOUT THE FUEL TO POWER IT.

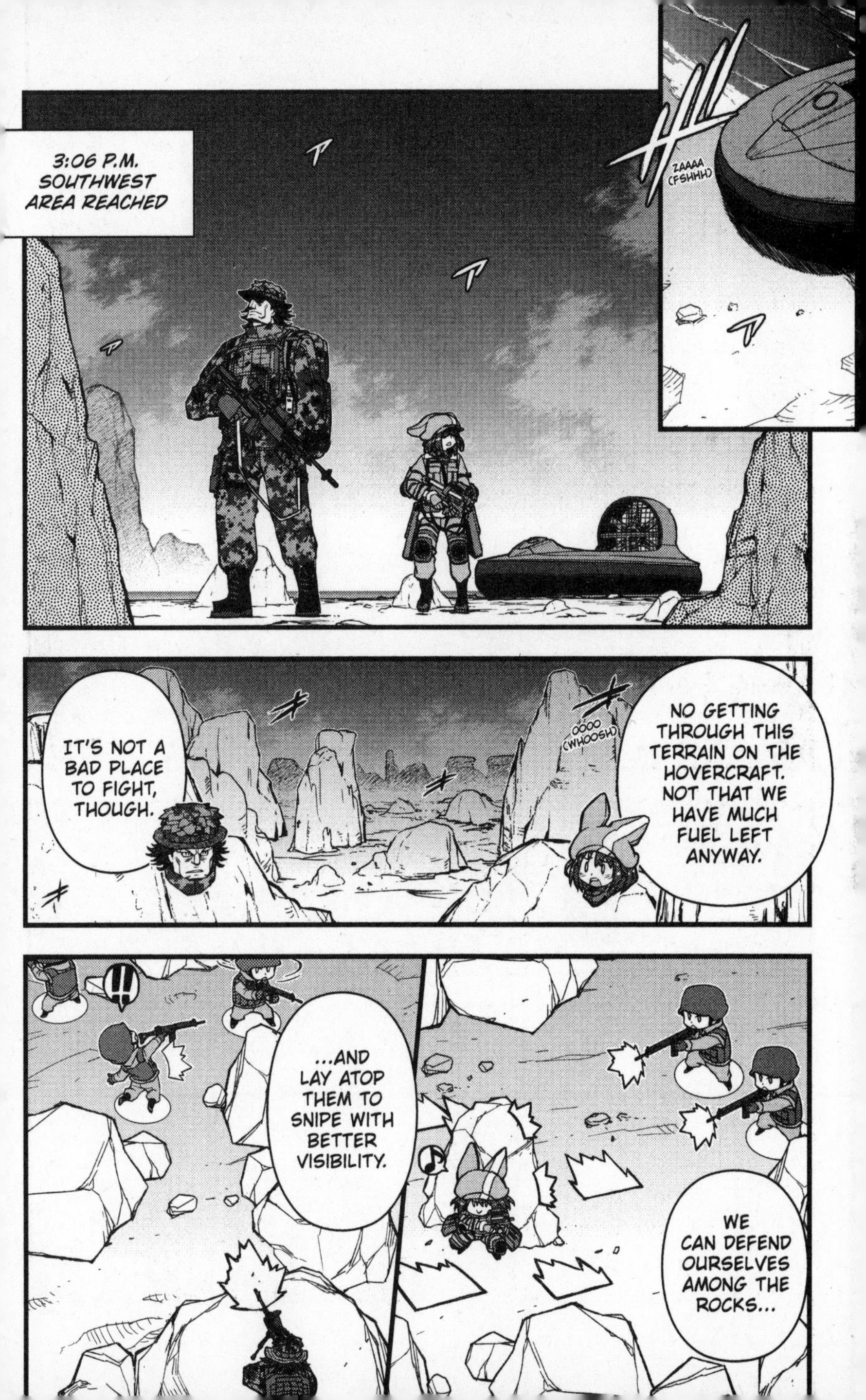
ZAAAA (FSHHH)
3:06 P.M. SOUTHWEST AREA REACHED
NO GETTING THROUGH THIS TERRAIN ON THE HOVERCRAFT. NOT THAT WE HAVE MUCH FUEL LEFT ANYWAY.
OOOO (WHOOSH)
IT'S NOT A BAD PLACE TO FIGHT, THOUGH.
WE CAN DEFEND OURSELVES AMONG THE ROCKS...
...AND LAY ATOP THEM TO SNIPE WITH BETTER VISIBILITY.

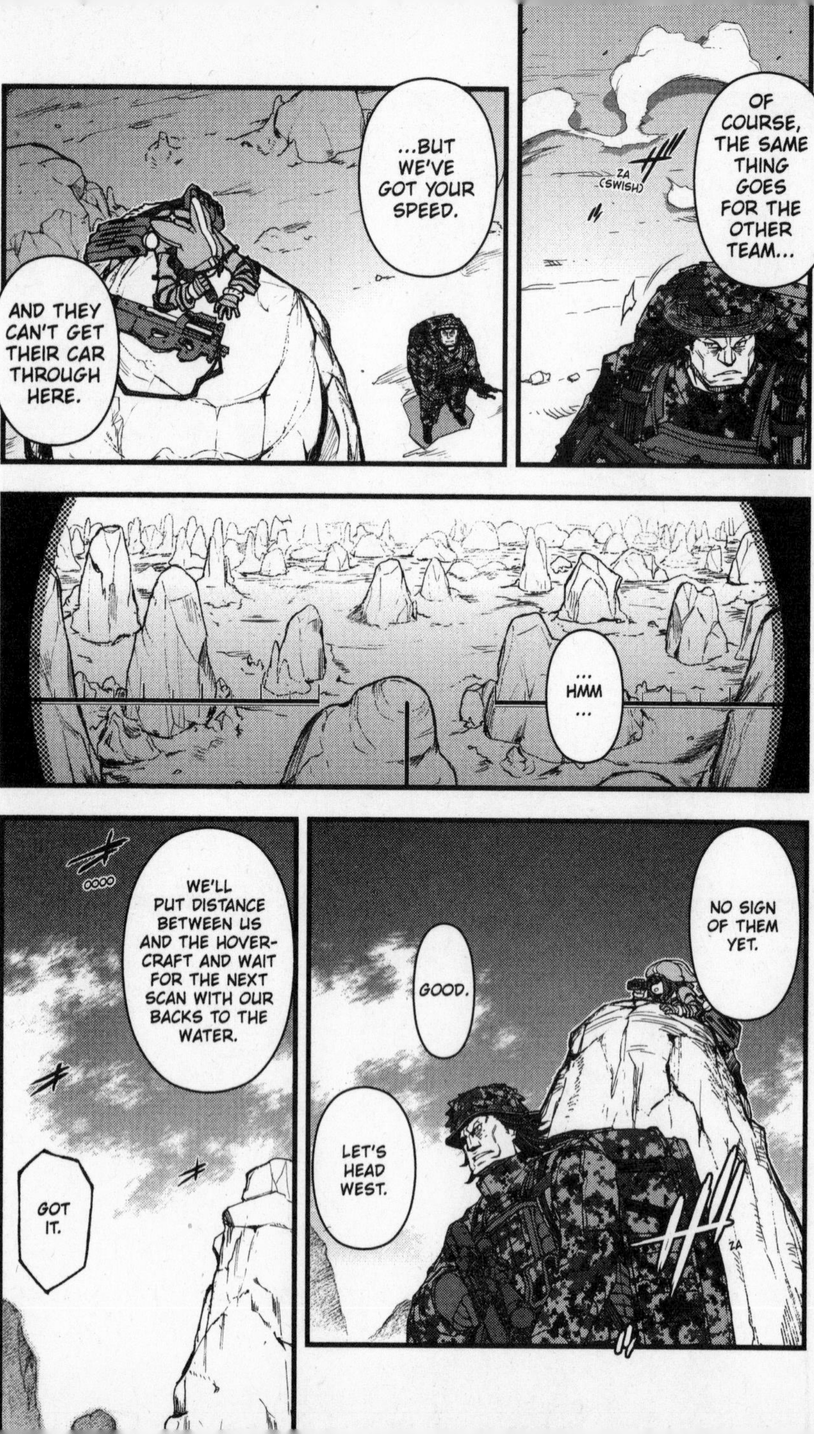
OF COURSE, THE SAME THING GOES FOR THE OTHER TEAM...
ZA (SWISH)
...BUT WE'VE GOT YOUR SPEED.
AND THEY CAN'T GET THEIR CAR THROUGH HERE.
... HMM ...
NO SIGN OF THEM YET.
GOOD.
LET'S HEAD WEST.
ZA
WE'LL PUT DISTANCE BETWEEN US AND THE HOVER-CRAFT AND WAIT FOR THE NEXT SCAN WITH OUR BACKS TO THE WATER.
GOT IT.

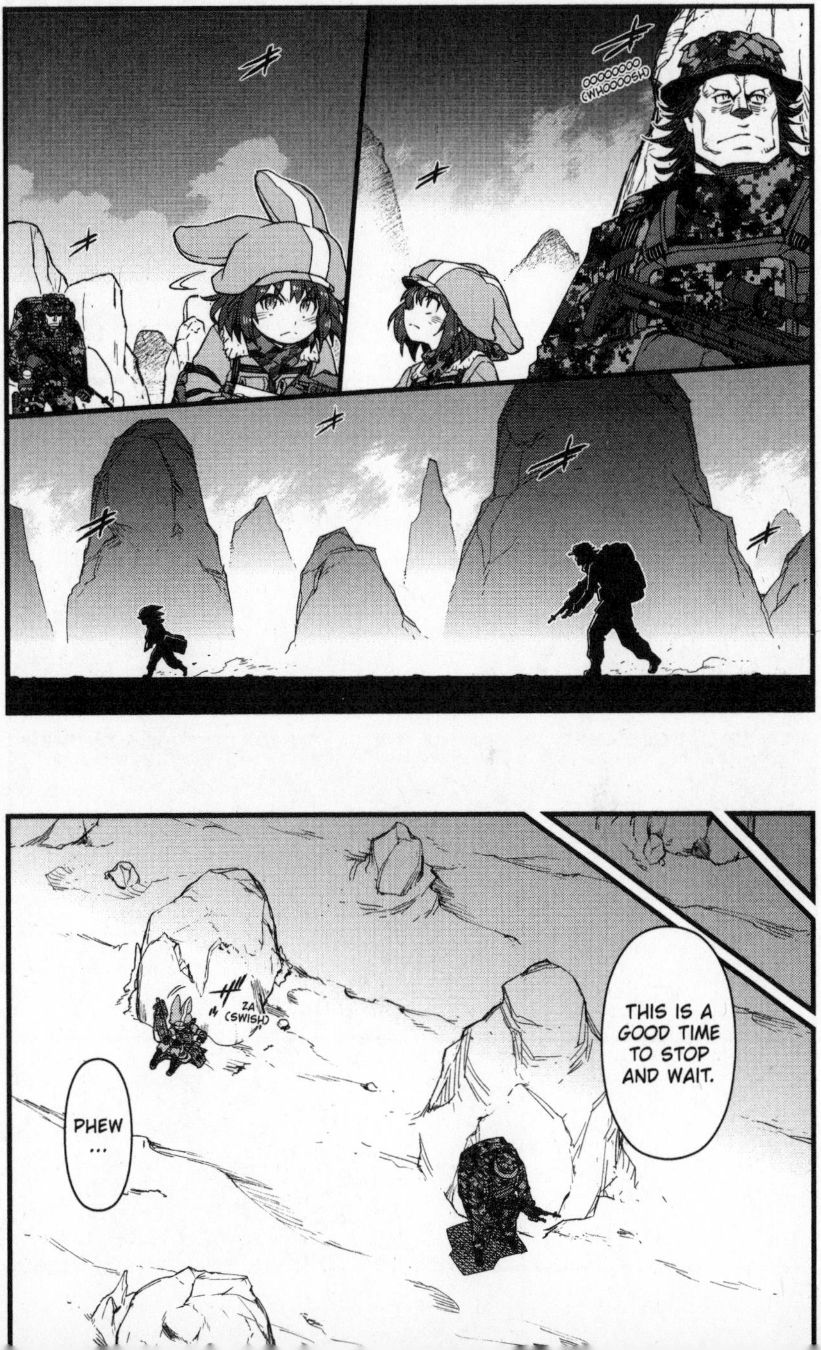
OOOOOOOO (WHOOOOSH)
THIS IS A GOOD TIME TO STOP AND WAIT.
ZA (SWISH)
PHEW ...

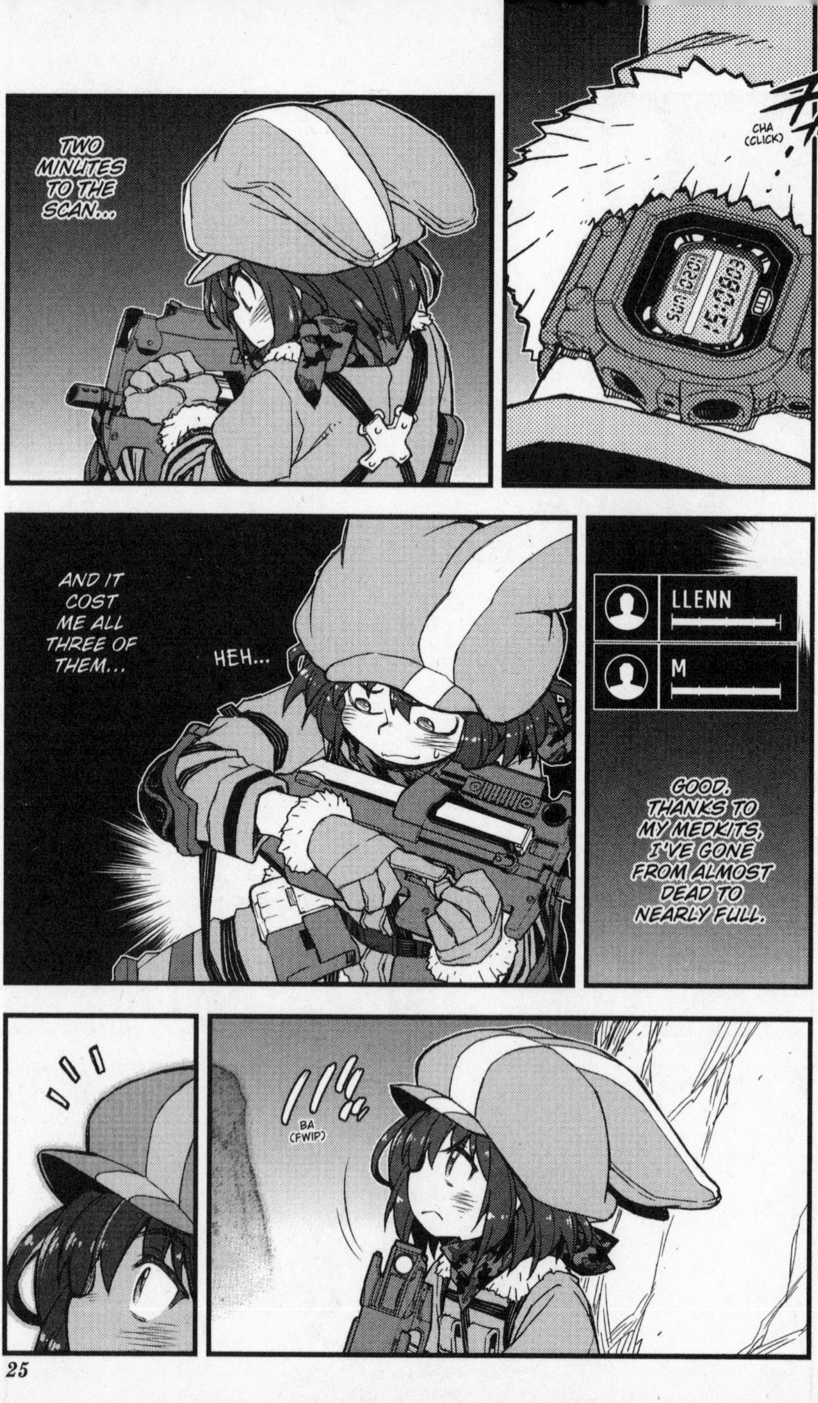
CHA (CLICK)
TWO MINUTES TO THE SCAN...
LLENN
M
GOOD. THANKS TO MY MEDKITS, I'VE GONE FROM ALMOST DEAD TO NEARLY FULL.
AND IT COST ME ALL THREE OF THEM...
HEH...
BA (FWIP)

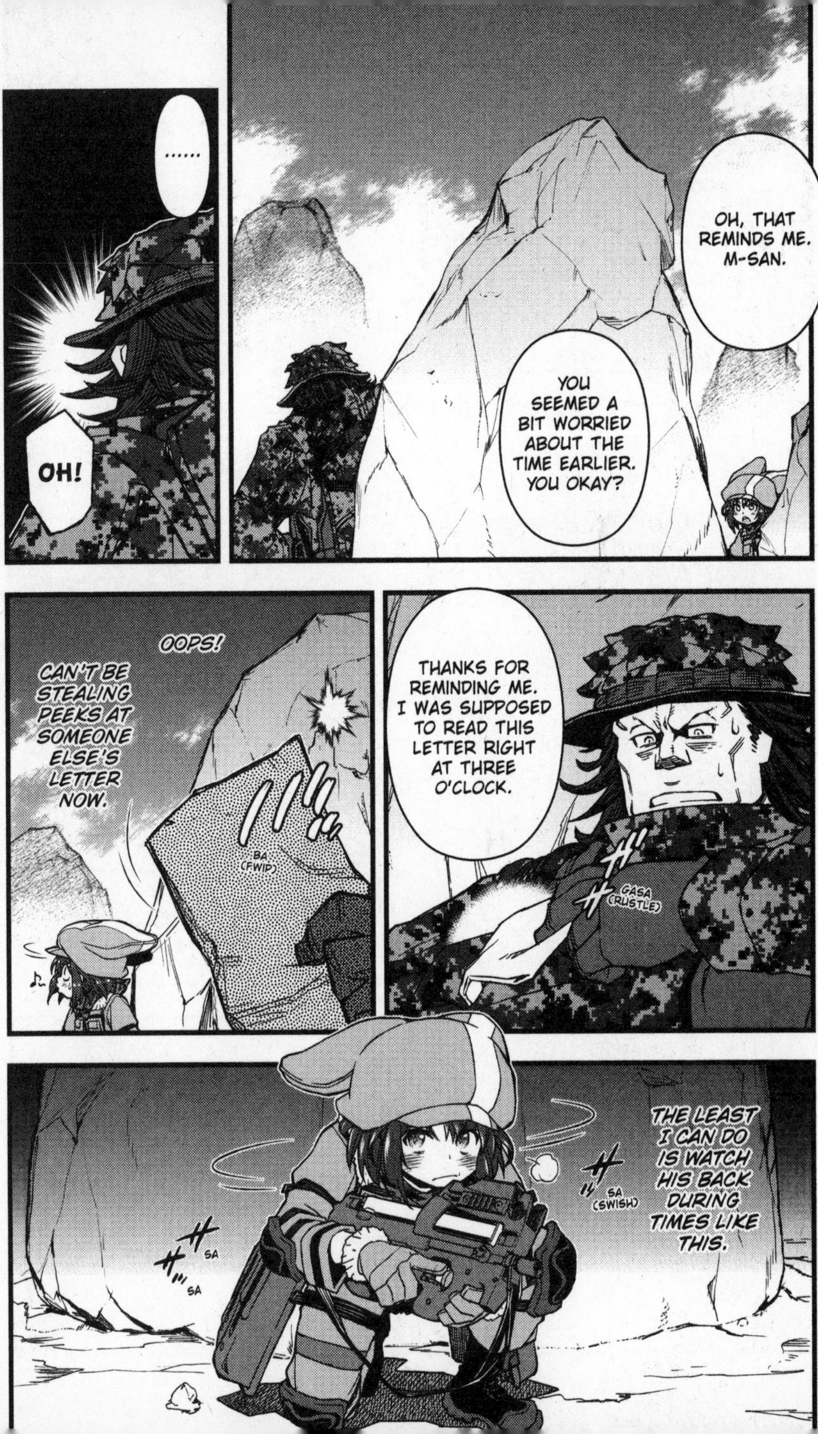
OH, THAT REMINDS ME. M-SAN.
YOU SEEMED A BIT WORRIED ABOUT THE TIME EARLIER. YOU OKAY?
......
OH!
THANKS FOR REMINDING ME. I WAS SUPPOSED TO READ THIS LETTER RIGHT AT THREE O'CLOCK.
GASA (RUSTLE)
OOPS!
CAN'T BE STEALING PEEKS AT SOMEONE ELSE'S LETTER NOW.
BA (FWIP)
THE LEAST I CAN DO IS WATCH HIS BACK DURING TIMES LIKE THIS.
SA (SWISH)
SA
SA

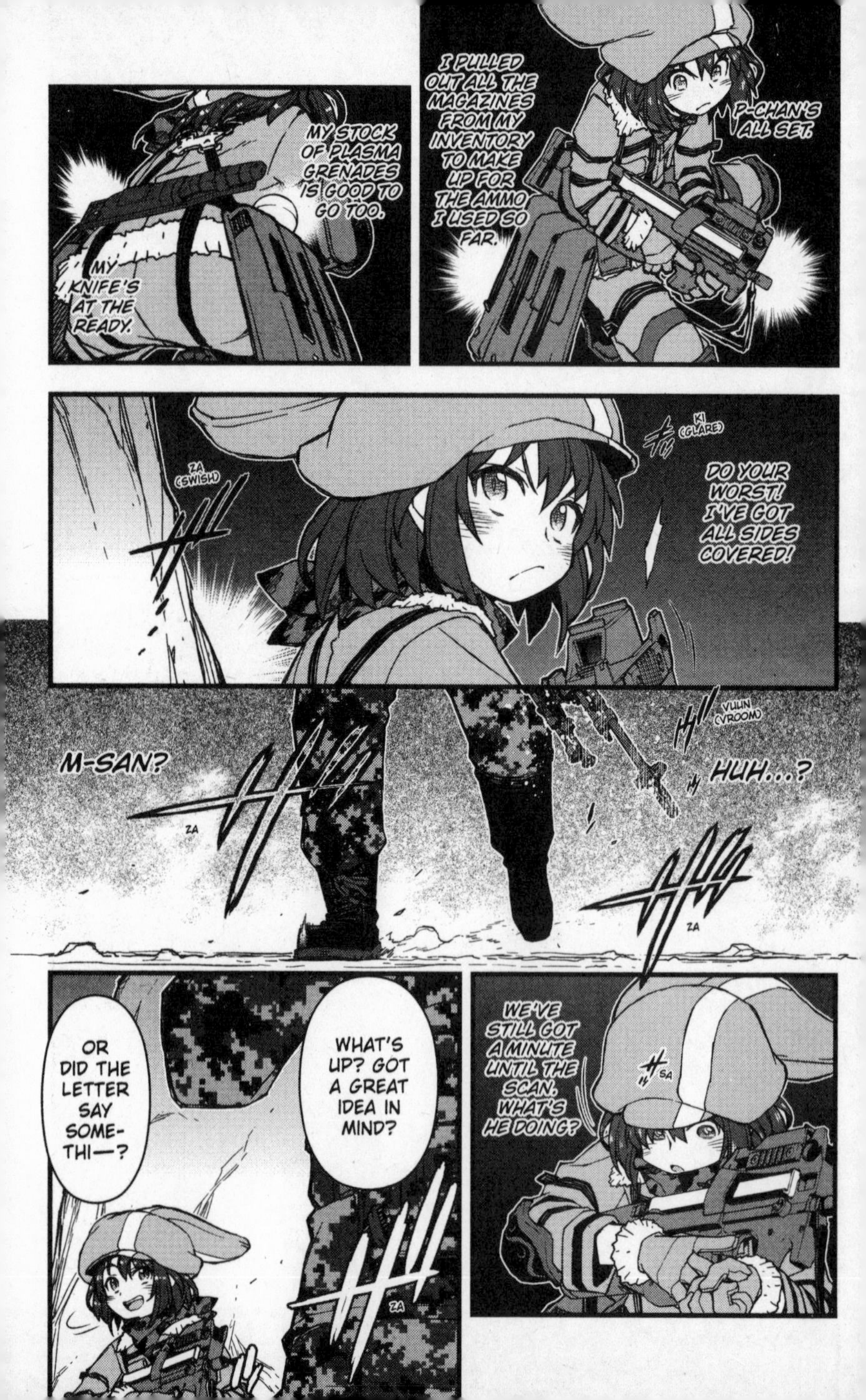
P-CHAN'S ALL SET.
I PULLED OUT ALL THE MAGAZINES FROM MY INVENTORY TO MAKE UP FOR THE AMMO I USED SO FAR.
MY STOCK OF PLASMA GRENADES IS GOOD TO GO TOO.
MY KNIFE'S AT THE READY.
KI (GLARE)
DO YOUR WORST! I'VE GOT ALL SIDES COVERED!
ZA (SWISH)
VUUN (VROOM)
HUH...?
M-SAN?
ZA
ZA
SA
WE'VE STILL GOT A MINUTE UNTIL THE SCAN. WHAT'S HE DOING?
WHAT'S UP? GOT A GREAT IDEA IN MIND?
OR DID THE LETTER SAY SOME-THI—?
ZA

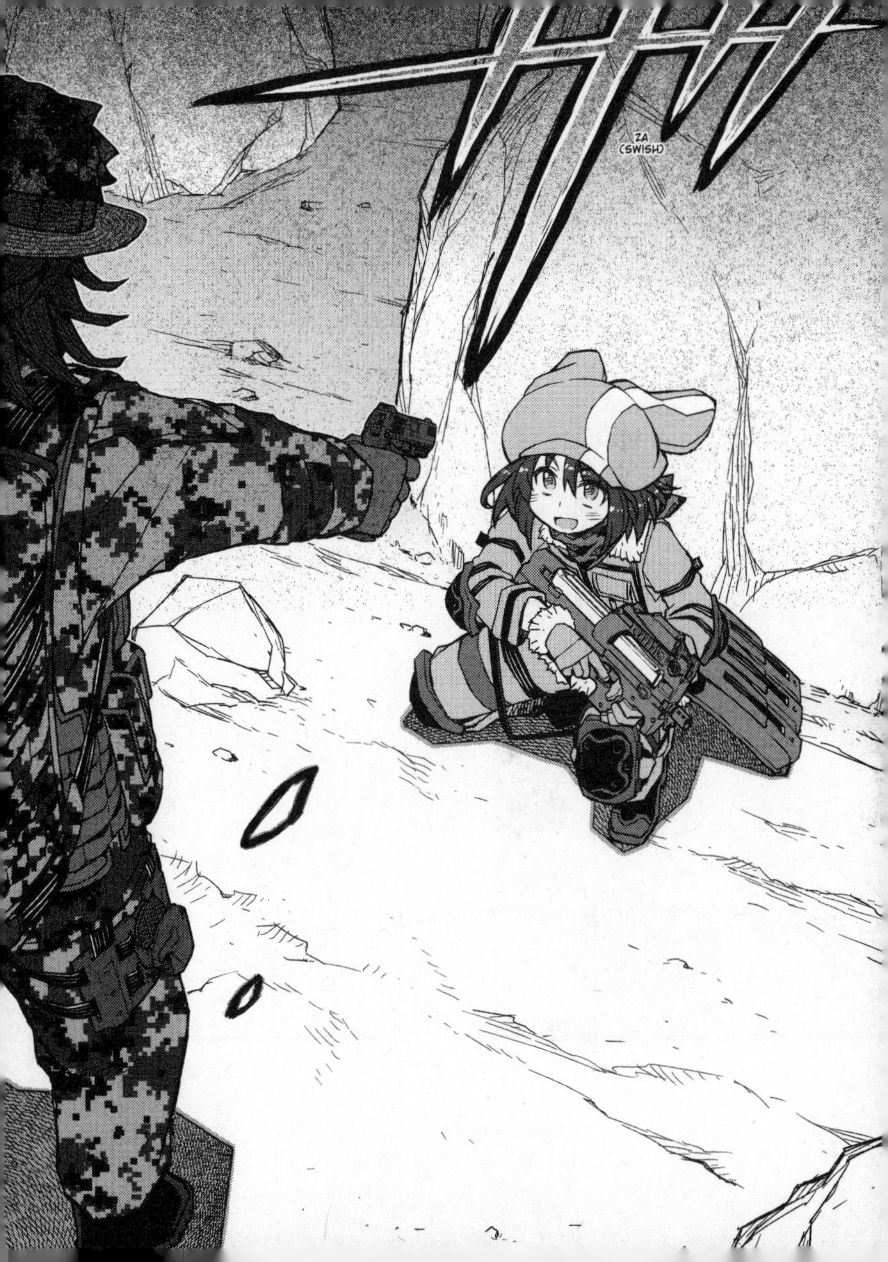
ZA
(SWISH)

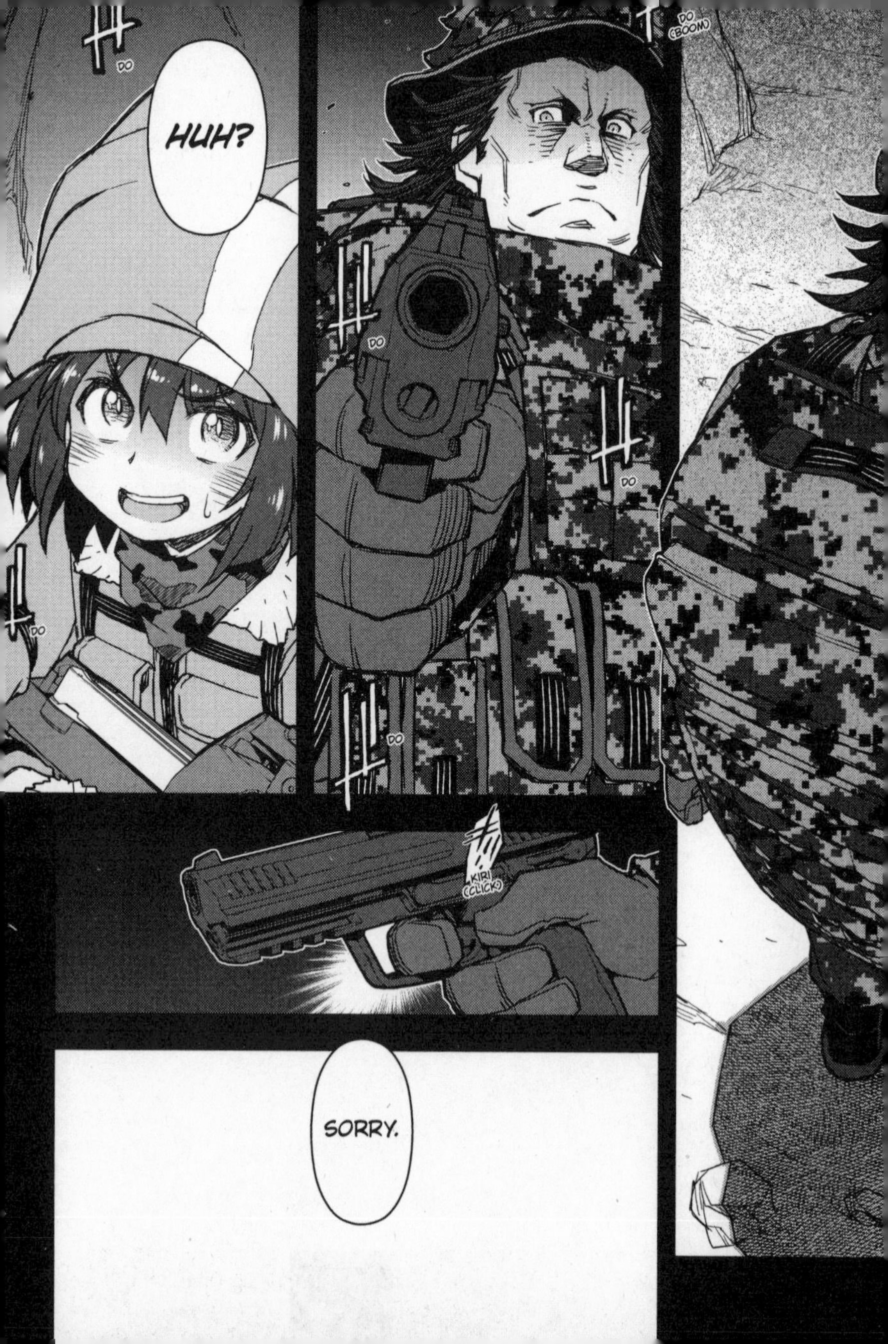
DO (BOOM)
DO
DO
DO
DO
HUH?
DO
KIRI (CLICK)
SORRY.

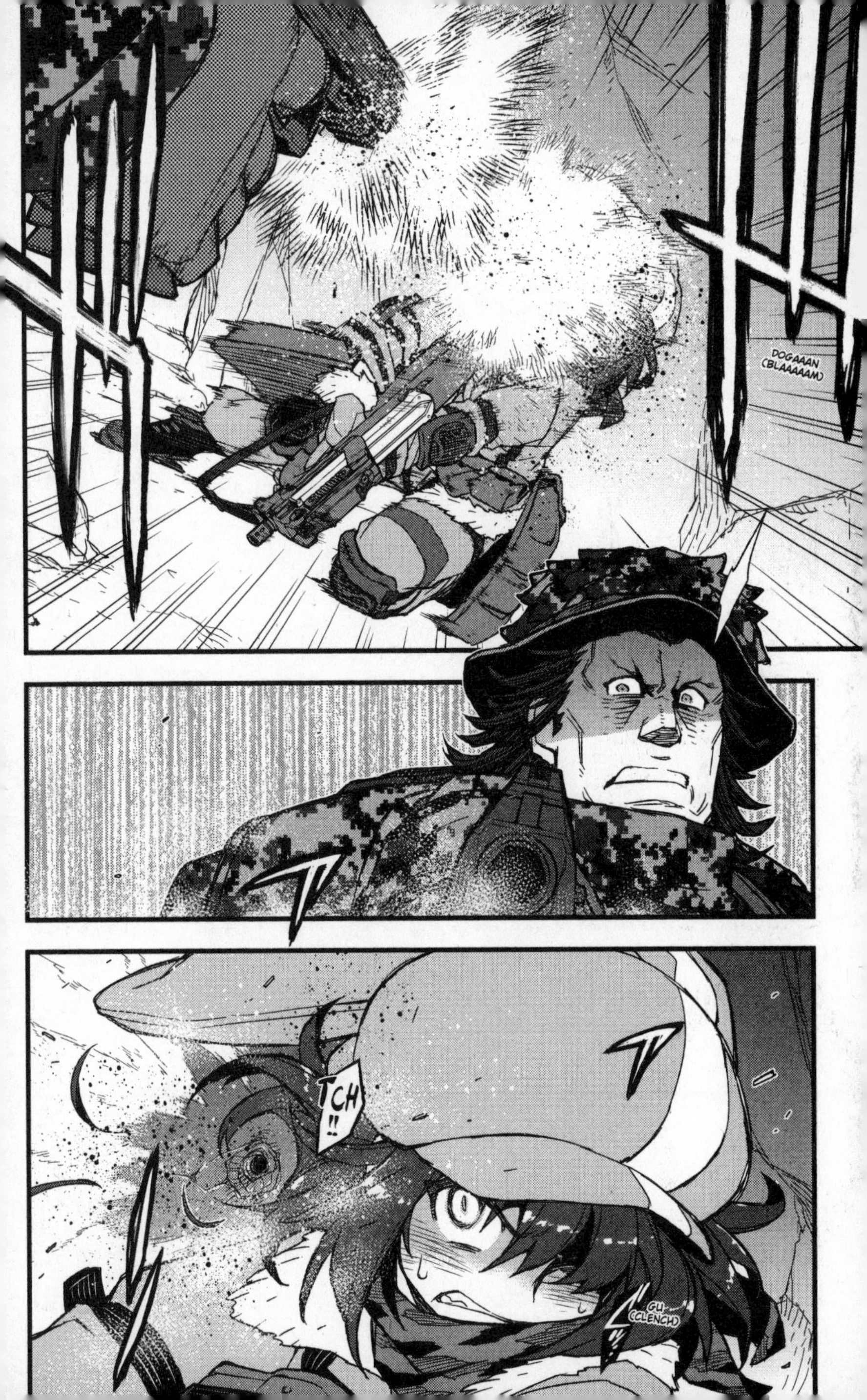
DOGAAAN (BLAAAAAM)
TCH!!
GU (CLENCH)

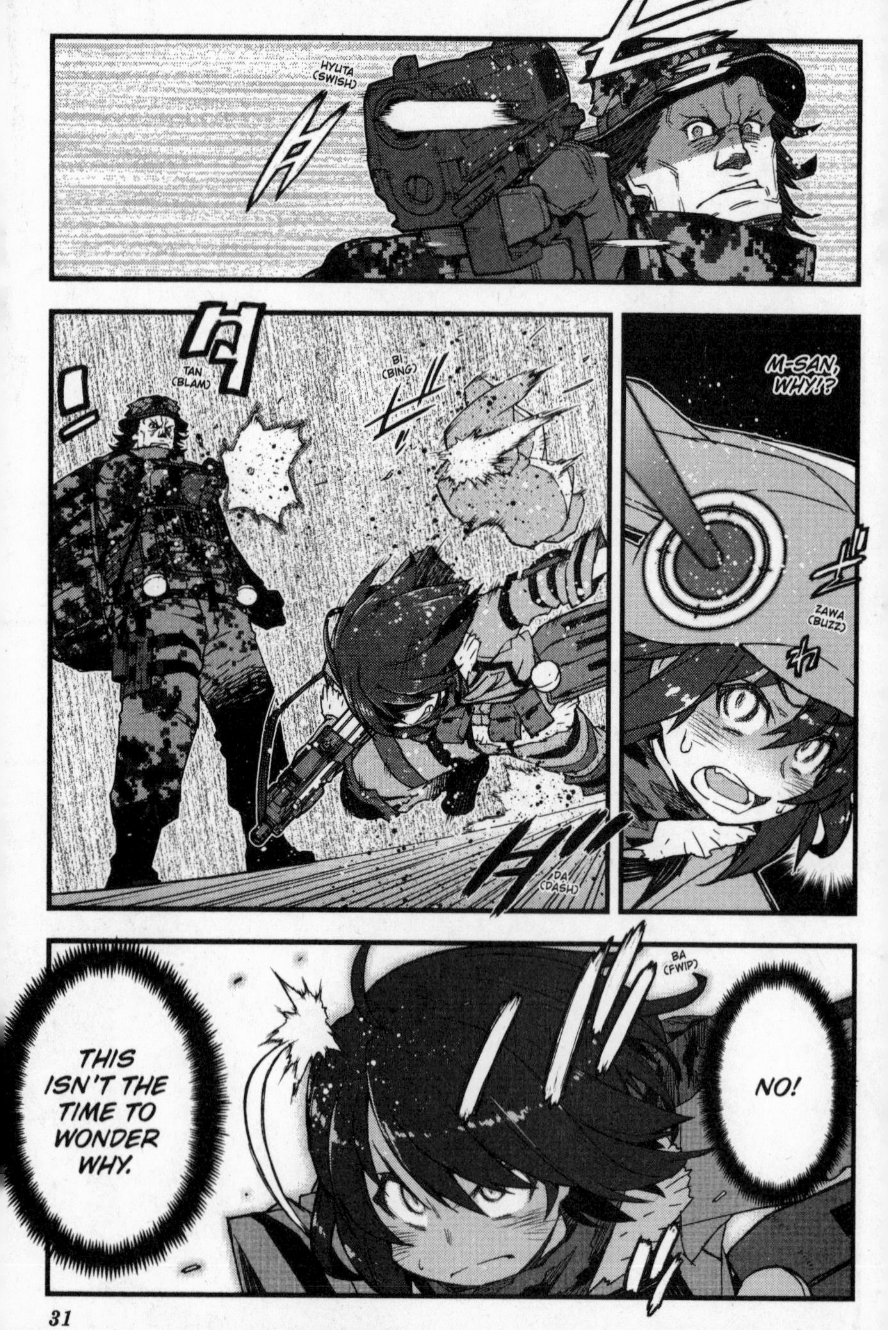
HYUTA (SWISH)
M-SAN, WHY!?
ZAWA (BUZZ)
BI (BING)
TAN (BLAM)
DA (DASH)
BA (FWIP)
NO!
THIS ISN'T THE TIME TO WONDER WHY.

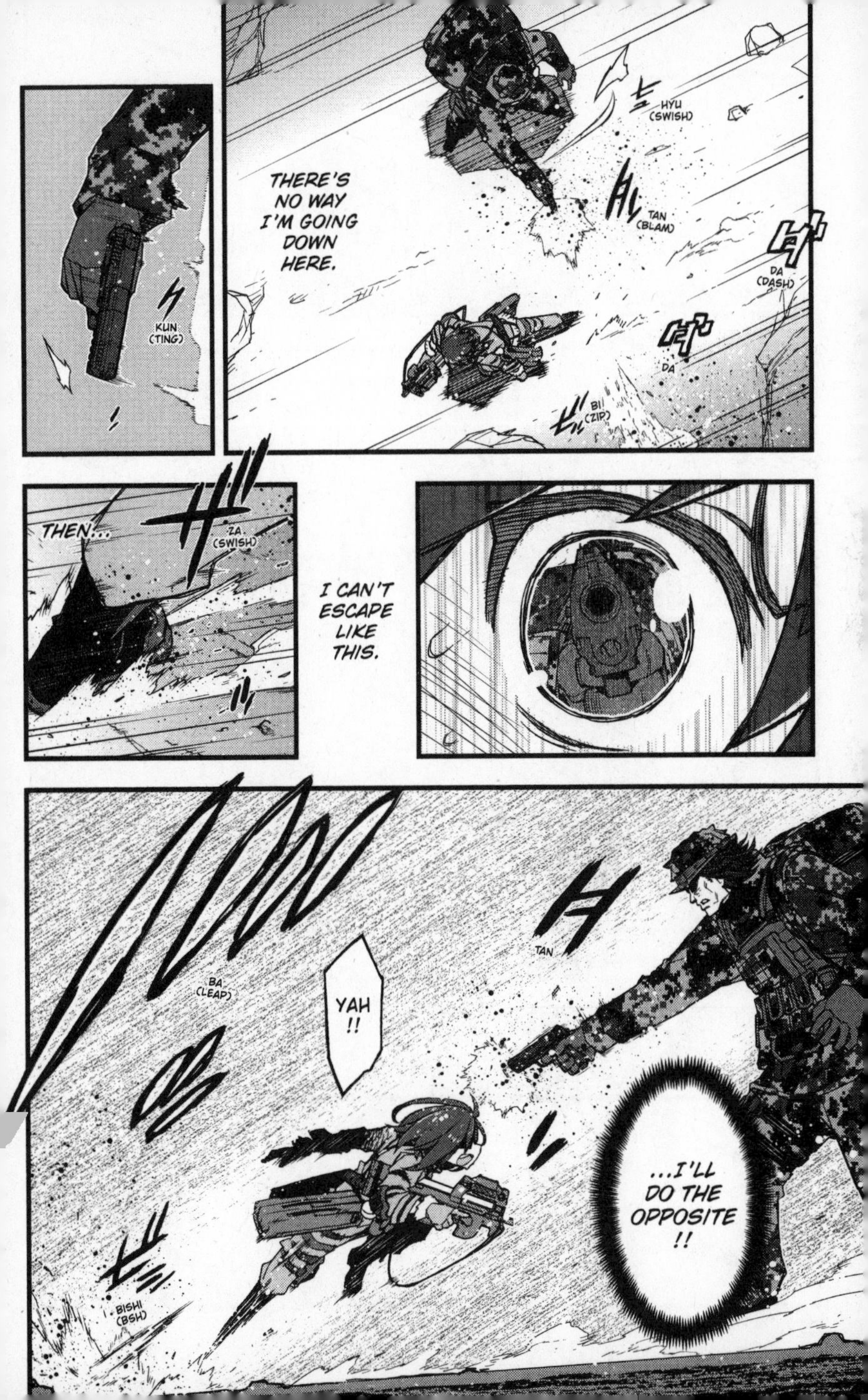
HYU (SWISH)
DA (DASH)
TAN (BLAM)
THERE'S NO WAY I'M GOING DOWN HERE.
DA
BI (ZIP)
KUN (TING)
I CAN'T ESCAPE LIKE THIS.
ZA (SWISH)
THEN...
TAN
...I'LL DO THE OPPOSITE!!
YAH!!
BA (LEAP)
BISHI (BSH)

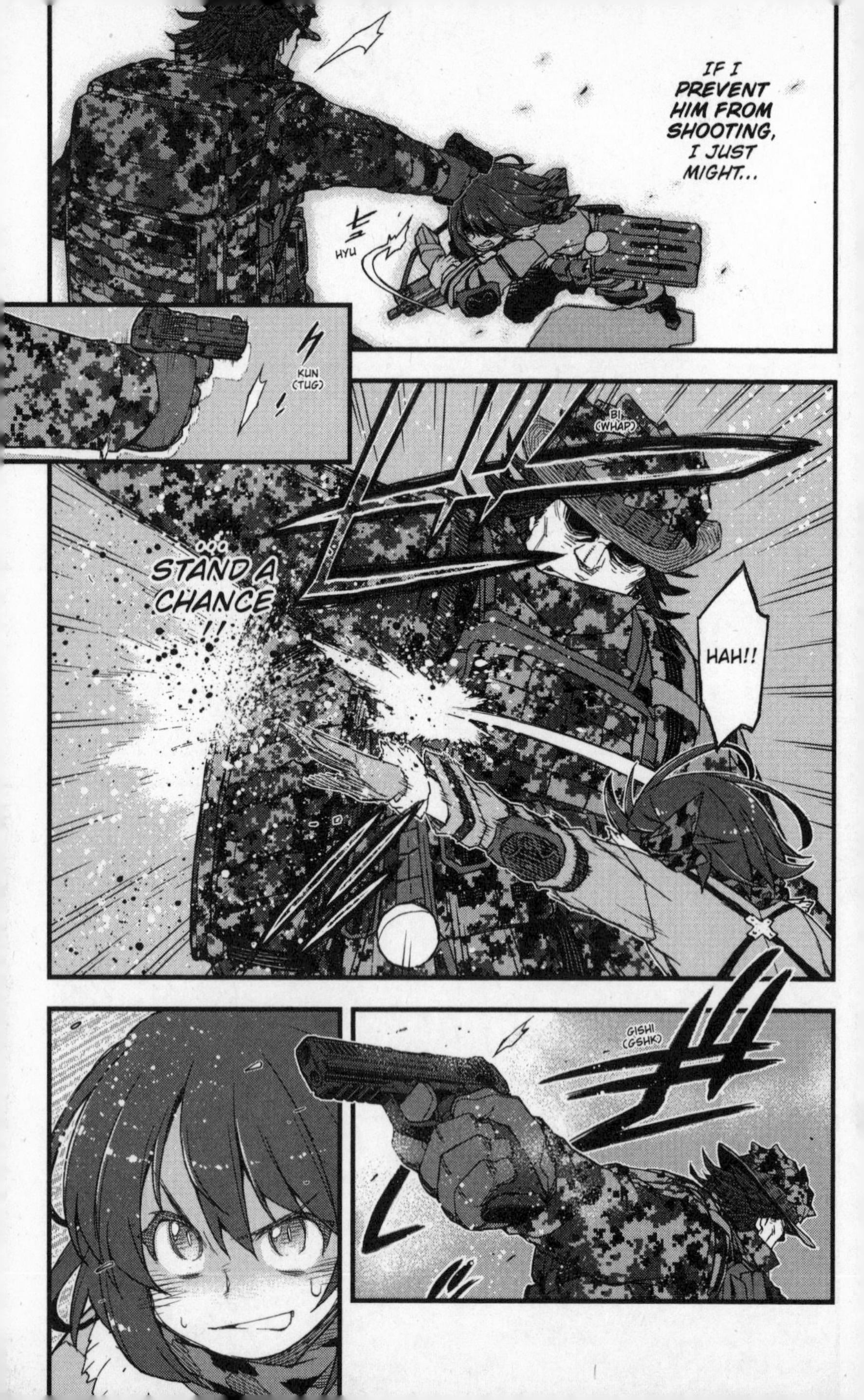
IF I PREVENT HIM FROM SHOOTING, I JUST MIGHT...
HYU
KUN (TUG)
...STAND A CHANCE!!
BI (WHAP)
HAH!!
GISHI (GSHK)

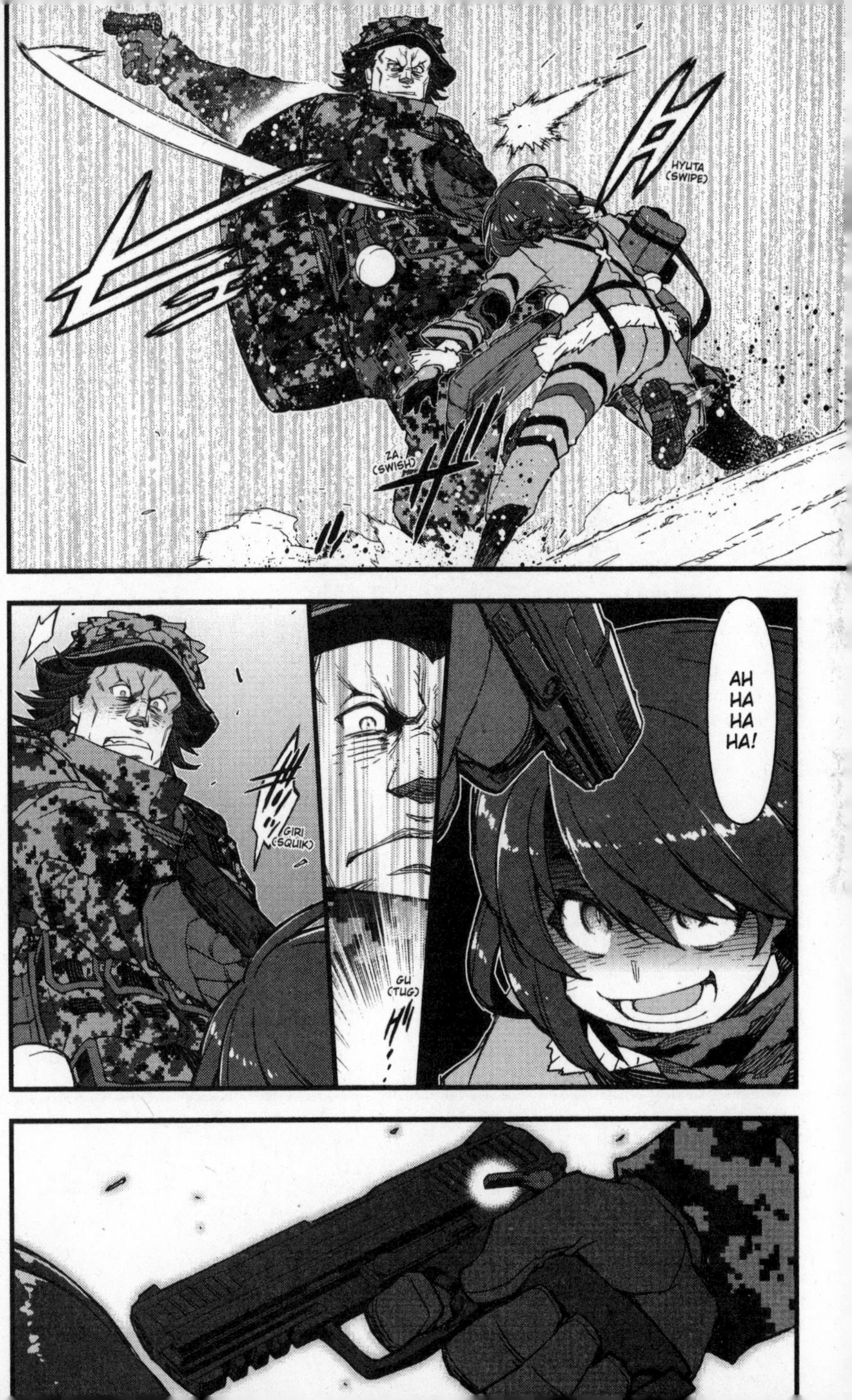
HYUTA (SWIPE)
ZA (SWISH)
AH HA HA HA HA!
GU (TUG)
GIRI (SQUIK)

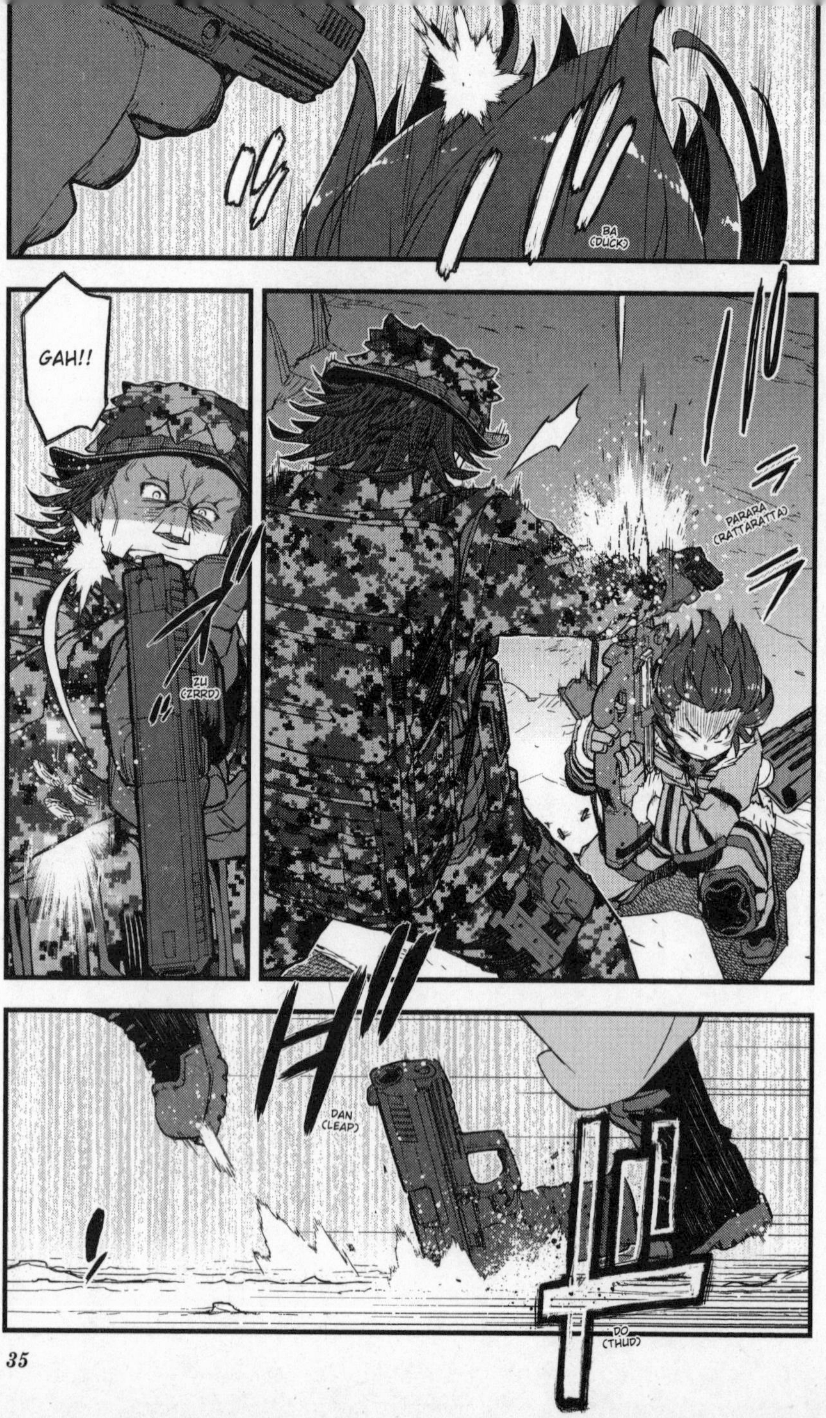
BA (DUCK)
PARARA (RATTARATTA)
GAH!!
ZU (ZRRD)
DO (THUD)
DAN (LEAP)

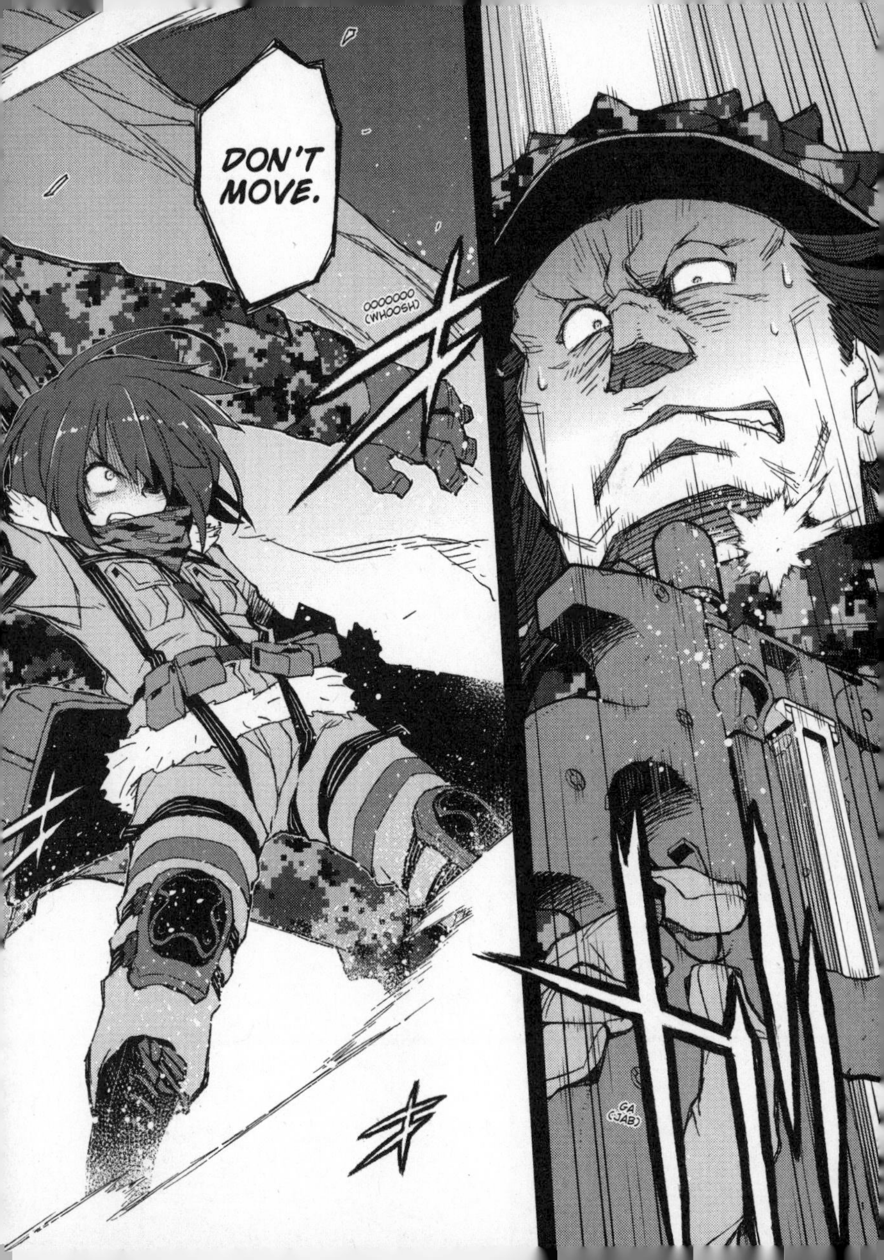
GA (JAB)
DON'T MOVE.
OOOOOOO (WHOOSH)

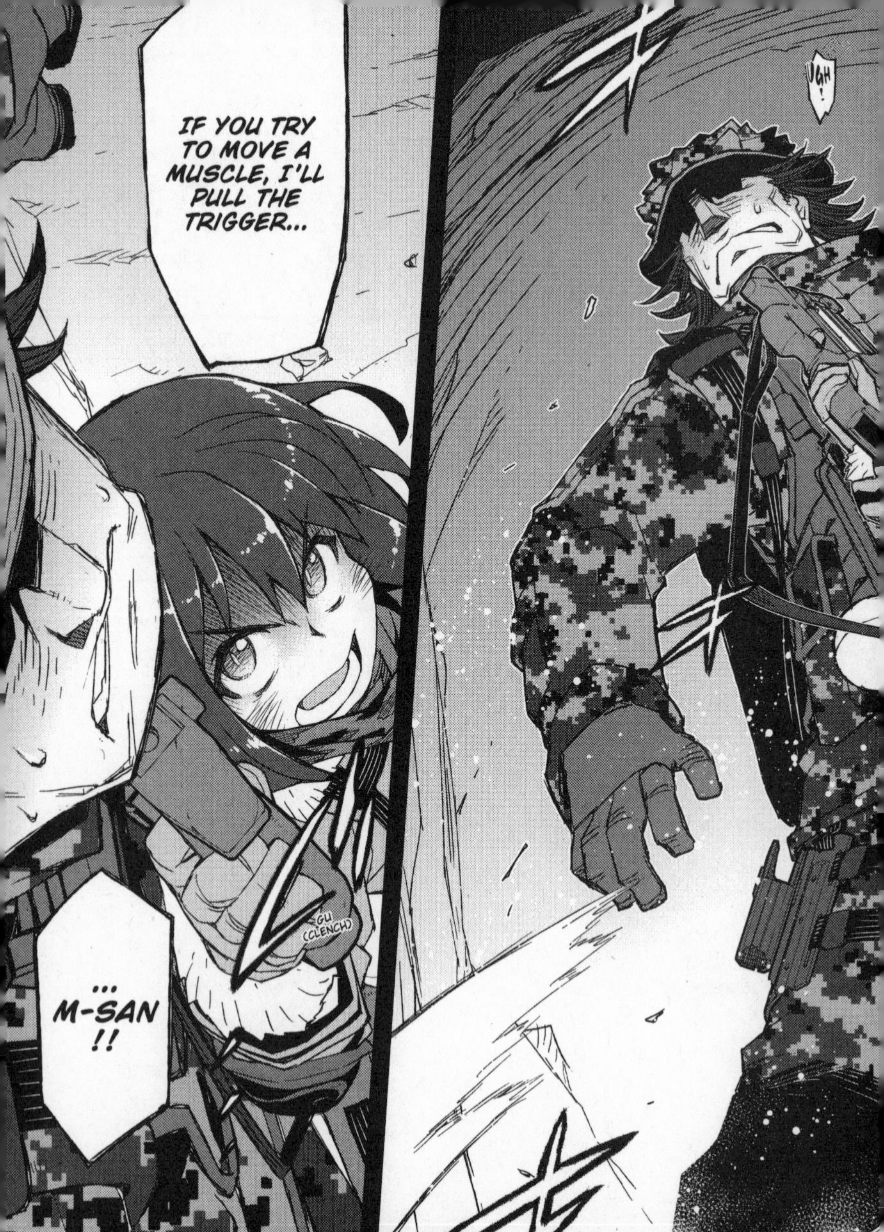
UGH!
IF YOU TRY TO MOVE A MUSCLE, I'LL PULL THE TRIGGER...
GU (CLENCH)
...M-SAN!!

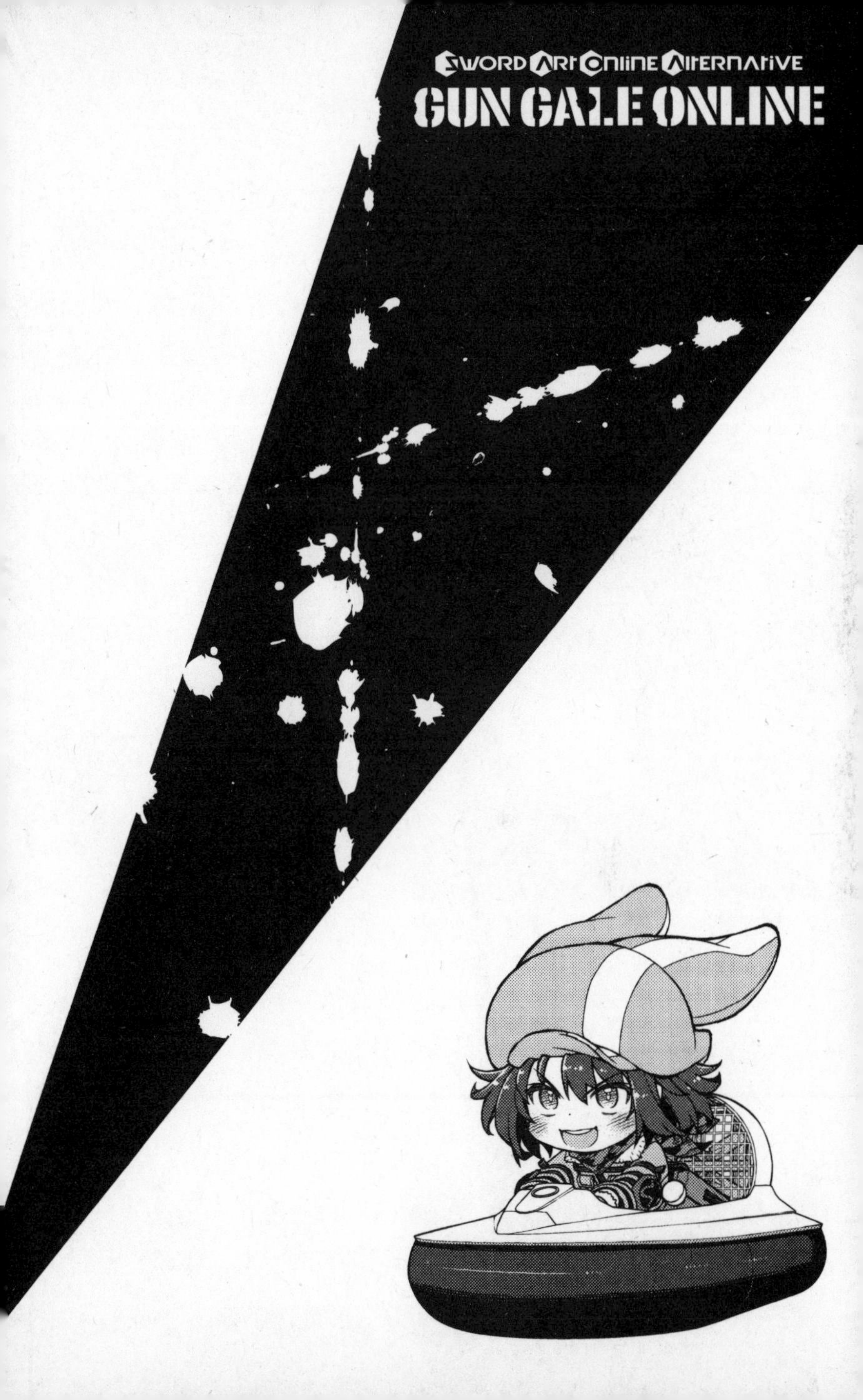
SWORD ART ONLINE ALTERNATIVE
GUN GALE ONLINE

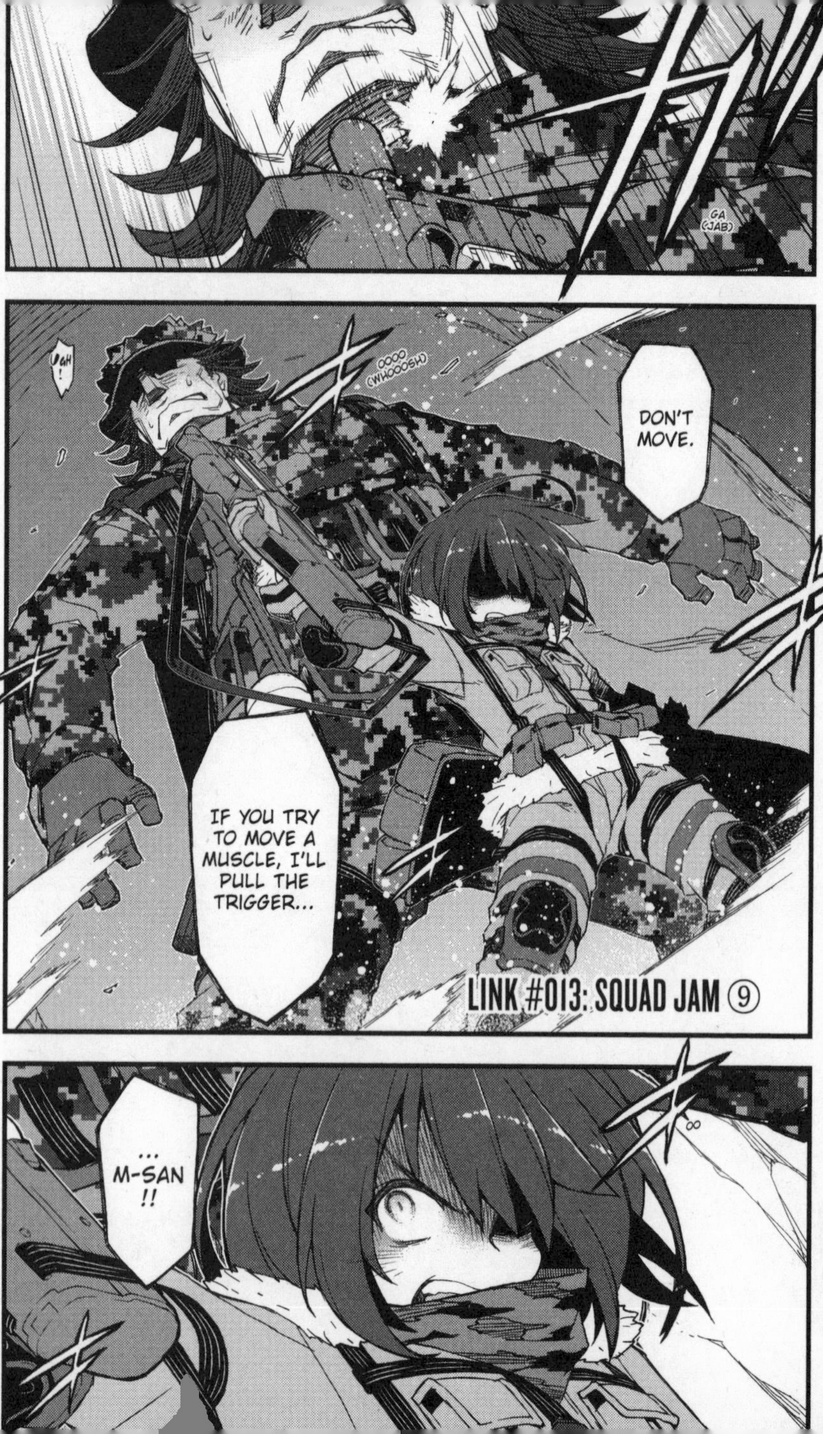
GA (JAB)
DON'T MOVE.
OOOO (WHOOOSH)
UGH!
IF YOU TRY TO MOVE A MUSCLE, I'LL PULL THE TRIGGER...
LINK #013: SQUAD JAM ⑨
... M-SAN!!

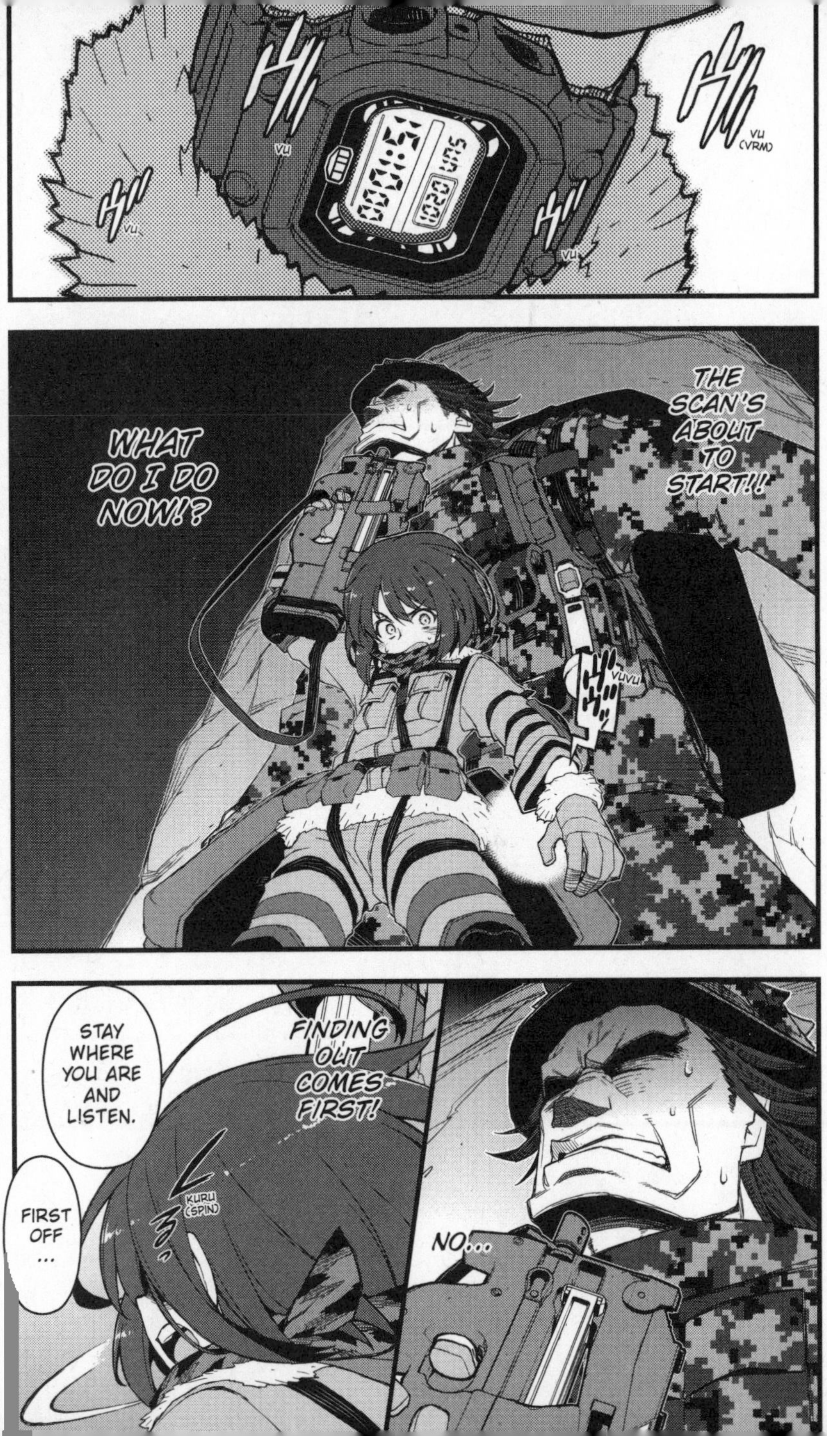
VU (VRM)
VU
VU
VU
THE SCAN'S ABOUT TO START!!
WHAT DO I DO NOW!?
VUVU
NO...
FINDING OUT COMES FIRST!
STAY WHERE YOU ARE AND LISTEN.
KURU (SPIN)
FIRST OFF ...

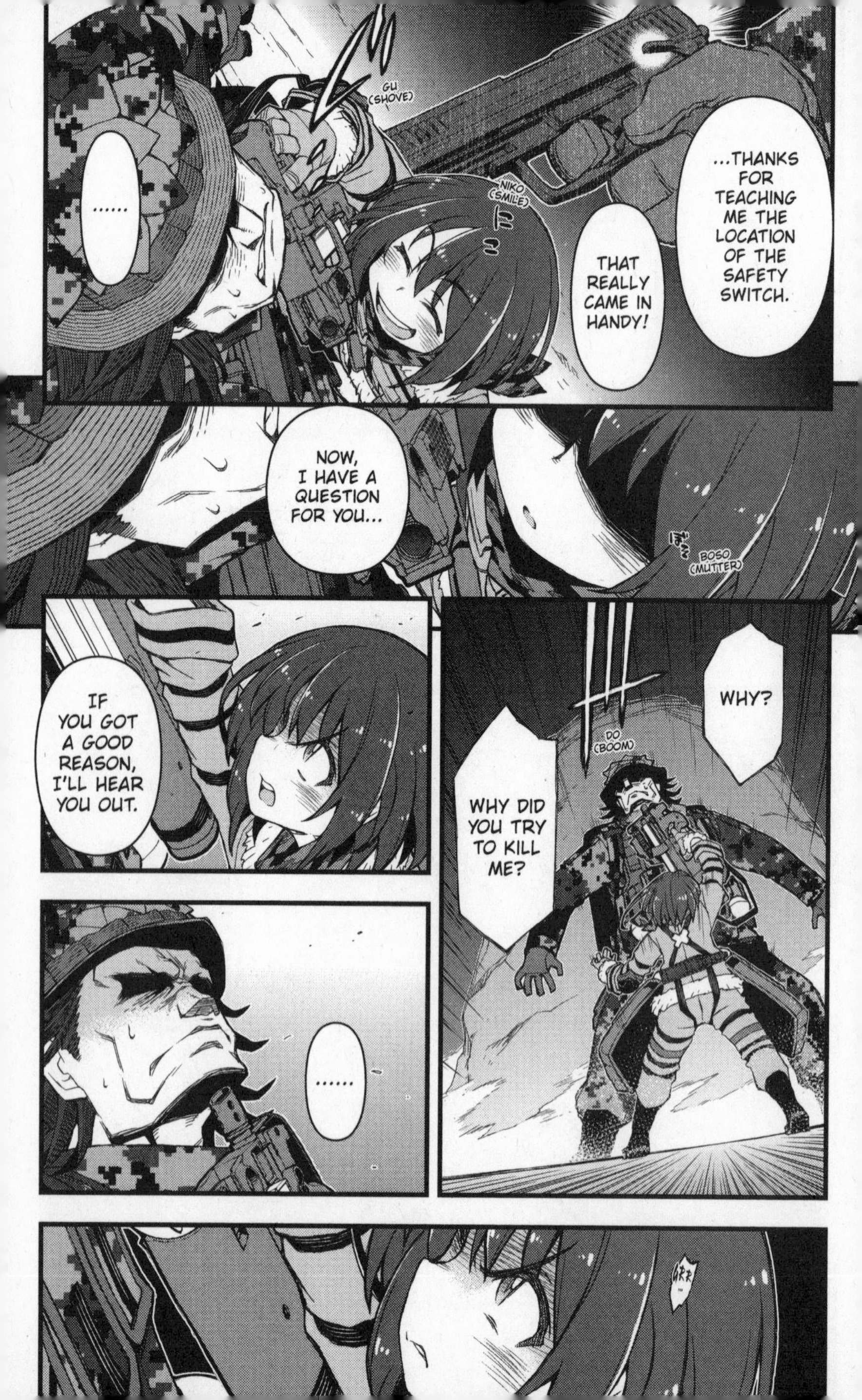
...THANKS FOR TEACHING ME THE LOCATION OF THE SAFETY SWITCH.
GU (SHOVE)
NIKO (SMILE)
THAT REALLY CAME IN HANDY!
......
BOSO (MUTTER)
NOW, I HAVE A QUESTION FOR YOU...
WHY?
DO (BOOM)
WHY DID YOU TRY TO KILL ME?
IF YOU GOT A GOOD REASON, I'LL HEAR YOU OUT.
......
GRR...

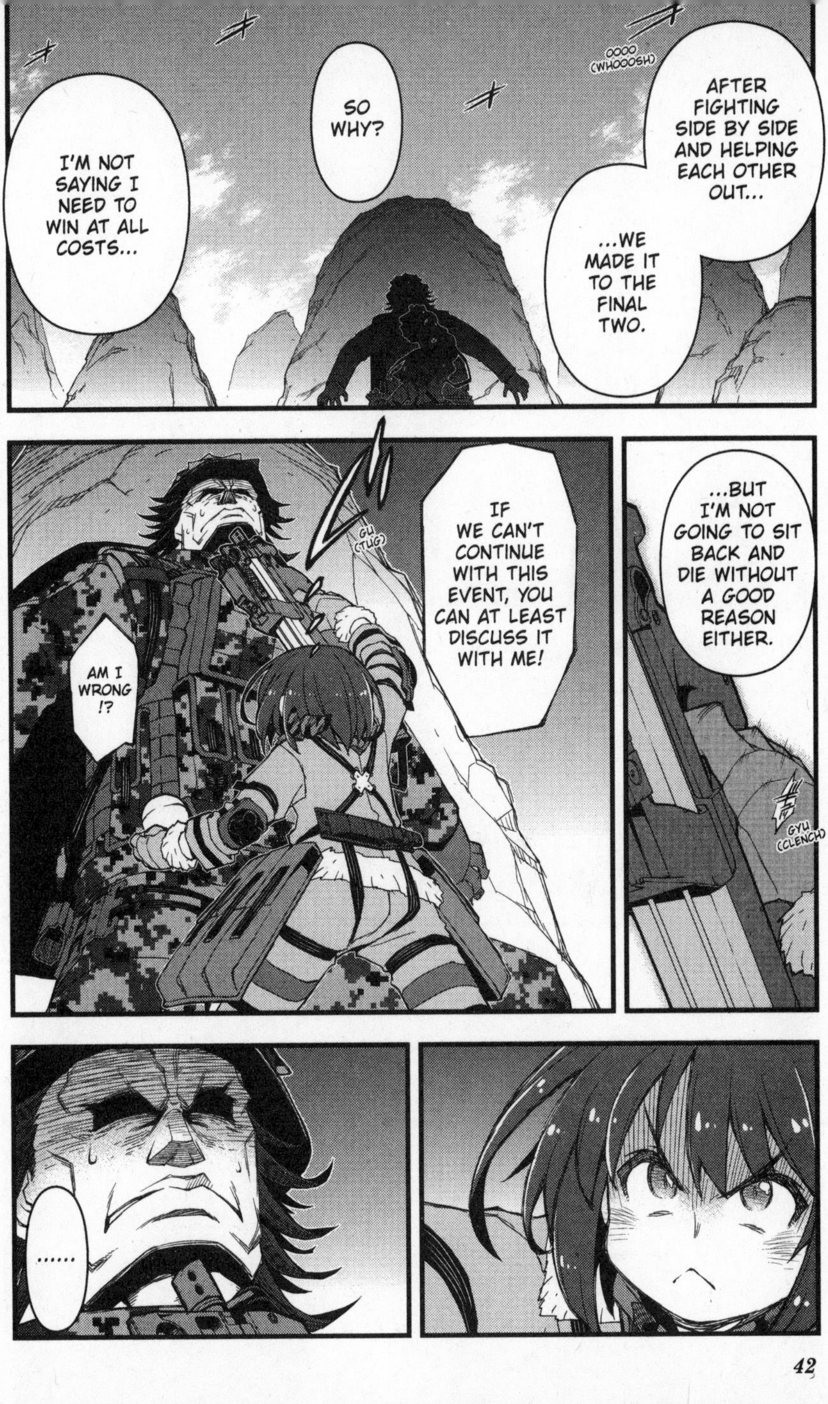
OOOO (WHOOOSH)
AFTER FIGHTING SIDE BY SIDE AND HELPING EACH OTHER OUT...
...WE MADE IT TO THE FINAL TWO.
SO WHY?
I'M NOT SAYING I NEED TO WIN AT ALL COSTS...
...BUT I'M NOT GOING TO SIT BACK AND DIE WITHOUT A GOOD REASON EITHER.
GYU (CLENCH)
GU (TUG)
IF WE CAN'T CONTINUE WITH THIS EVENT, YOU CAN AT LEAST DISCUSS IT WITH ME!
AM I WRONG!?
......

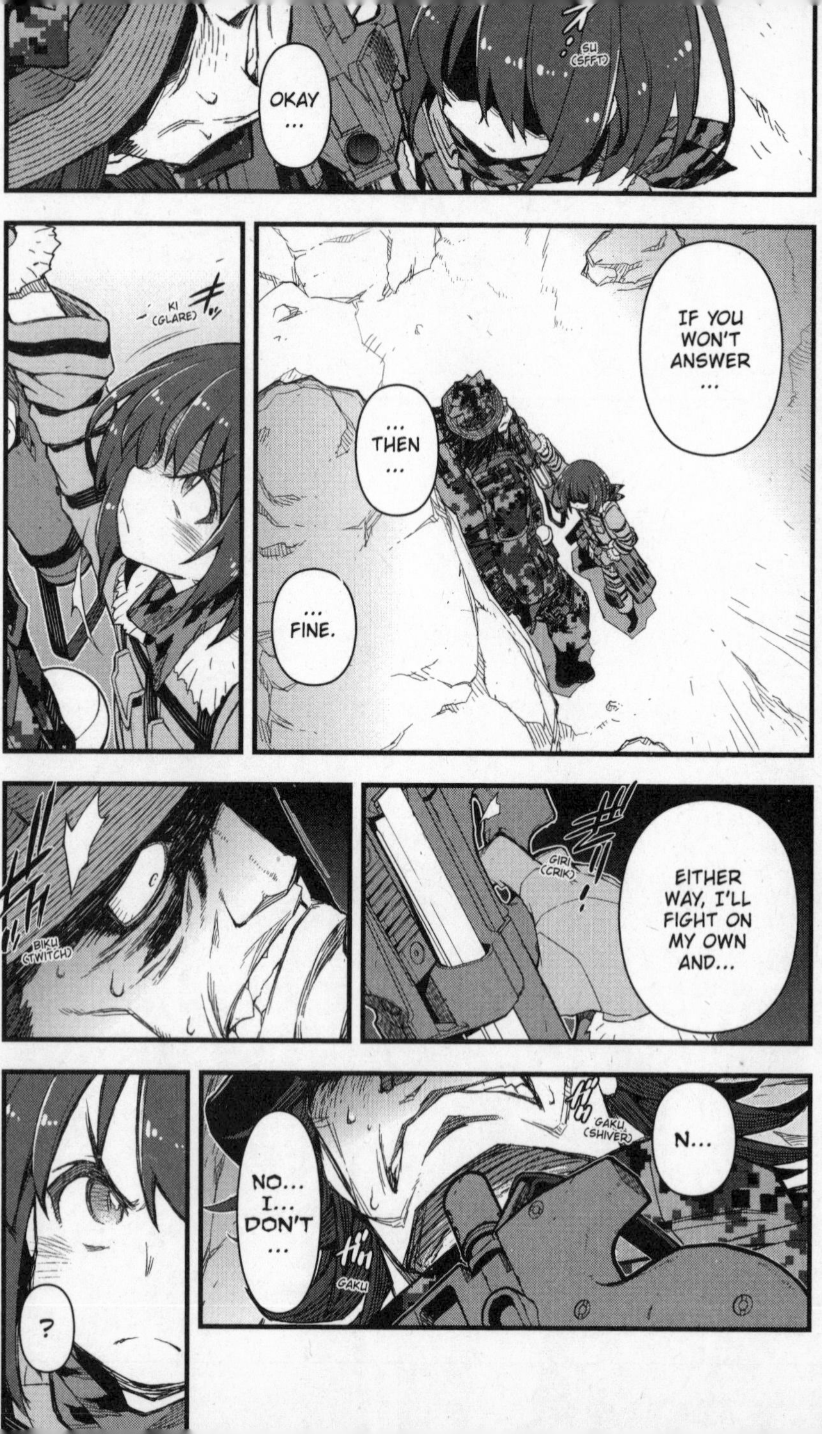
SU (SFFT)
OKAY...
IF YOU WON'T ANSWER...
...THEN...
...FINE.
KI (GLARE)
GIRI (CRIK)
EITHER WAY, I'LL FIGHT ON MY OWN AND...
BIKU (TWITCH)
N...
GAKU (SHIVER)
NO... I... DON'T...
GAKU
?

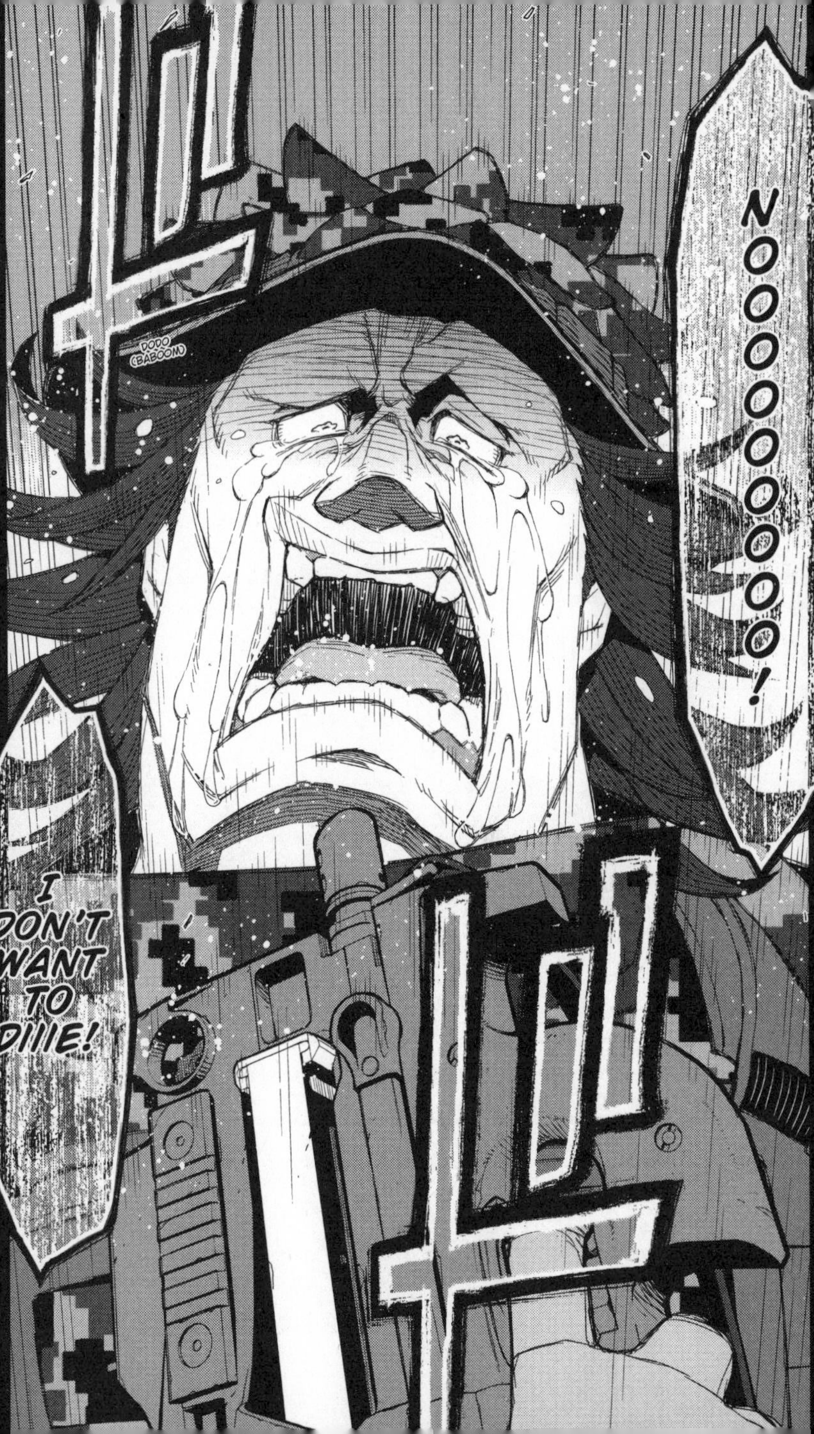
NOOOOOOOOOOO!
DODO (BABOOM)
I DON'T WANT TO DIIIE!

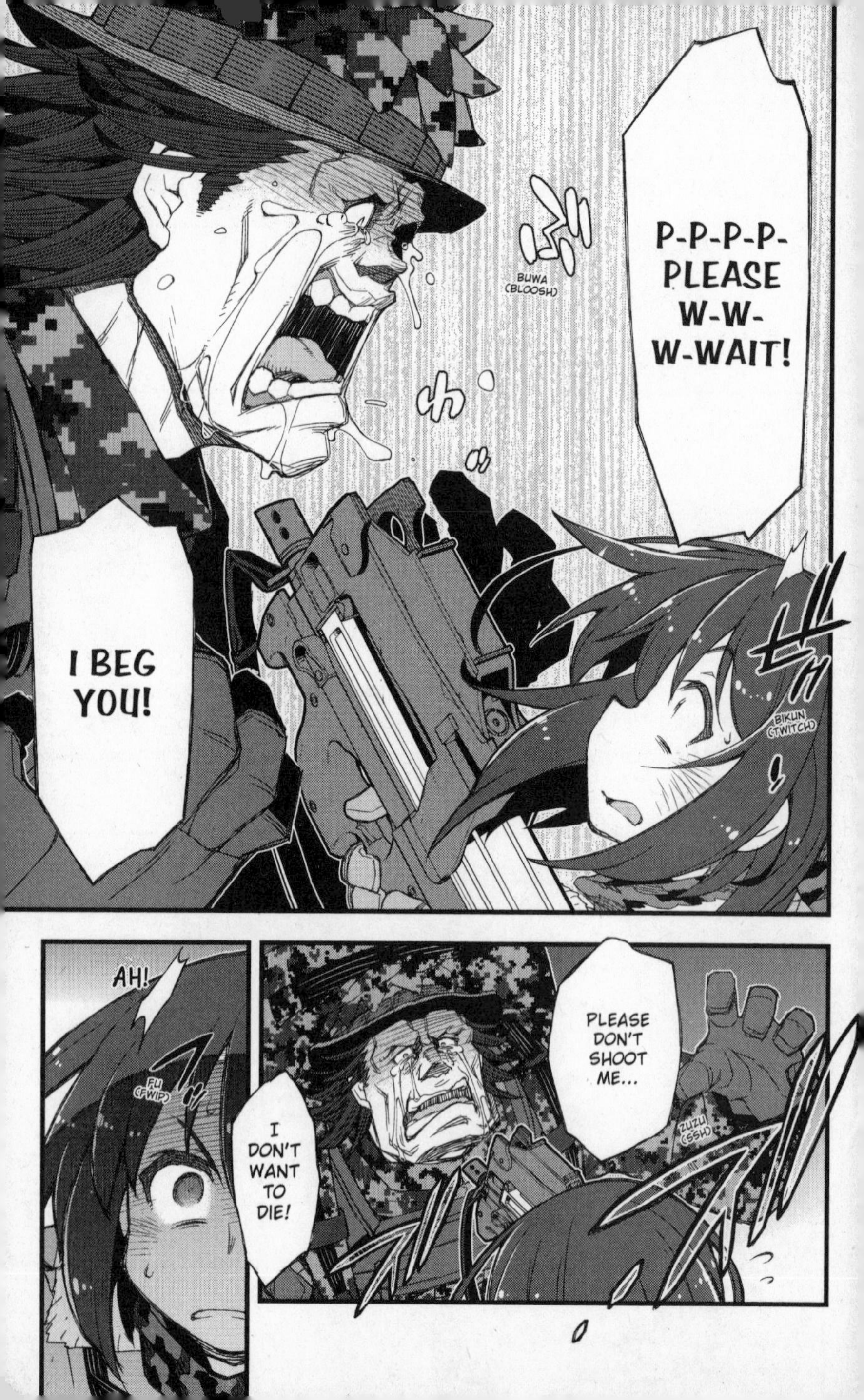
P-P-P-P-PLEASE W-W-W-WAIT!
BUWA (BLOOSH)
BIKUN (TWITCH)
I BEG YOU!
PLEASE DON'T SHOOT ME...
ZUZU (SSH)
I DON'T WANT TO DIE!
AH!
FU (FWIP)

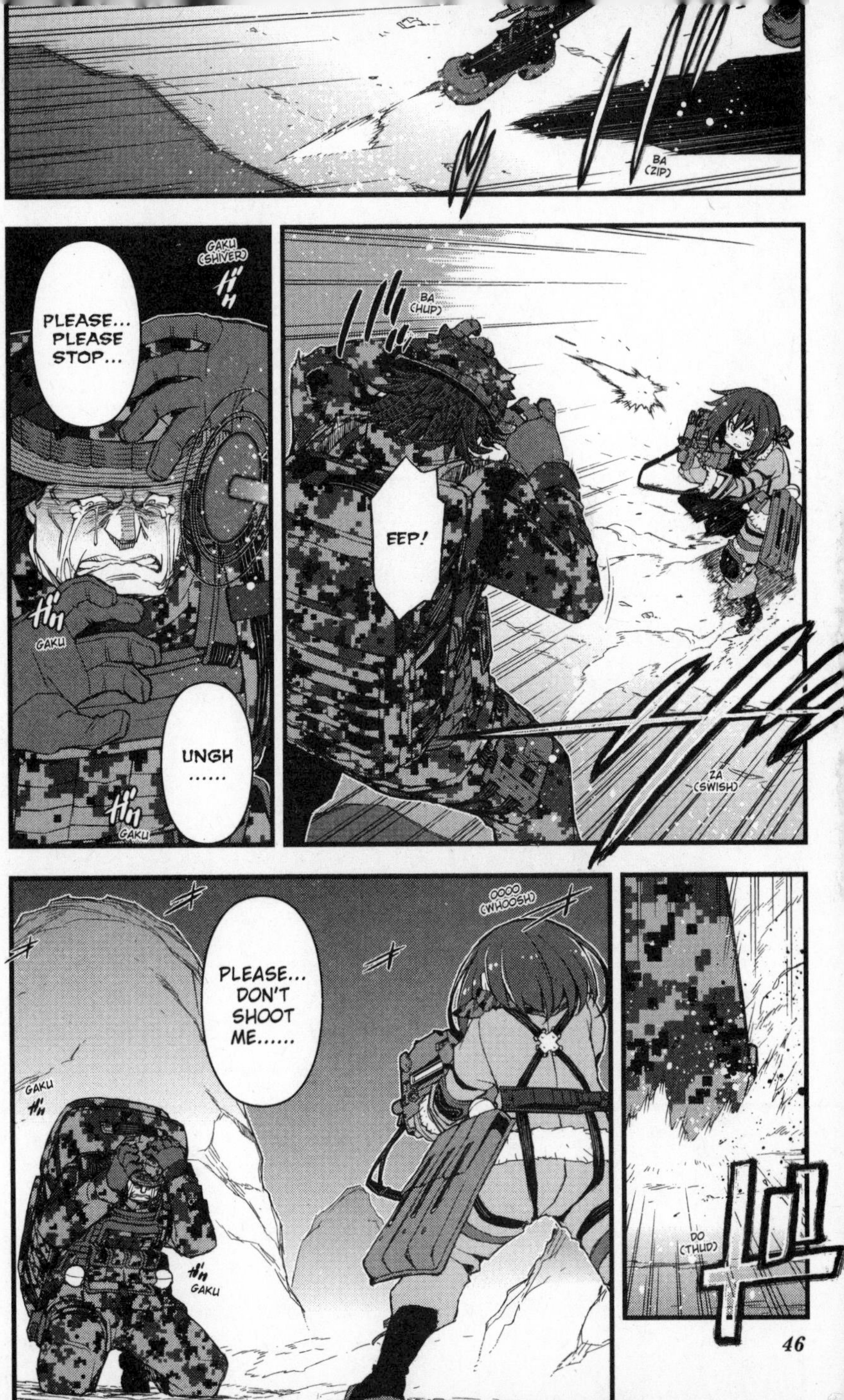
BA
(ZIP)
BA
(HUP)
EEP!
ZA
(SWISH)
GAKU
(SHIVER)
PLEASE... PLEASE STOP...
GAKU
UNGH ......
GAKU
DO
(THUD)
OOOO
(WHOOSH)
PLEASE... DON'T SHOOT ME......
GAKU
GAKU

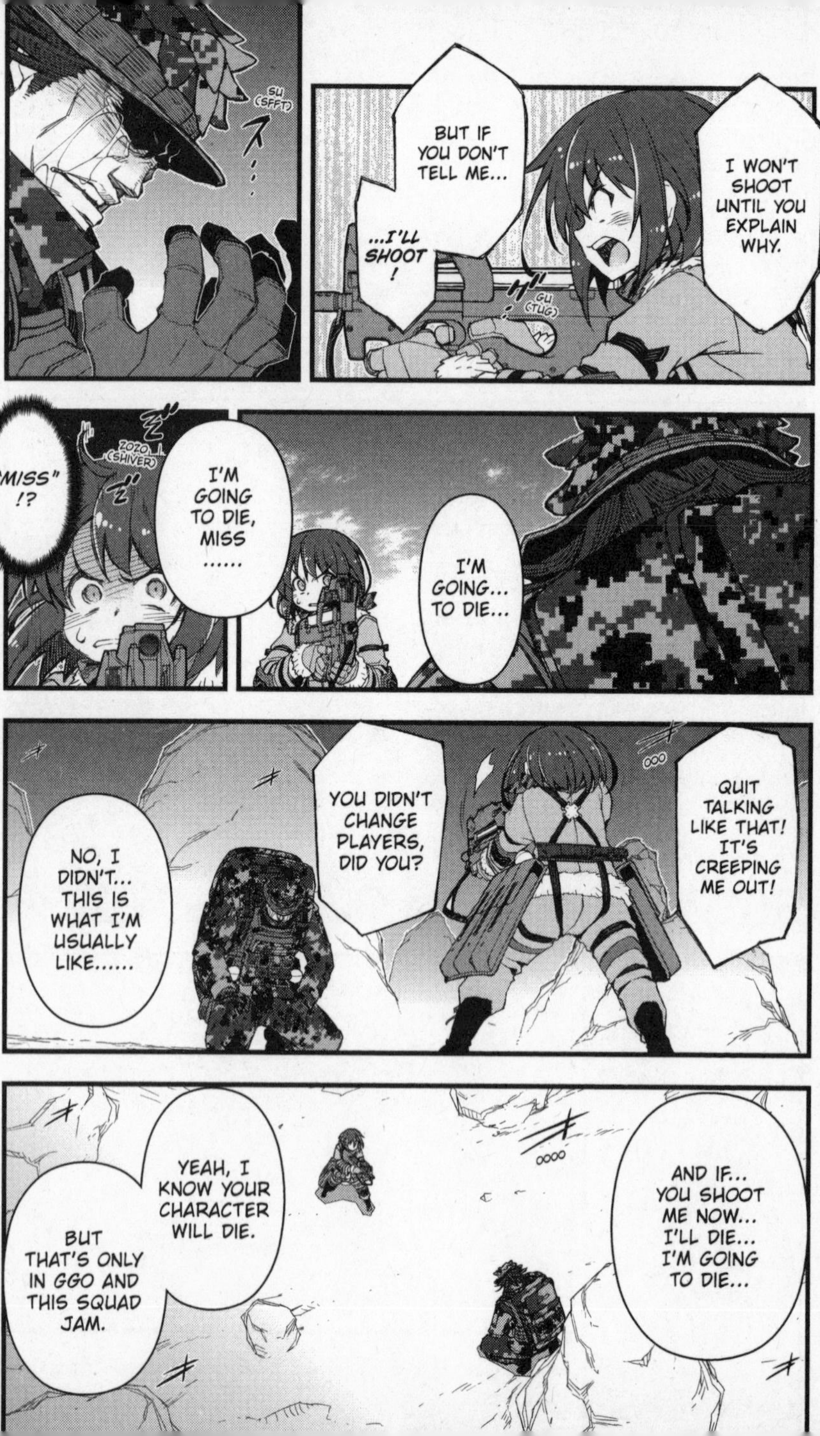
I WON'T SHOOT UNTIL YOU EXPLAIN WHY.
BUT IF YOU DON'T TELL ME...
...I'LL SHOOT!
GU (TUG)
SU (SFFT)
I'M GOING... TO DIE...
I'M GOING TO DIE, MISS ......
ZOZO (SHIVER)
"MISS" !?
QUIT TALKING LIKE THAT! IT'S CREEPING ME OUT!
YOU DIDN'T CHANGE PLAYERS, DID YOU?
NO, I DIDN'T... THIS IS WHAT I'M USUALLY LIKE......
AND IF... YOU SHOOT ME NOW... I'LL DIE... I'M GOING TO DIE...
YEAH, I KNOW YOUR CHARACTER WILL DIE.
BUT THAT'S ONLY IN GGO AND THIS SQUAD JAM.

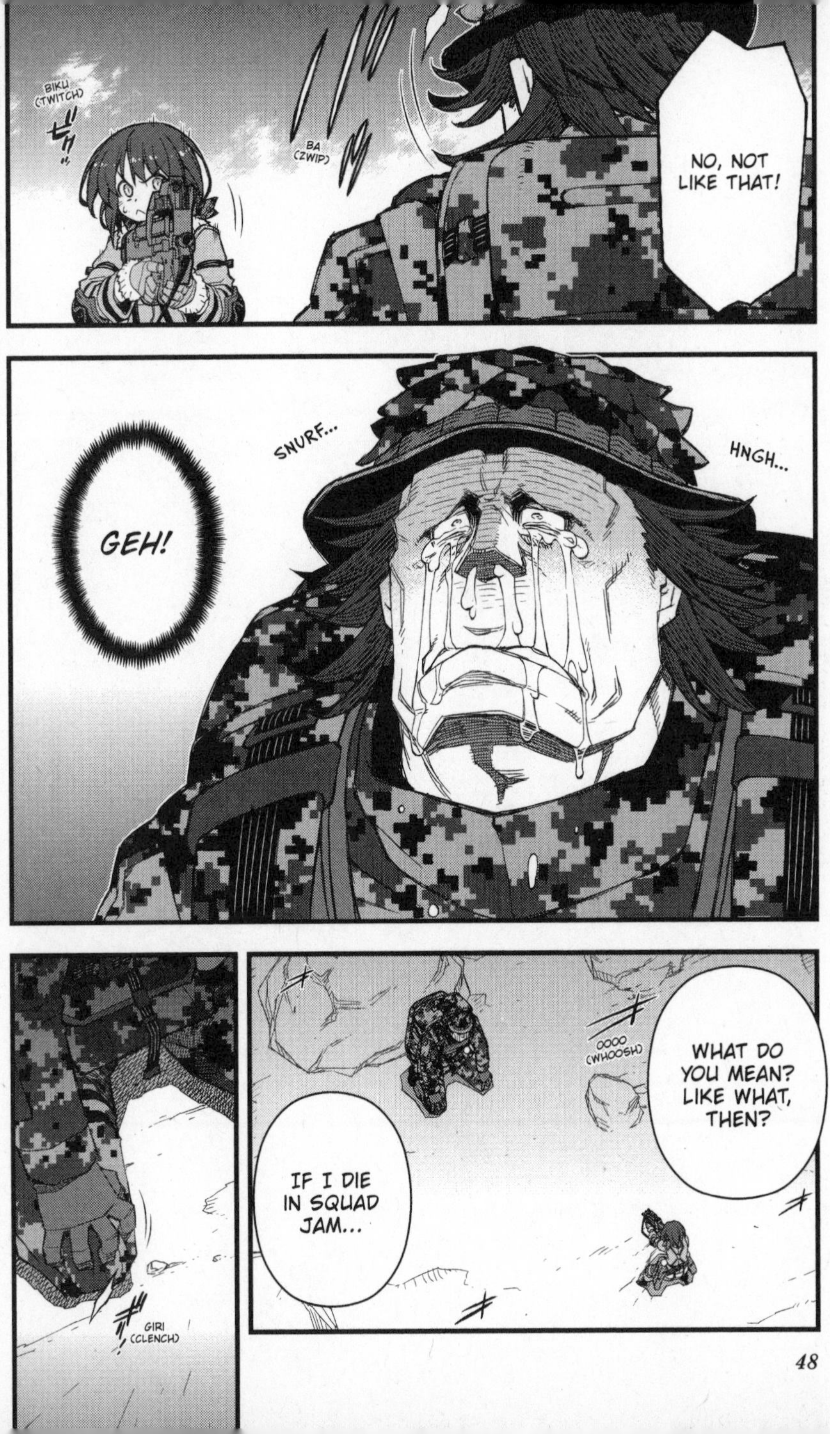
NO, NOT LIKE THAT!
BA (ZWIP)
BIKU (TWITCH)
HNGH...
SNURF...
GEH!
WHAT DO YOU MEAN? LIKE WHAT, THEN?
OOOO (WHOOSH)
IF I DIE IN SQUAD JAM...
GIRI (CLENCH)

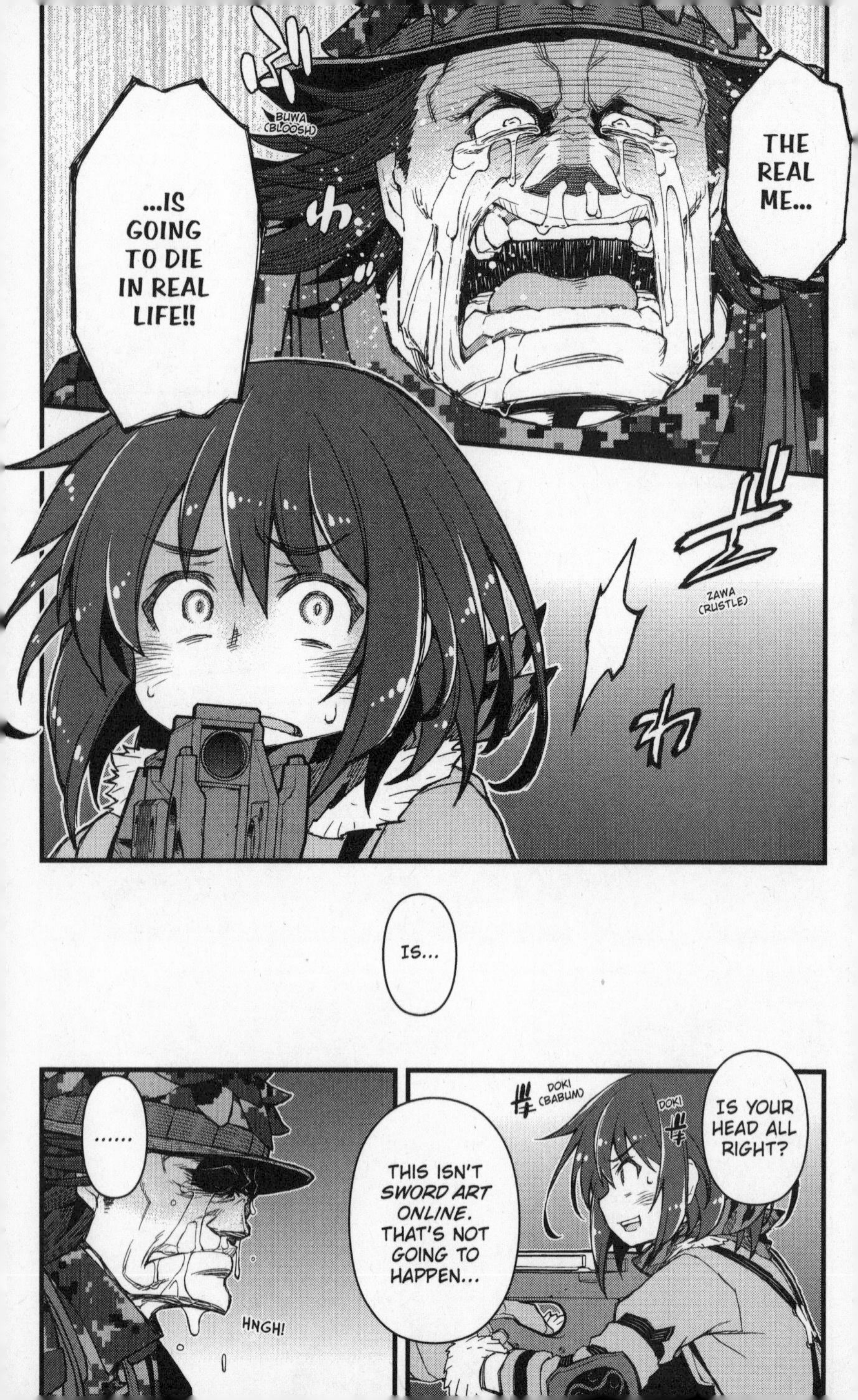
THE REAL ME...
BUWA (BLOOSH)
...IS GOING TO DIE IN REAL LIFE!!
ZAWA (RUSTLE)
IS...
IS YOUR HEAD ALL RIGHT?
DOKI
DOKI (BABUM)
THIS ISN'T *SWORD ART ONLINE*. THAT'S NOT GOING TO HAPPEN...
......
HNGH!

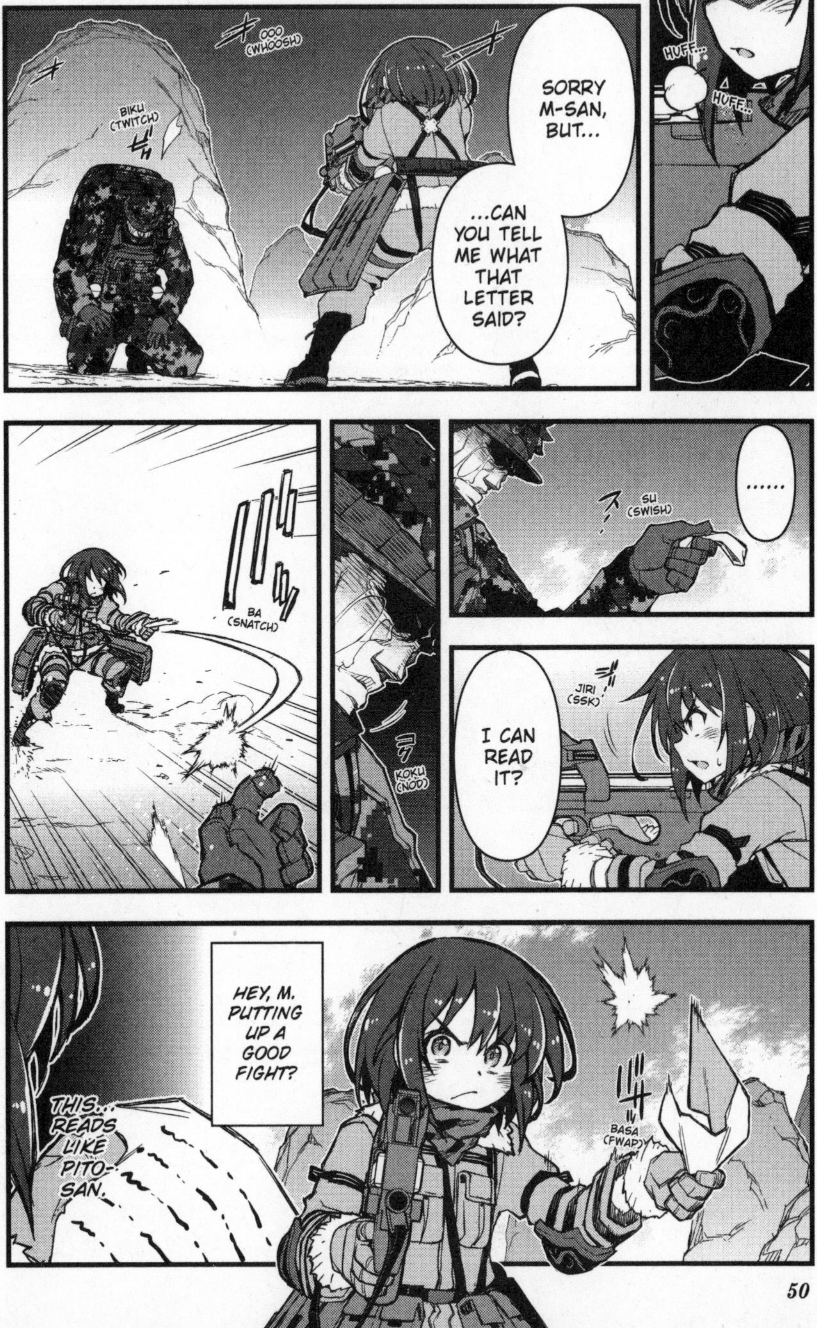
HUFF...
HUFF...
SORRY M-SAN, BUT...
...CAN YOU TELL ME WHAT THAT LETTER SAID?
OOO (WHOOSH)
BIKU (TWITCH)
......
SU (SWISH)
JIRI (SSK)
I CAN READ IT?
KOKU (NOD)
BA (SNATCH)
BASA (FWAP)
HEY, M. PUTTING UP A GOOD FIGHT?
THIS... READS LIKE PITO-SAN.

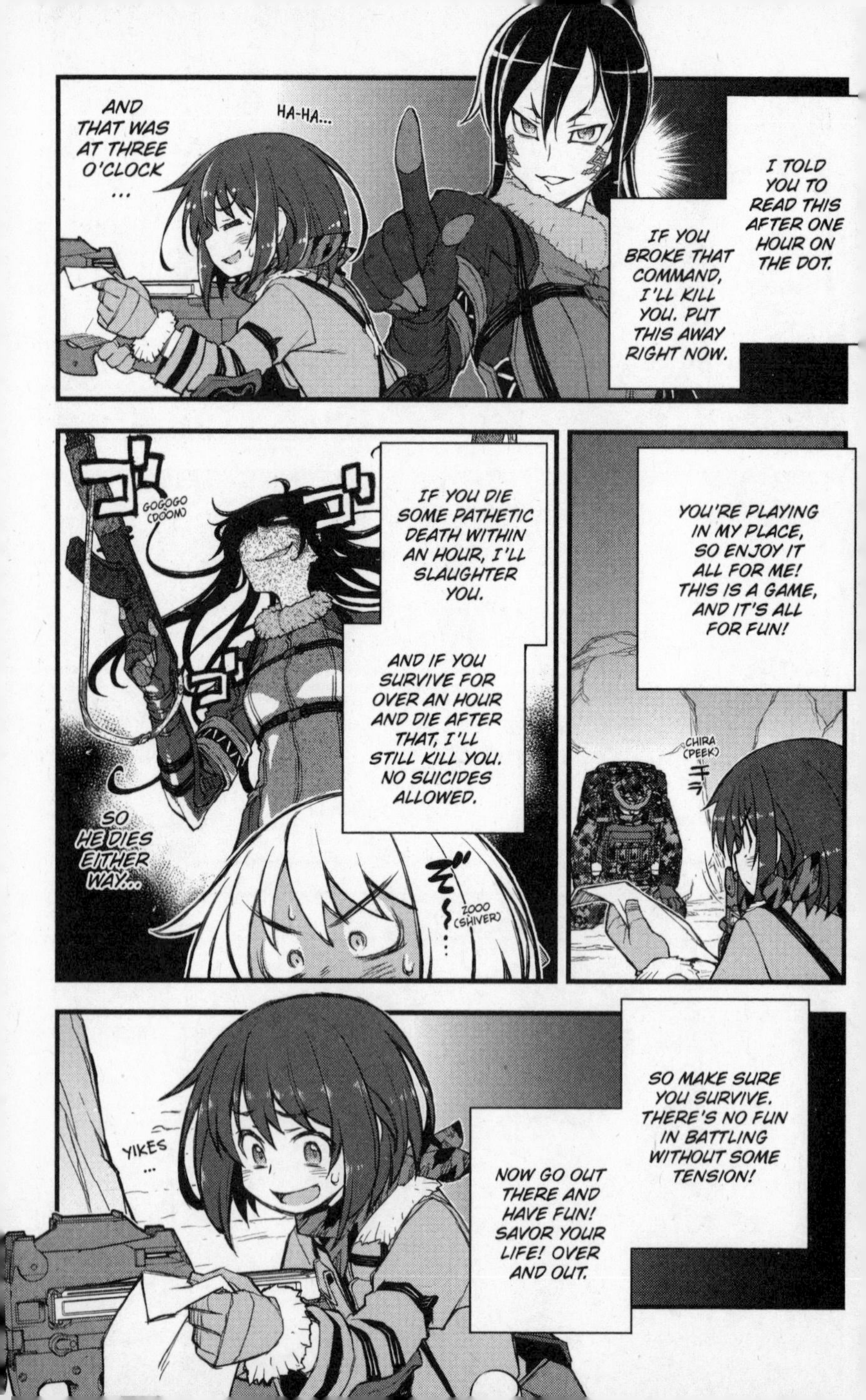
I TOLD YOU TO READ THIS AFTER ONE HOUR ON THE DOT.
IF YOU BROKE THAT COMMAND, I'LL KILL YOU. PUT THIS AWAY RIGHT NOW.
HA-HA...
AND THAT WAS AT THREE O'CLOCK ...
YOU'RE PLAYING IN MY PLACE, SO ENJOY IT ALL FOR ME! THIS IS A GAME, AND IT'S ALL FOR FUN!
CHIRA (PEEK)
IF YOU DIE SOME PATHETIC DEATH WITHIN AN HOUR, I'LL SLAUGHTER YOU.
AND IF YOU SURVIVE FOR OVER AN HOUR AND DIE AFTER THAT, I'LL STILL KILL YOU. NO SUICIDES ALLOWED.
GOGOGO (DOOM)
SO HE DIES EITHER WAY...
ZOOO (SHIVER)
SO MAKE SURE YOU SURVIVE. THERE'S NO FUN IN BATTLING WITHOUT SOME TENSION!
NOW GO OUT THERE AND HAVE FUN! SAVOR YOUR LIFE! OVER AND OUT.
YIKES ...

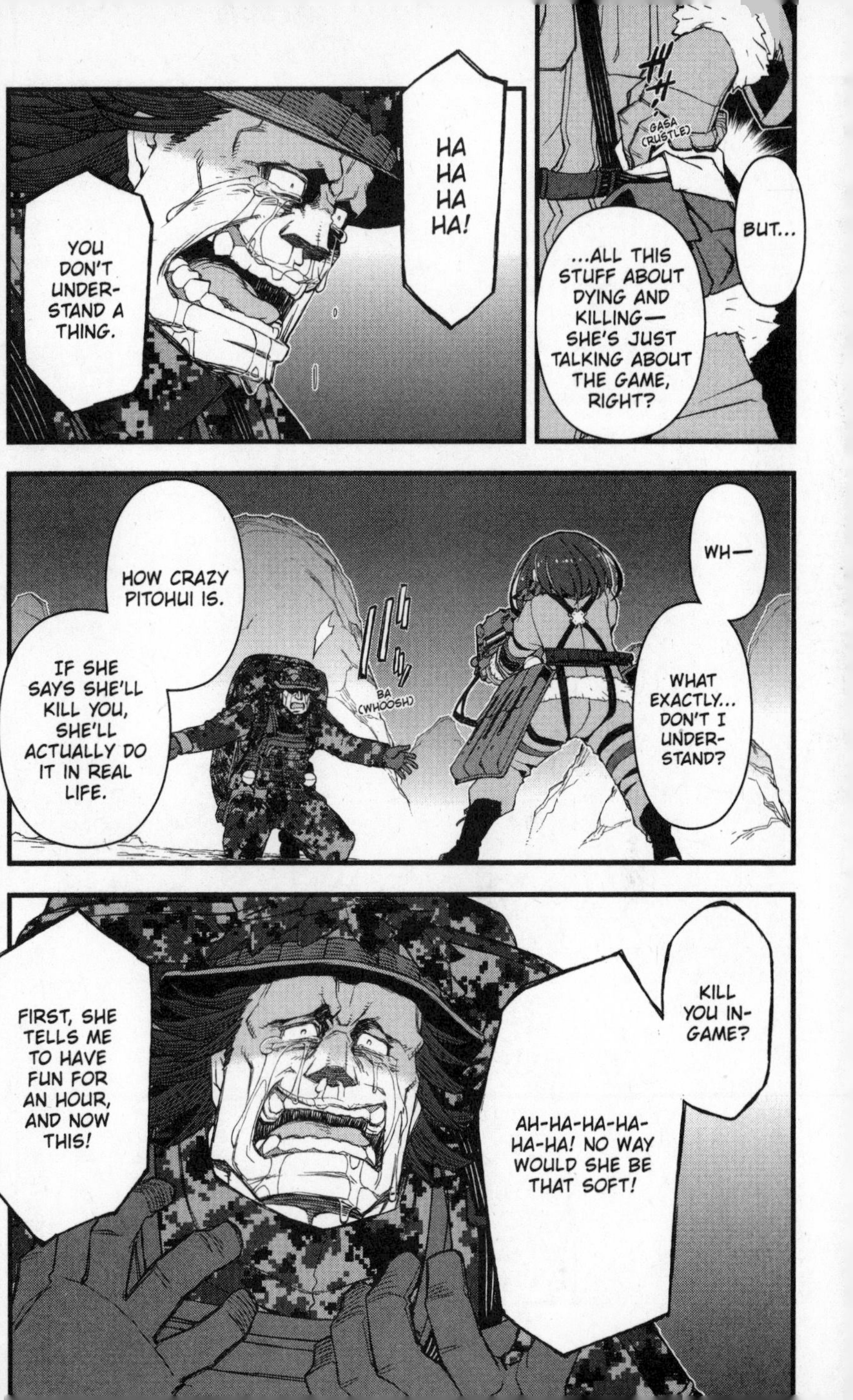

GASA (RUSTLE)
BUT...
...ALL THIS STUFF ABOUT DYING AND KILLING—SHE'S JUST TALKING ABOUT THE GAME, RIGHT?
HA HA HA HA!
YOU DON'T UNDER-STAND A THING.
WH—
WHAT EXACTLY... DON'T I UNDER-STAND?
BA (WHOOSH)
HOW CRAZY PITOHUI IS.
IF SHE SAYS SHE'LL KILL YOU, SHE'LL ACTUALLY DO IT IN REAL LIFE.
KILL YOU IN-GAME?
AH-HA-HA-HA-HA-HA! NO WAY WOULD SHE BE THAT SOFT!
FIRST, SHE TELLS ME TO HAVE FUN FOR AN HOUR, AND NOW THIS!

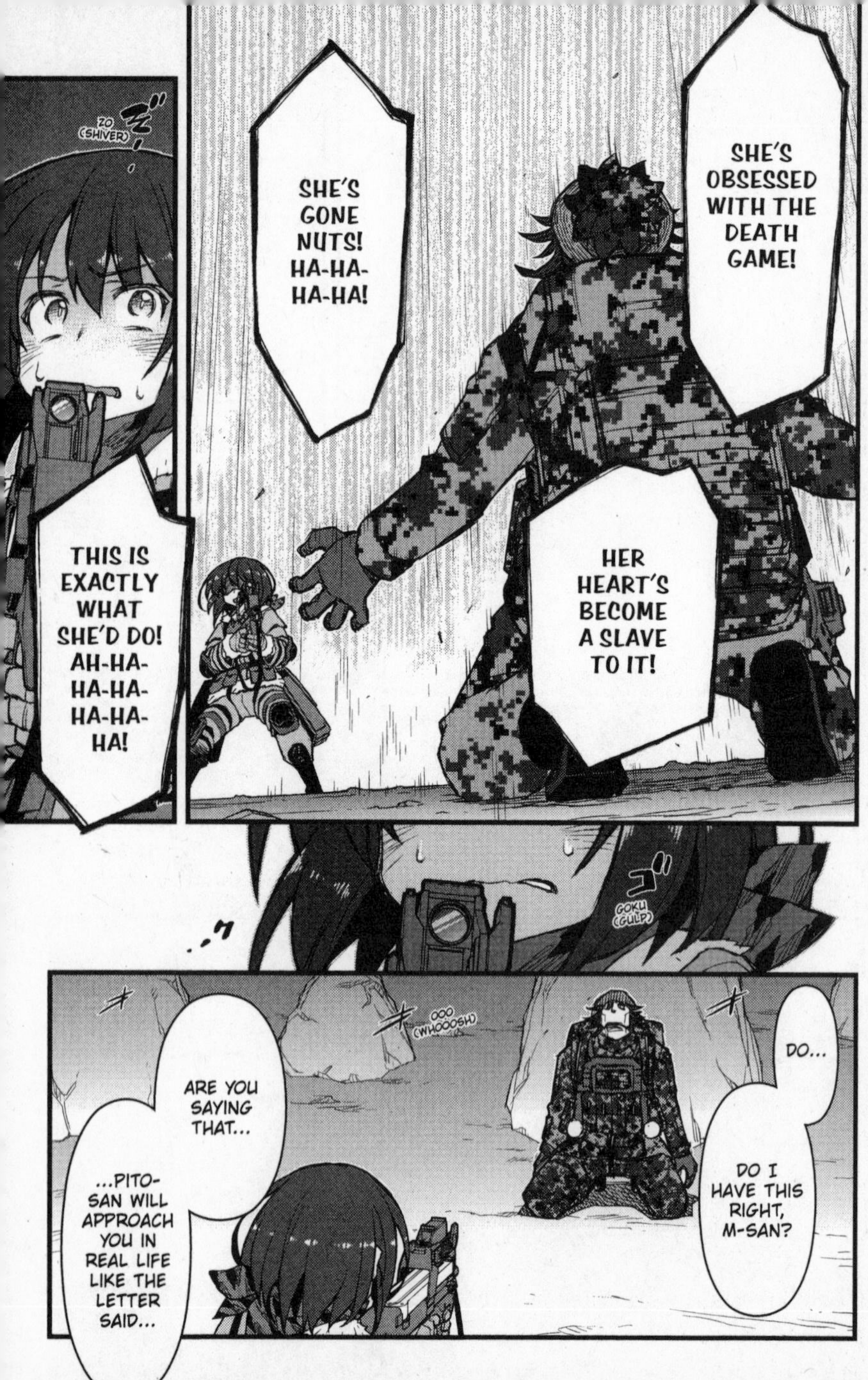
SHE'S OBSESSED WITH THE DEATH GAME!
SHE'S GONE NUTS! HA-HA-HA-HA!
HER HEART'S BECOME A SLAVE TO IT!
ZO (SHIVER)
THIS IS EXACTLY WHAT SHE'D DO! AH-HA-HA-HA-HA-HA-HA!
GOKU (GULP)
DO...
DO I HAVE THIS RIGHT, M-SAN?
OOO (WHOOOSH)
ARE YOU SAYING THAT...
...PITO-SAN WILL APPROACH YOU IN REAL LIFE LIKE THE LETTER SAID...

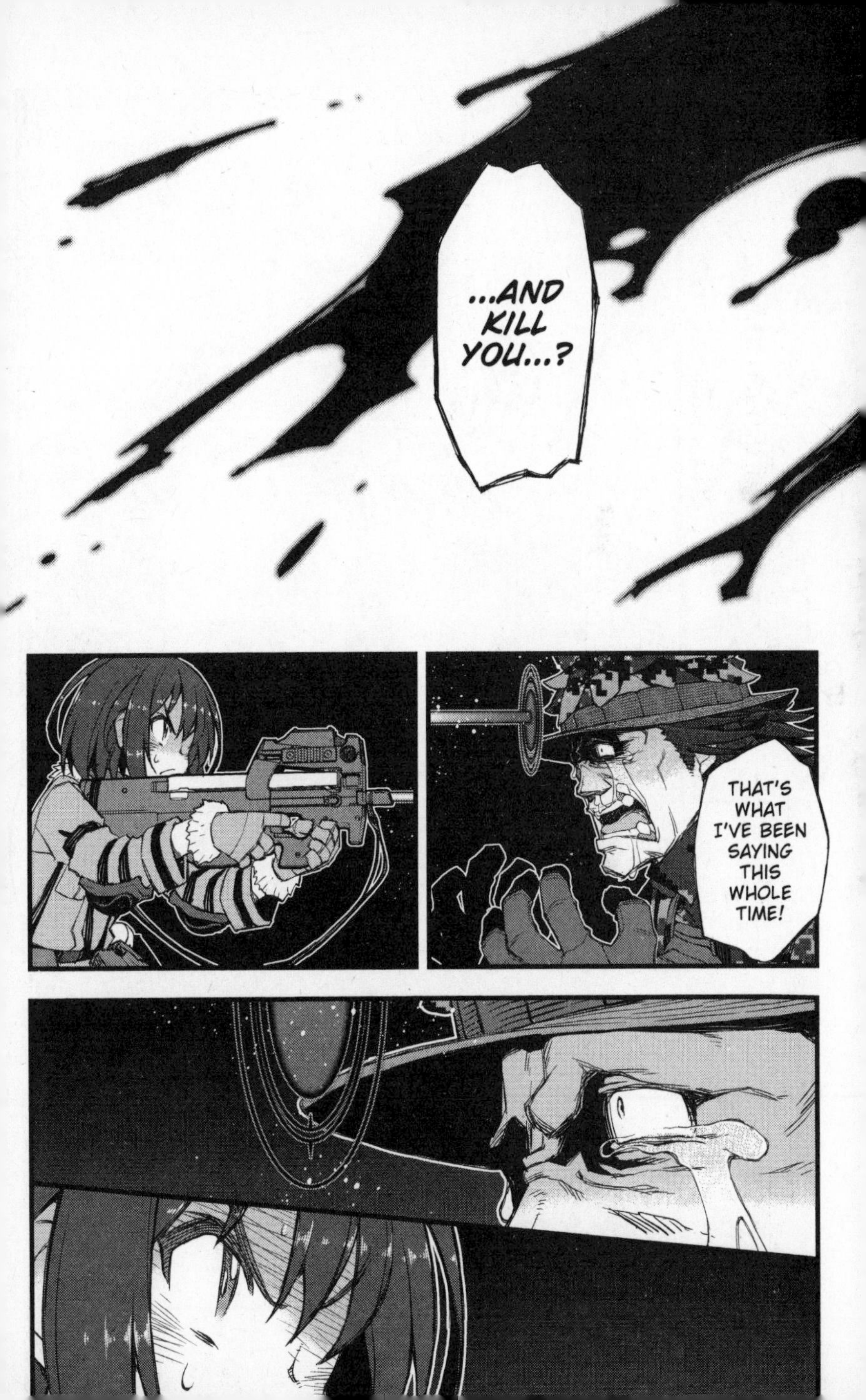
...AND KILL YOU...?
THAT'S WHAT I'VE BEEN SAYING THIS WHOLE TIME!

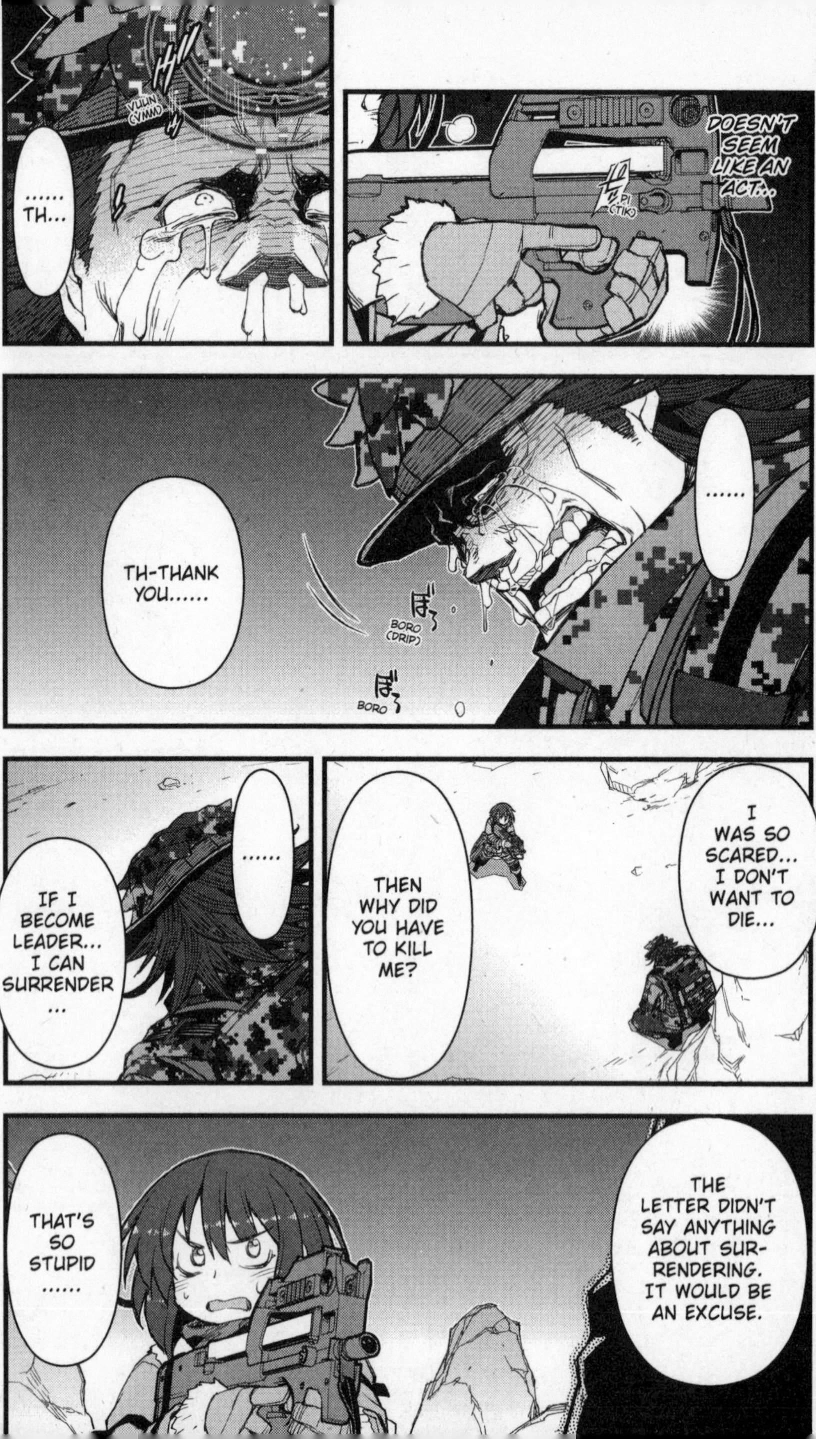
DOESN'T SEEM LIKE AN ACT...
PI (TIK)
VUUN (VMM)
...... TH...
......
TH-THANK YOU......
ぼろ
BORO (DRIP)
ぼろ
BORO
I WAS SO SCARED... I DON'T WANT TO DIE...
THEN WHY DID YOU HAVE TO KILL ME?
......
IF I BECOME LEADER... I CAN SURRENDER ...
THE LETTER DIDN'T SAY ANYTHING ABOUT SUR-RENDERING. IT WOULD BE AN EXCUSE.
THAT'S SO STUPID ......

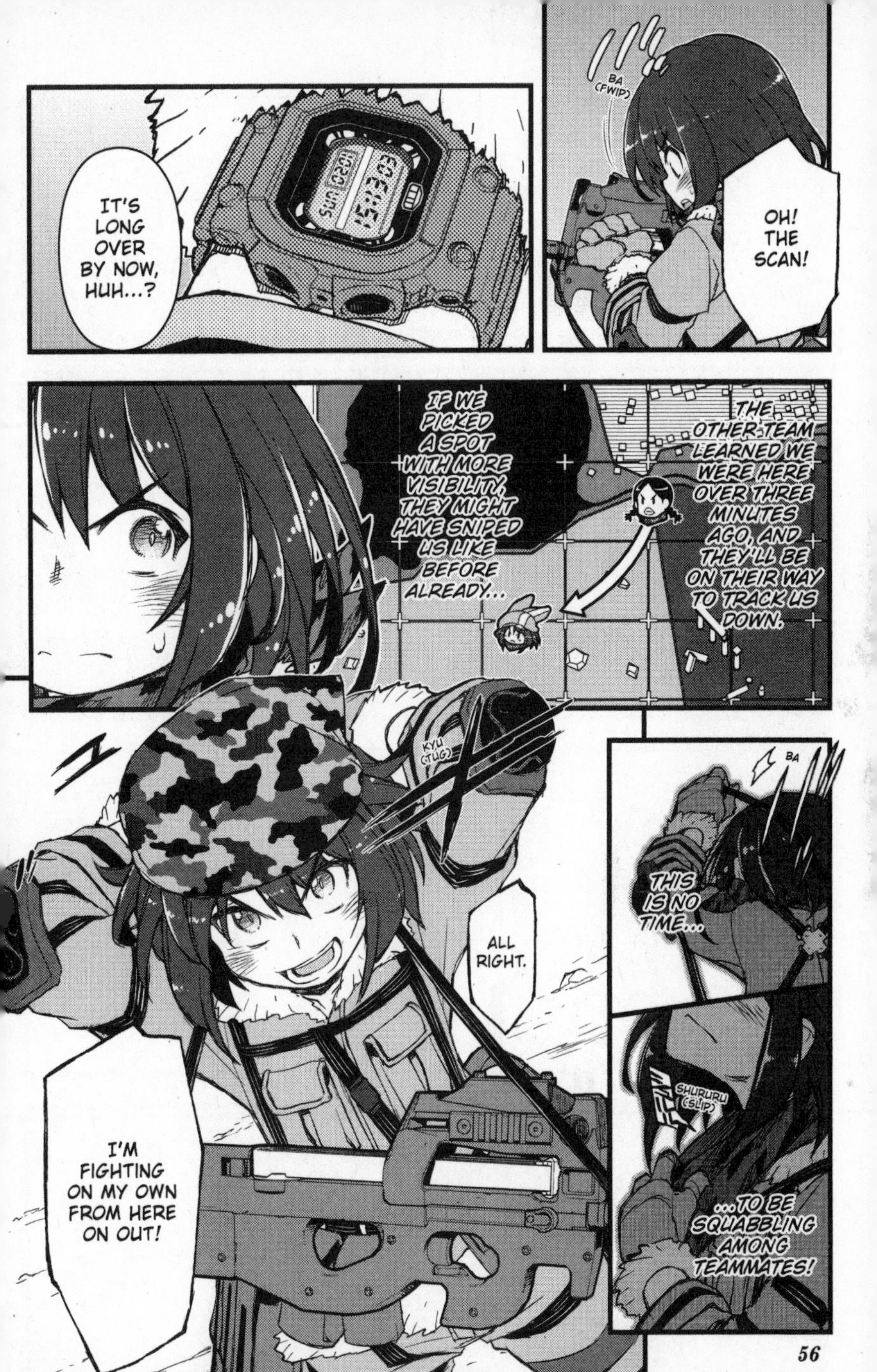
BA (FWIP)
OH! THE SCAN!
IT'S LONG OVER BY NOW, HUH...?
THE OTHER TEAM LEARNED WE WERE HERE OVER THREE MINUTES AGO, AND THEY'LL BE ON THEIR WAY TO TRACK US DOWN.
IF WE PICKED A SPOT WITH MORE VISIBILITY, THEY MIGHT HAVE SNIPED US LIKE BEFORE ALREADY...
BA
THIS IS NO TIME...
SHURURU (SLIP)
...TO BE SQUABBLING AMONG TEAMMATES!
KYU (TUG)
ALL RIGHT.
I'M FIGHTING ON MY OWN FROM HERE ON OUT!

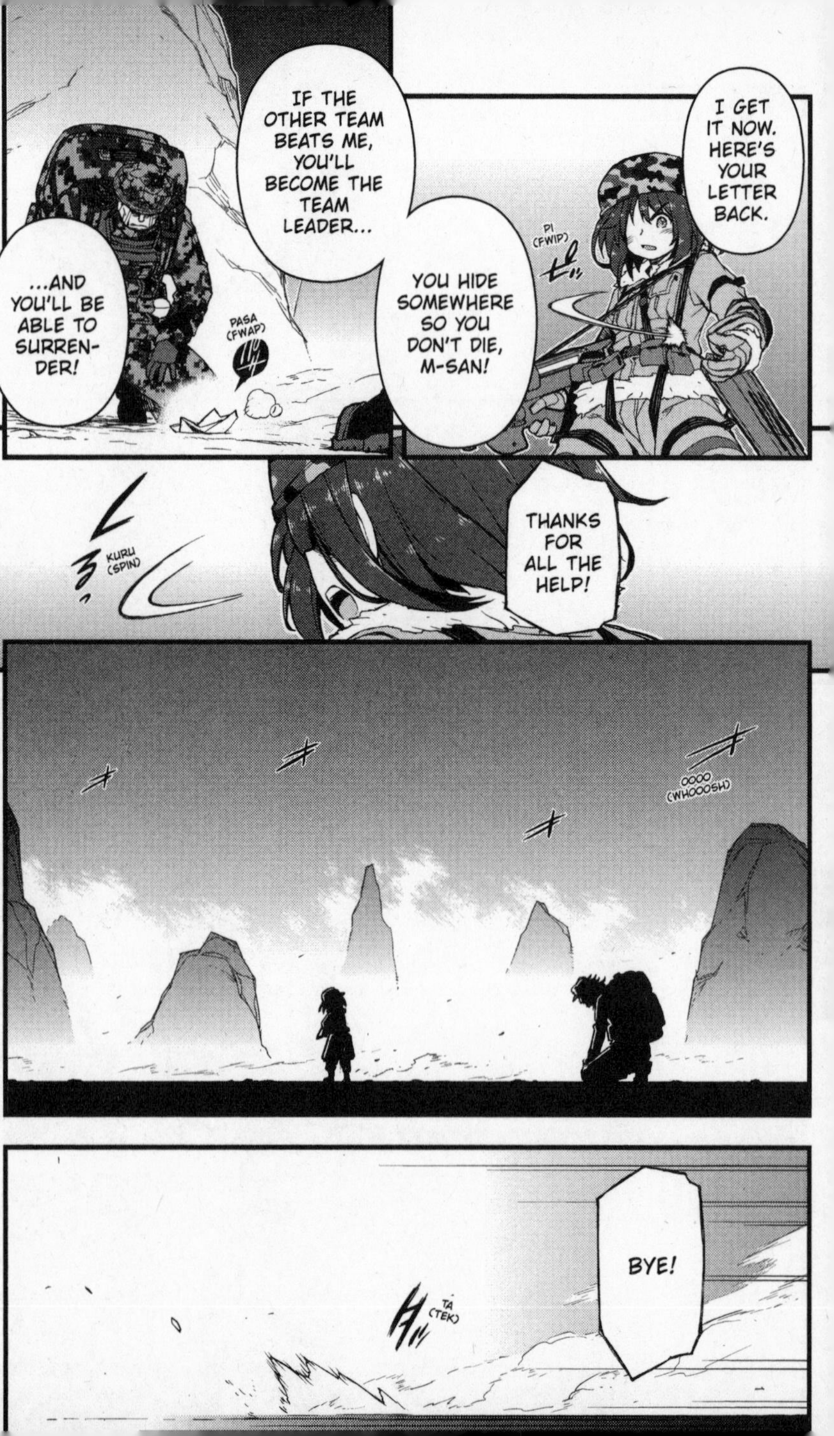
I GET IT NOW. HERE'S YOUR LETTER BACK.
PI (FWIP)
YOU HIDE SOMEWHERE SO YOU DON'T DIE, M-SAN!
IF THE OTHER TEAM BEATS ME, YOU'LL BECOME THE TEAM LEADER...
...AND YOU'LL BE ABLE TO SURREN-DER!
PASA (FWAP)
THANKS FOR ALL THE HELP!
KURU (SPIN)
OOOO (WHOOOSH)
BYE!
TA (TEK)

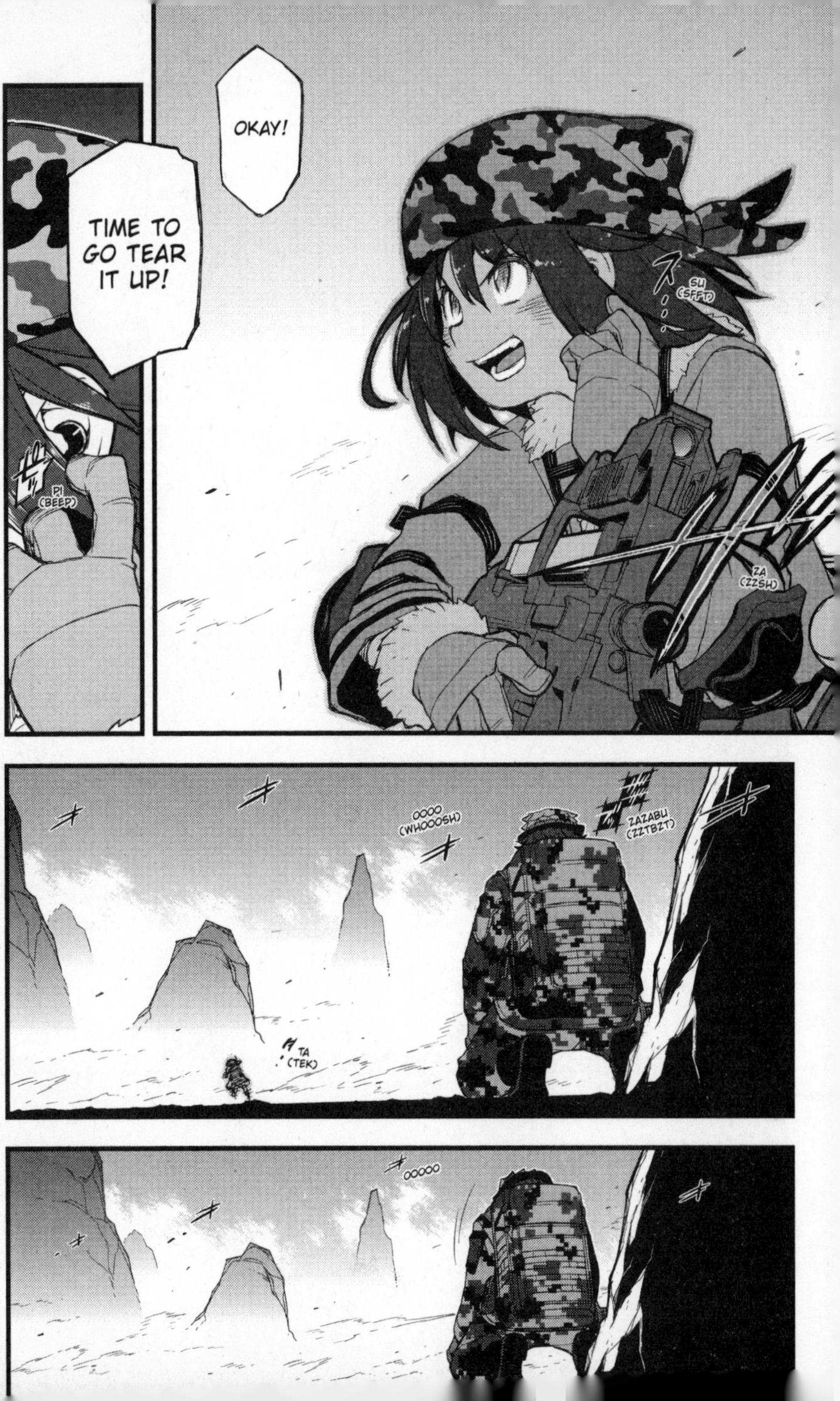
OKAY!
SU (SFFT)
ZA (ZZSH)
TIME TO GO TEAR IT UP!
PI (BEEP)
ZAZABU (ZZTBZT)
OOOO (WHOOOSH)
TA (TEK)
OOOOO

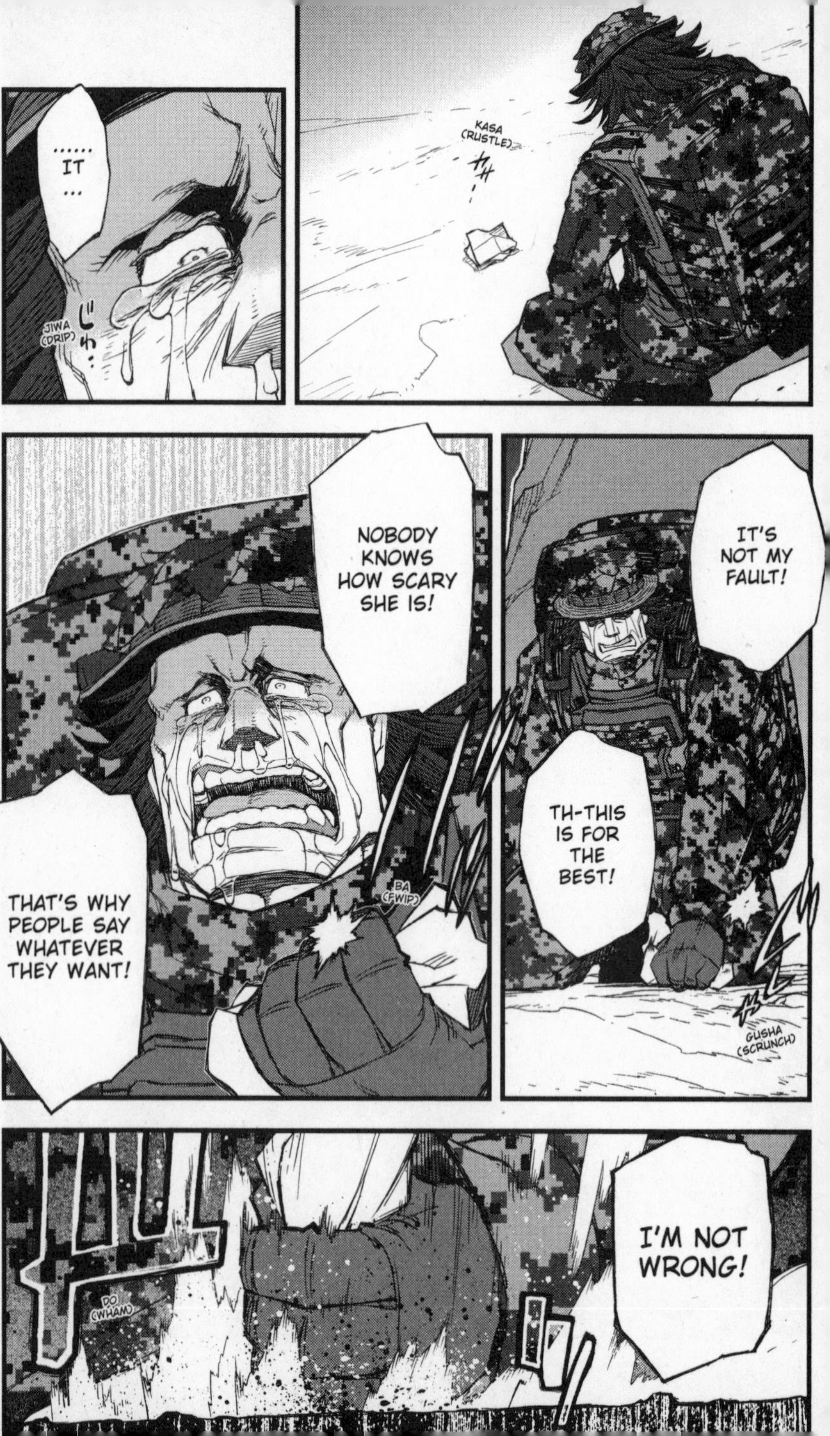
KASA (RUSTLE)
...... IT ...
JIWA (DRIP)
IT'S NOT MY FAULT!
TH-THIS IS FOR THE BEST!
GUSHA (SCRUNCH)
NOBODY KNOWS HOW SCARY SHE IS!
BA (FWIP)
THAT'S WHY PEOPLE SAY WHATEVER THEY WANT!
I'M NOT WRONG!
DO (WHAM)

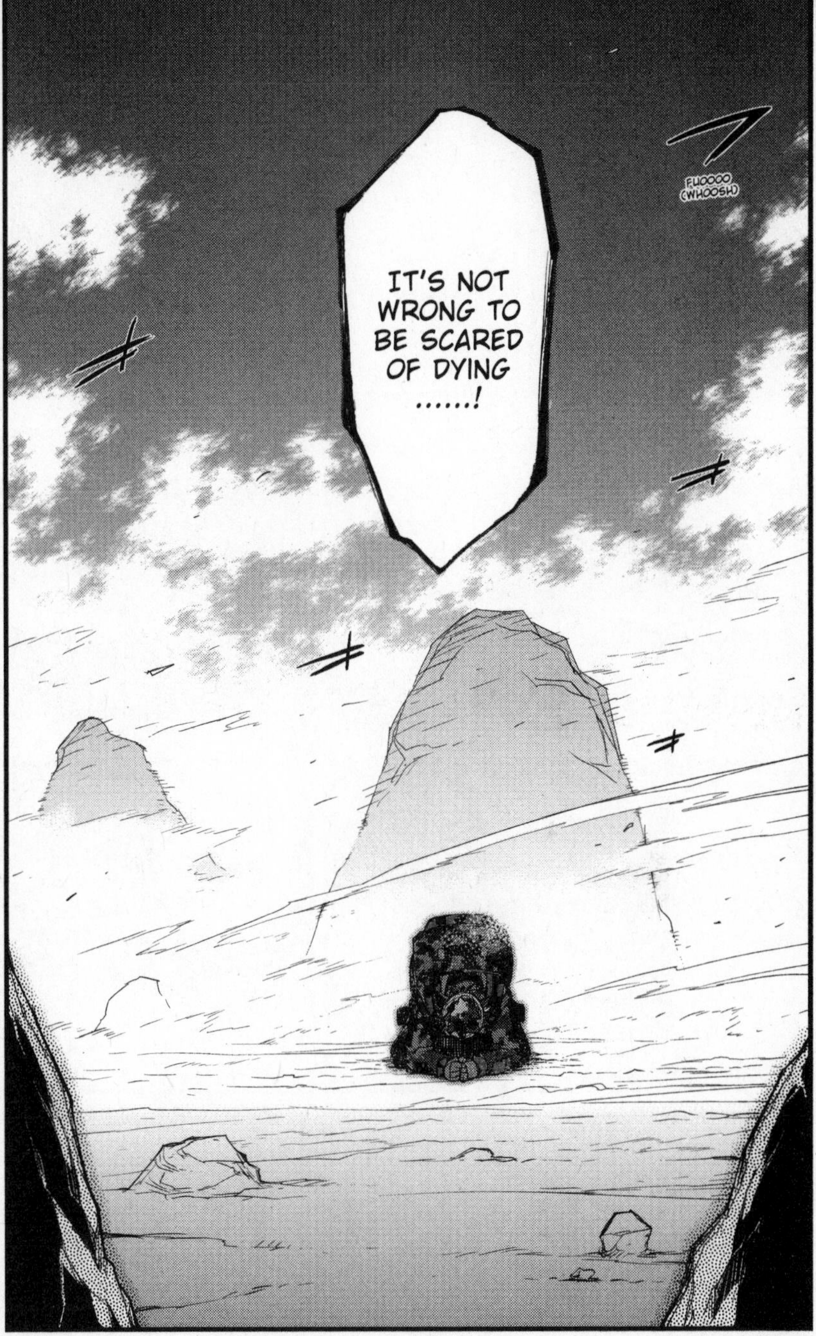
IT'S NOT WRONG TO BE SCARED OF DYING ......!
FUOOOO (WHOOSH)

LINK #014: SQUAD JAM ⑩

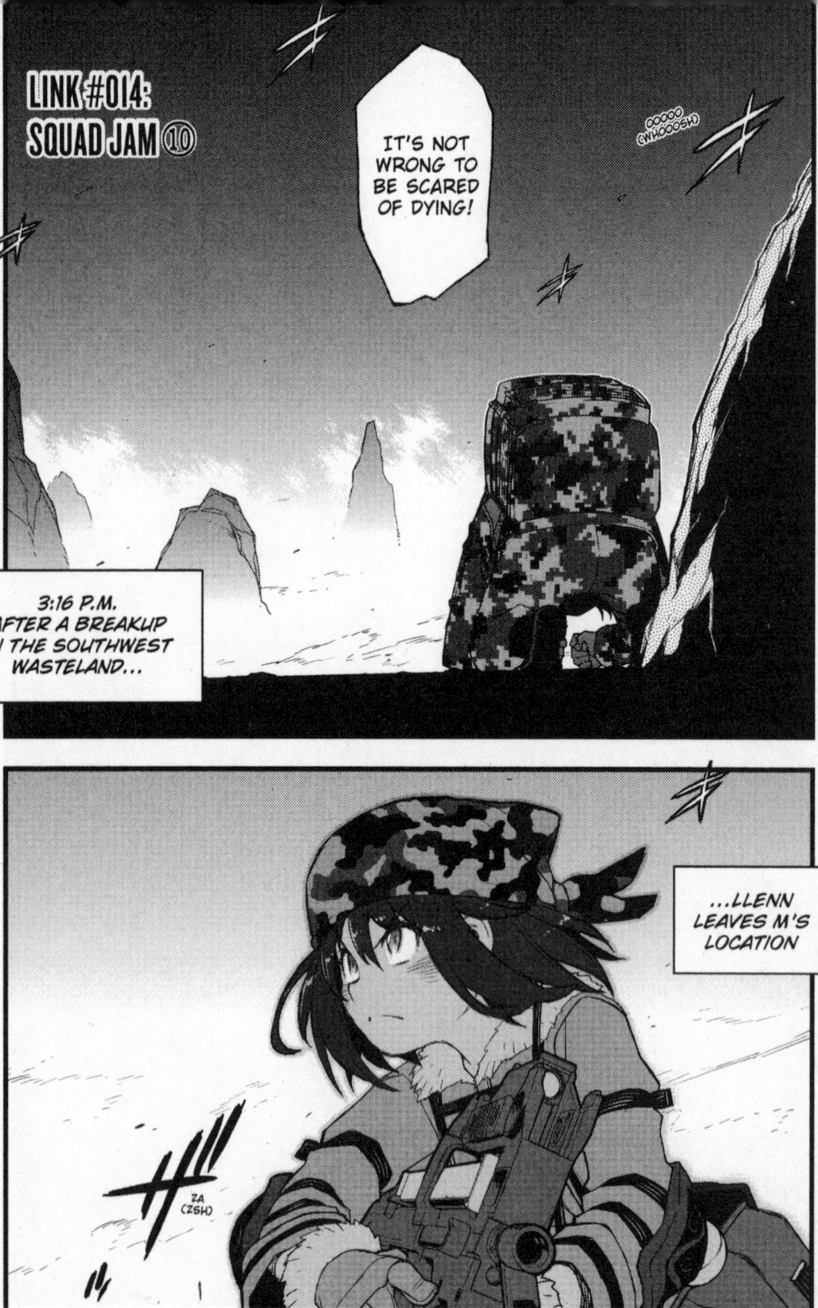

OOOOO (WHOOOSH)
IT'S NOT WRONG TO BE SCARED OF DYING!
3:16 P.M. AFTER A BREAKUP IN THE SOUTHWEST WASTELAND...
...LLENN LEAVES M'S LOCATION
ZA (ZSH)

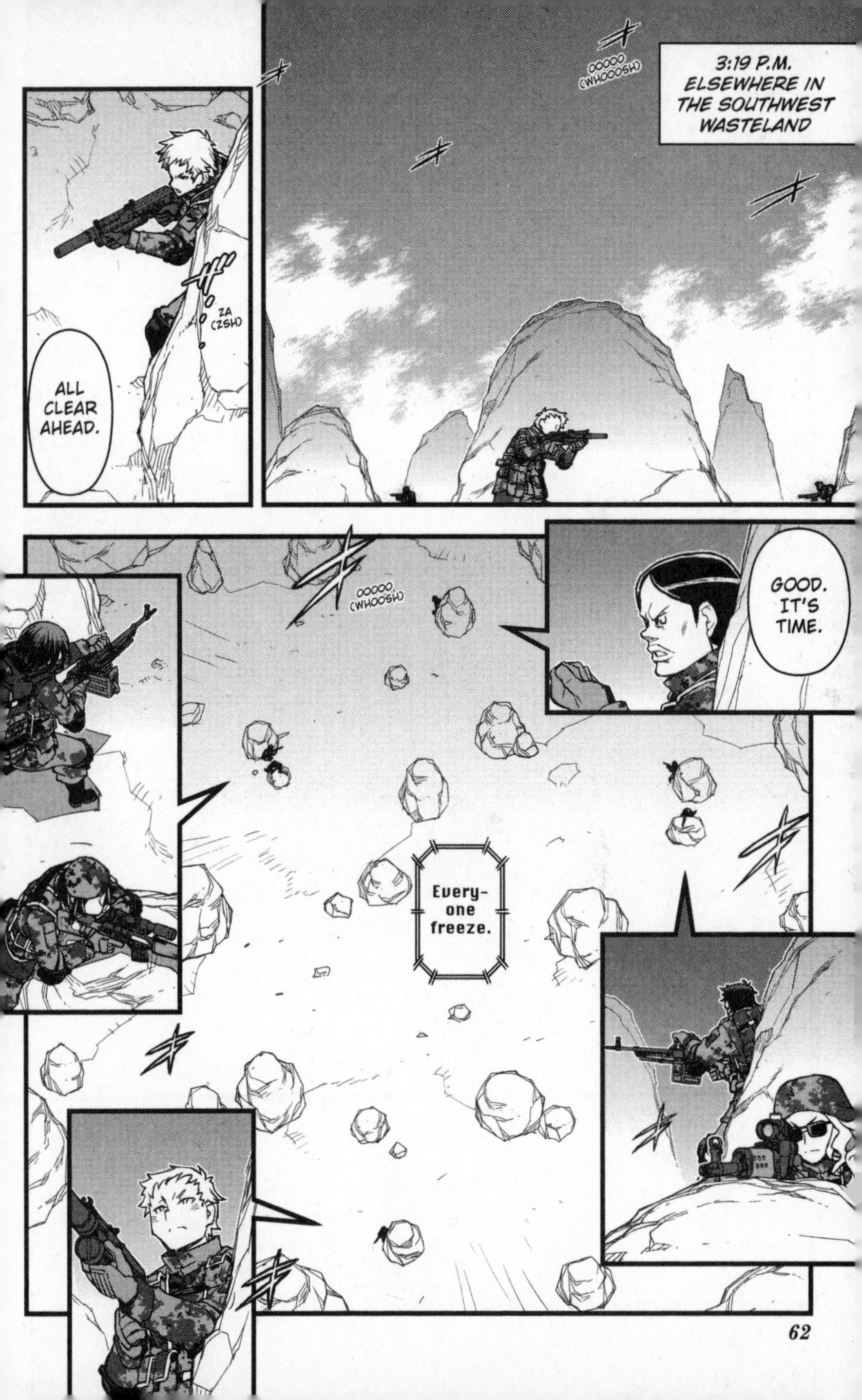
3:19 P.M. ELSEWHERE IN THE SOUTHWEST WASTELAND
OOOOO (WHOOOSH)
ZA (ZSH)
ALL CLEAR AHEAD.
GOOD. IT'S TIME.
OOOOO (WHOOSH)
Every-one freeze.

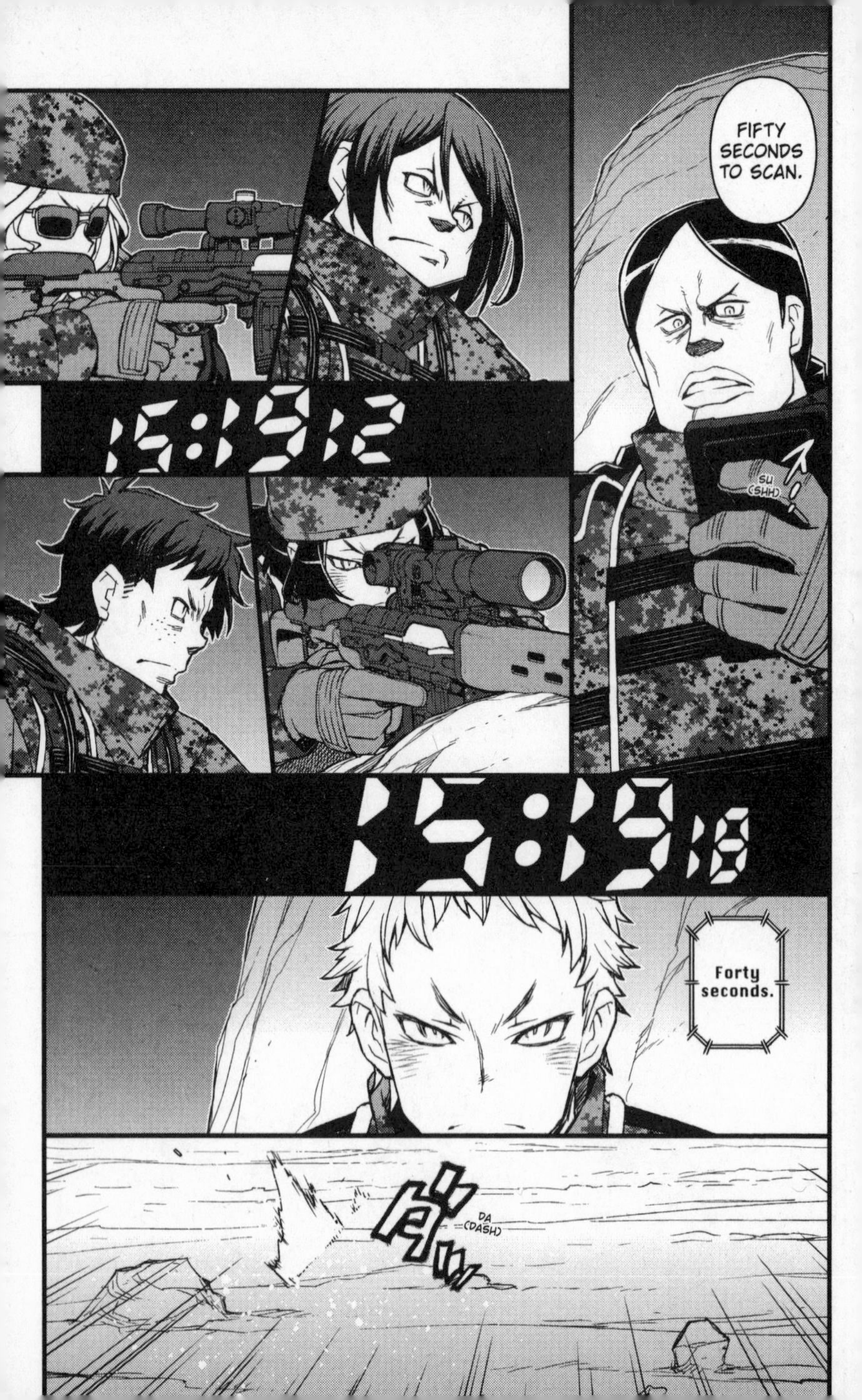
FIFTY SECONDS TO SCAN.
SU (SHH)
15:19:12
15:19:18
Forty seconds.
DA (DASH)

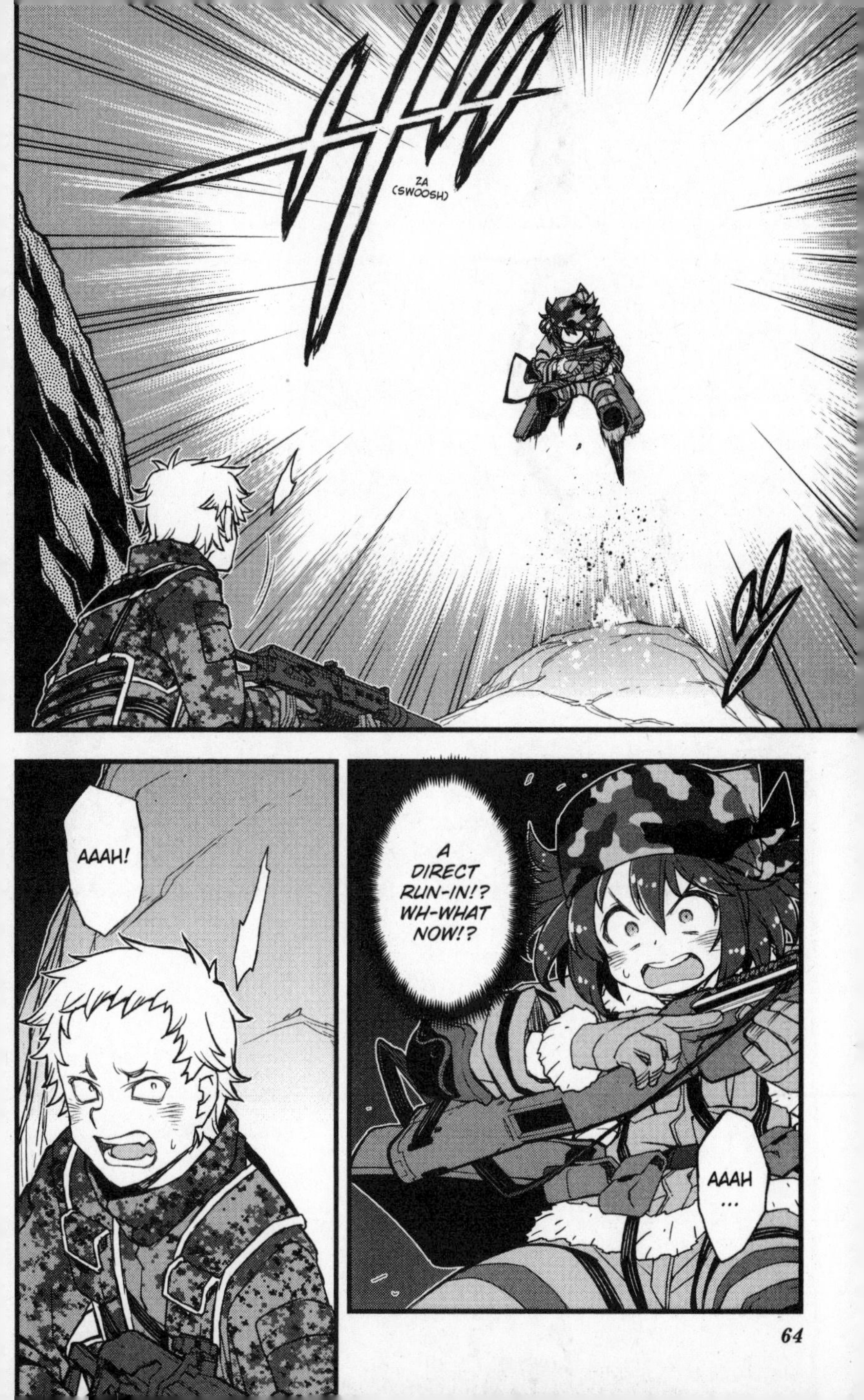
ZA
(SWOOSH)
A DIRECT RUN-IN!? WH-WHAT NOW!?
AAAH ...
AAAH!

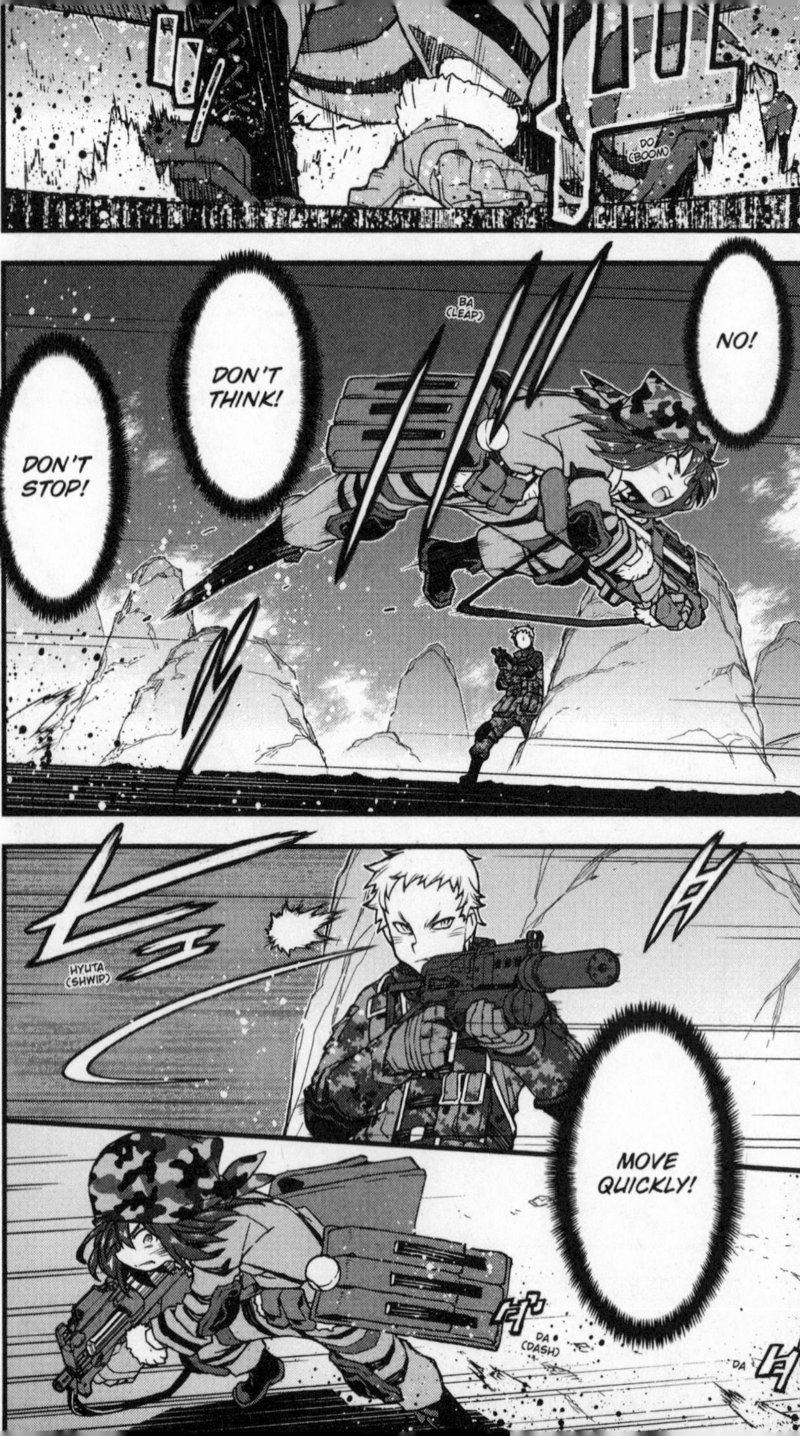
DO
(BOOM)
NO!
BA
(LEAP)
DON'T THINK!
DON'T STOP!
HYUTA
(SHWIP)
MOVE QUICKLY!
DA
(DASH)
DA

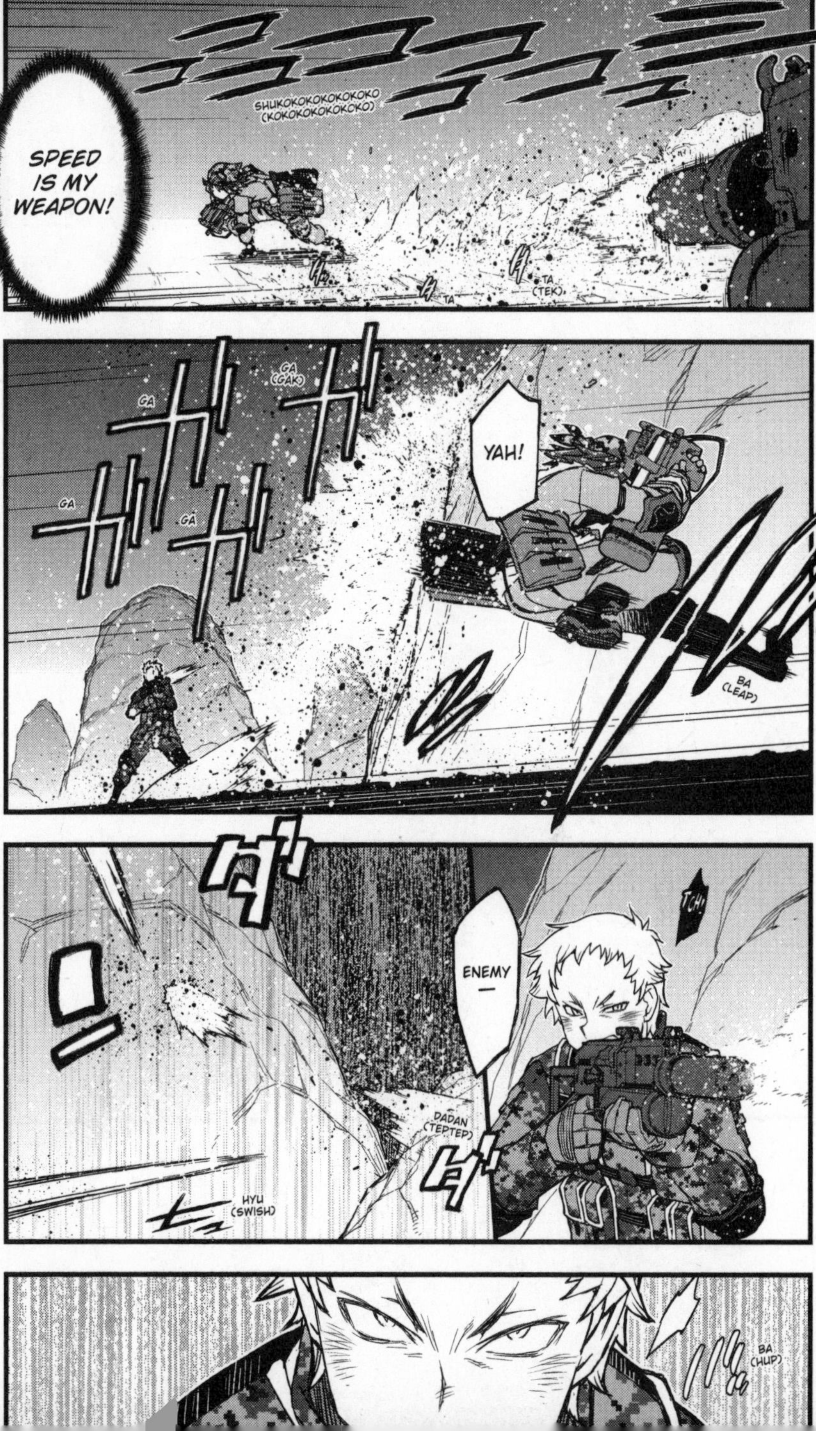
SHUKOKOKOKOKOKOKO
(KOKOKOKOKOKO)
SPEED IS MY WEAPON!
TA
(TEK)
TA
YAH!
BA
(LEAP)
GA
(GAK)
GA
GA
GA
TCH!
ENEMY
—
DADAN
(TEPTEP)
HYU
(SWISH)
BA
(HUP)

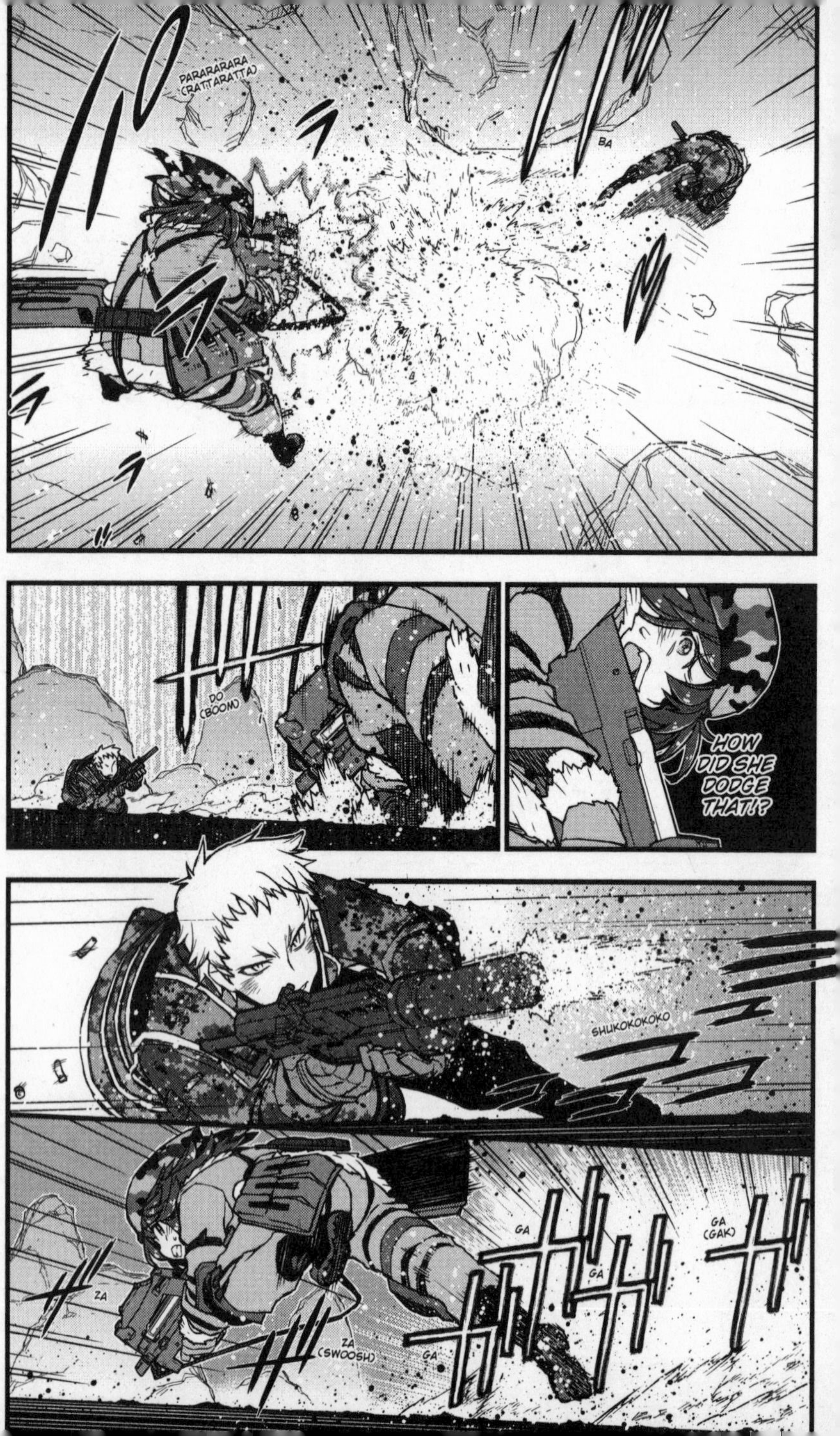
BA
PARARARARA (RATTARATTA)
HOW DID SHE DODGE THAT!?
DO (BOOM)
SHUKOKOKOKO
GA (GAK)
GA
GA
GA
ZA (SWOOSH)
ZA

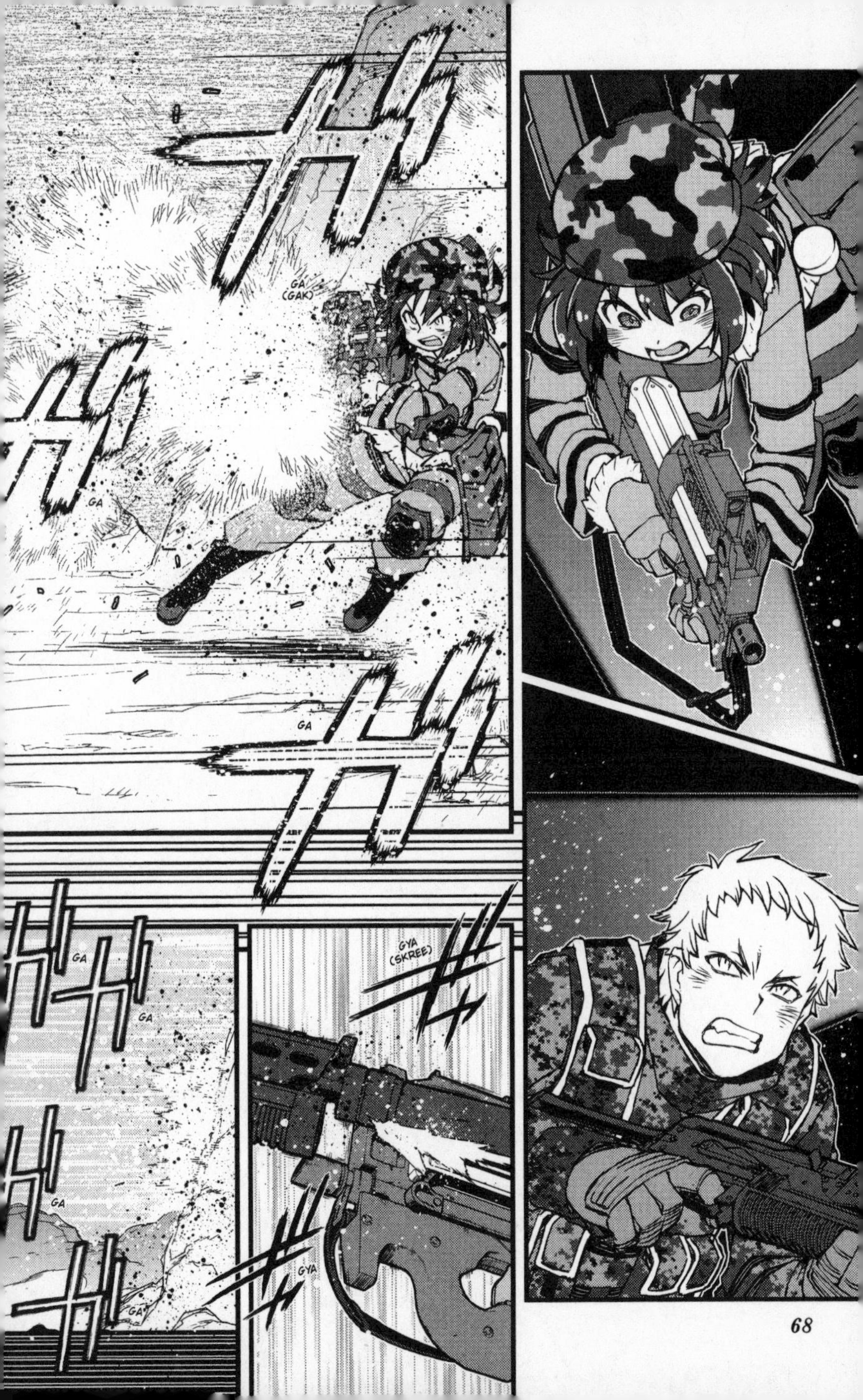
GA
(GAK)
GA
GA
GYA
(SKREE)
GYA
GA
GA
GA
GA

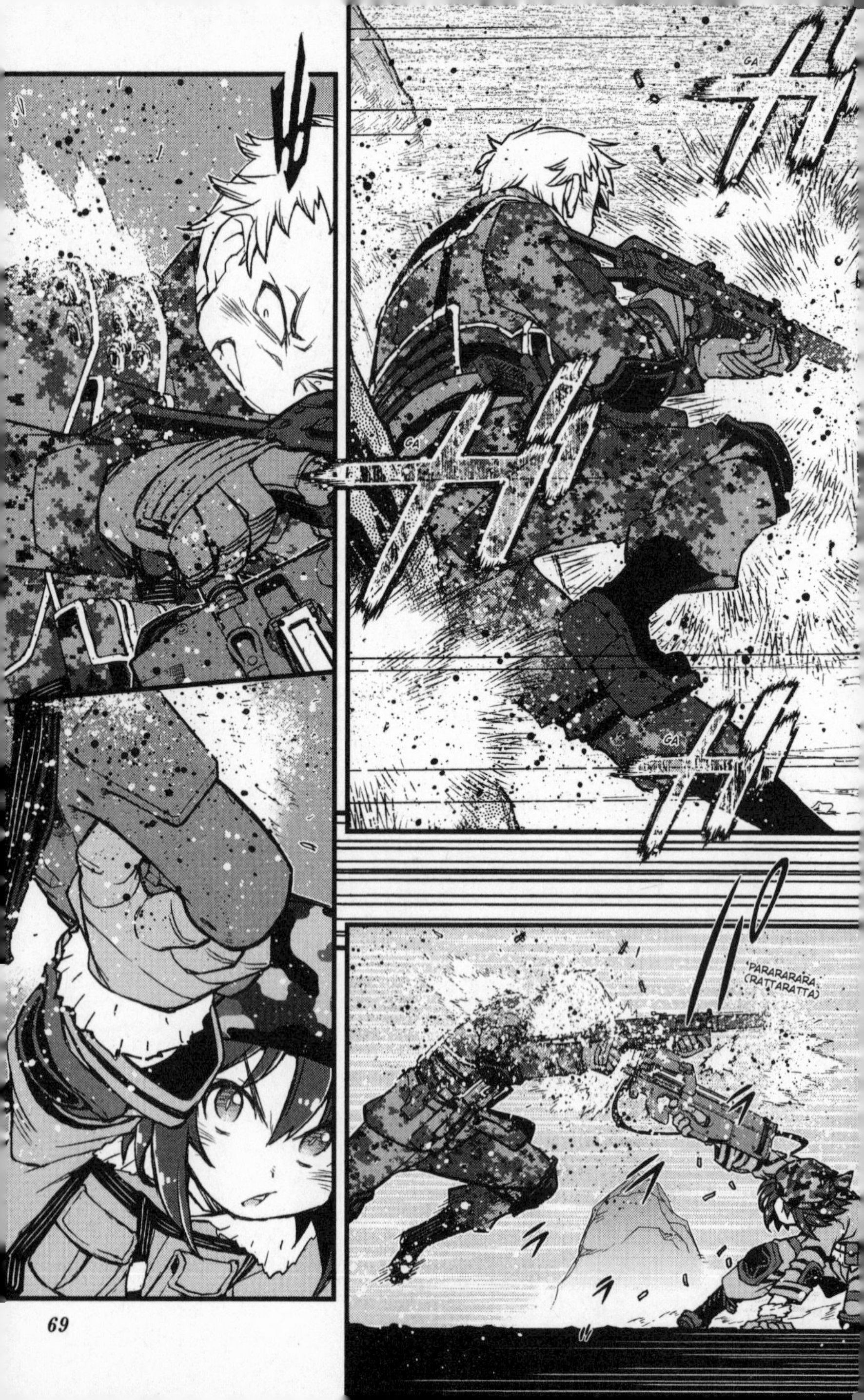
GA
GA
GA
PARARARARA
(RATTARATTA)

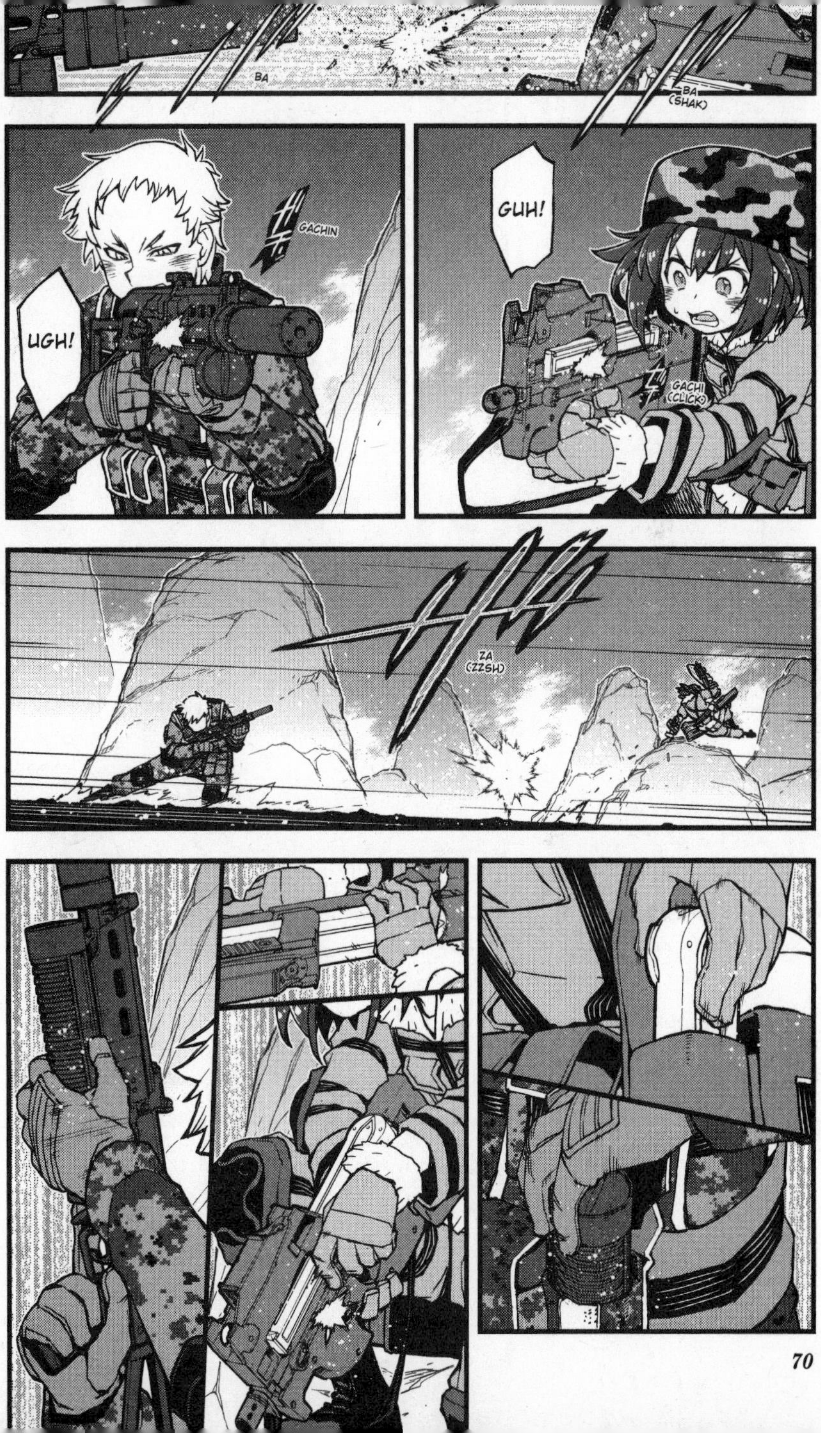
BA
BA
(SHAK)
GUH!
GACHI
(CLICK)
UGH!
GACHIN
ZA
(ZZSH)

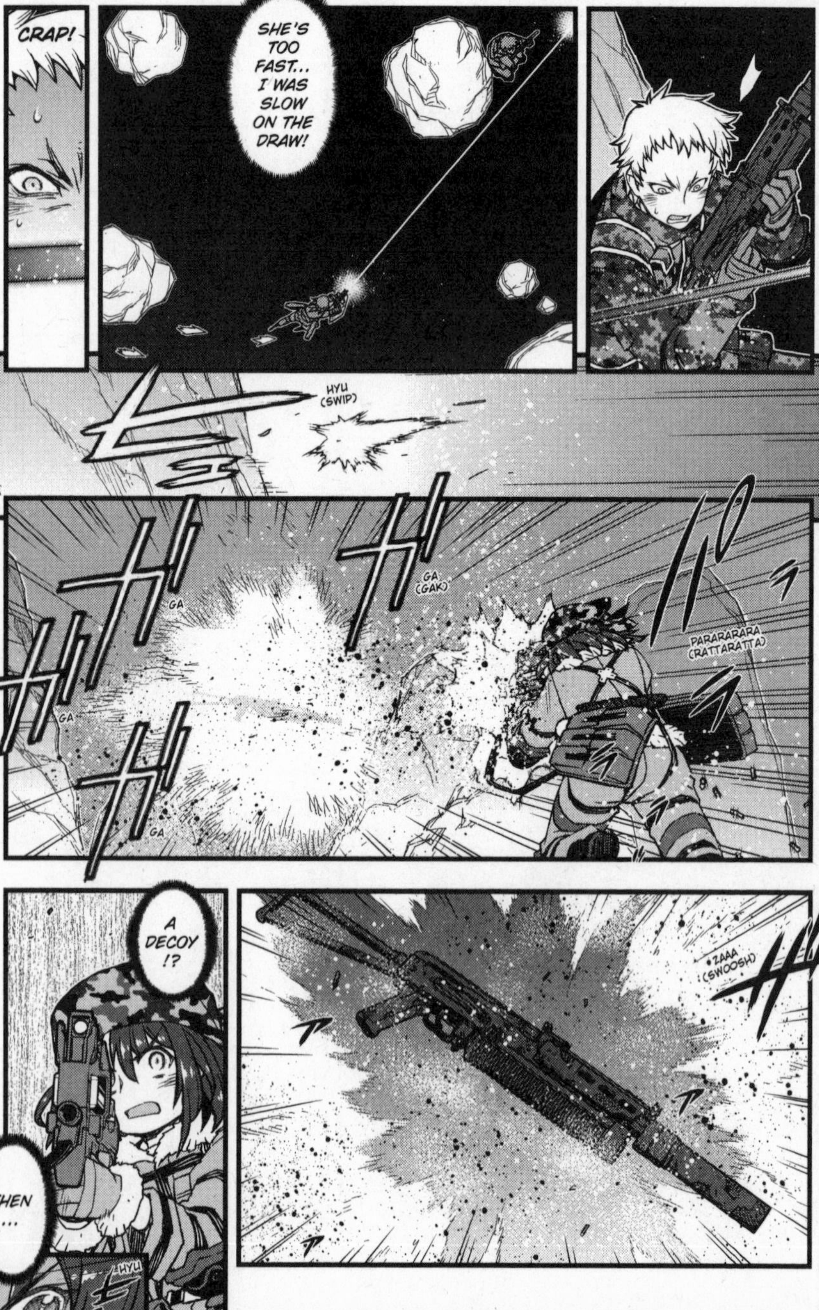
SHE'S TOO FAST... I WAS SLOW ON THE DRAW!
CRAP!
HYU (SWIP)
PARARARARA (RATTARATTA)
GA (GAK)
GA
GA
GA
ZAAA (SWOOSH)
A DECOY !?
THEN ...
HYU

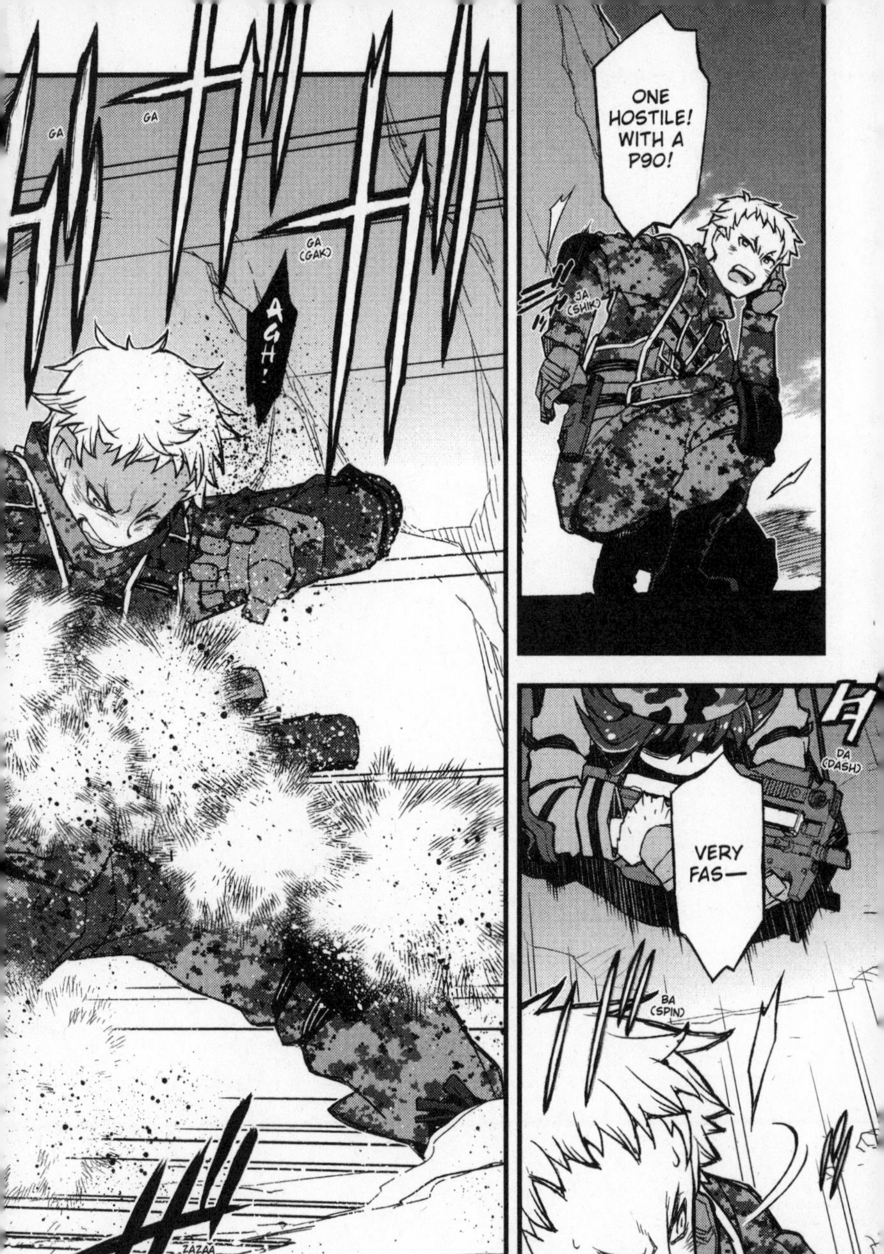
ONE HOSTILE! WITH A P90!
JA (SHIK)
DA (DASH)
VERY FAS—
BA (SPIN)
GA
GA
GA (GAK)
AGH!
ZAZAA (SLIDE)

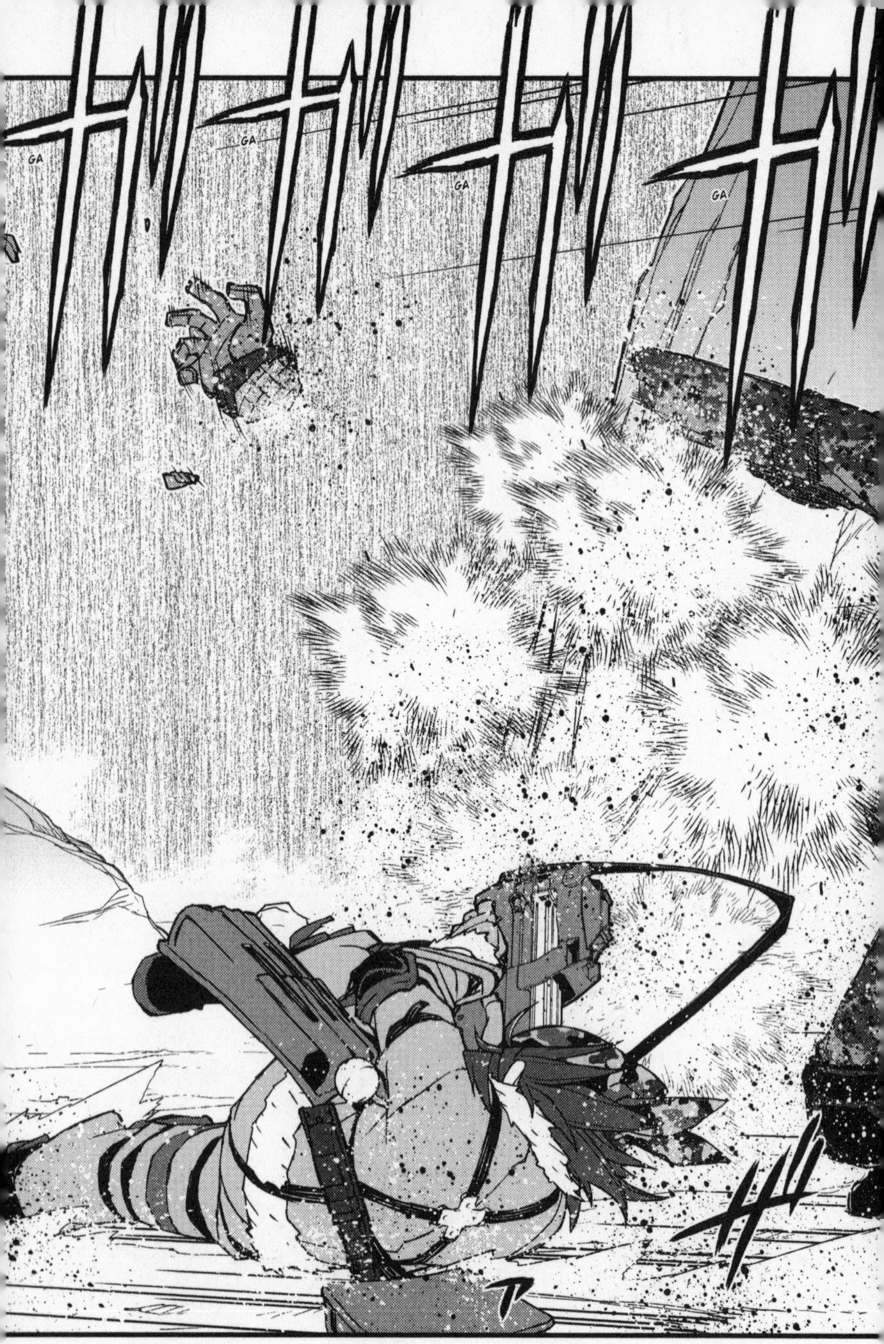
GA
GA
GA
GA

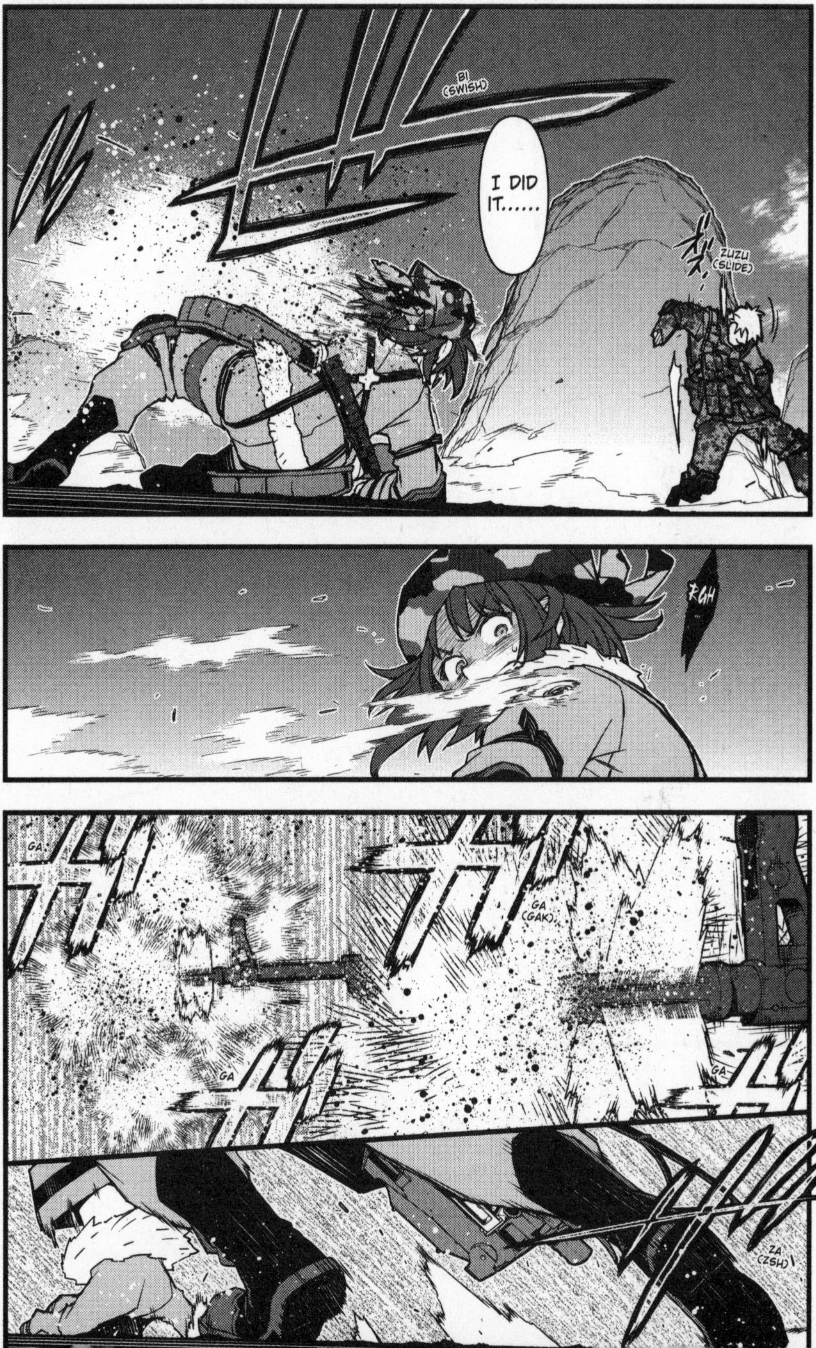
BI (SWISH)
I DID IT......
ZUZU (SLIDE)
RGH
GA (GAK)
GA
GA
GA
ZA (ZSH)

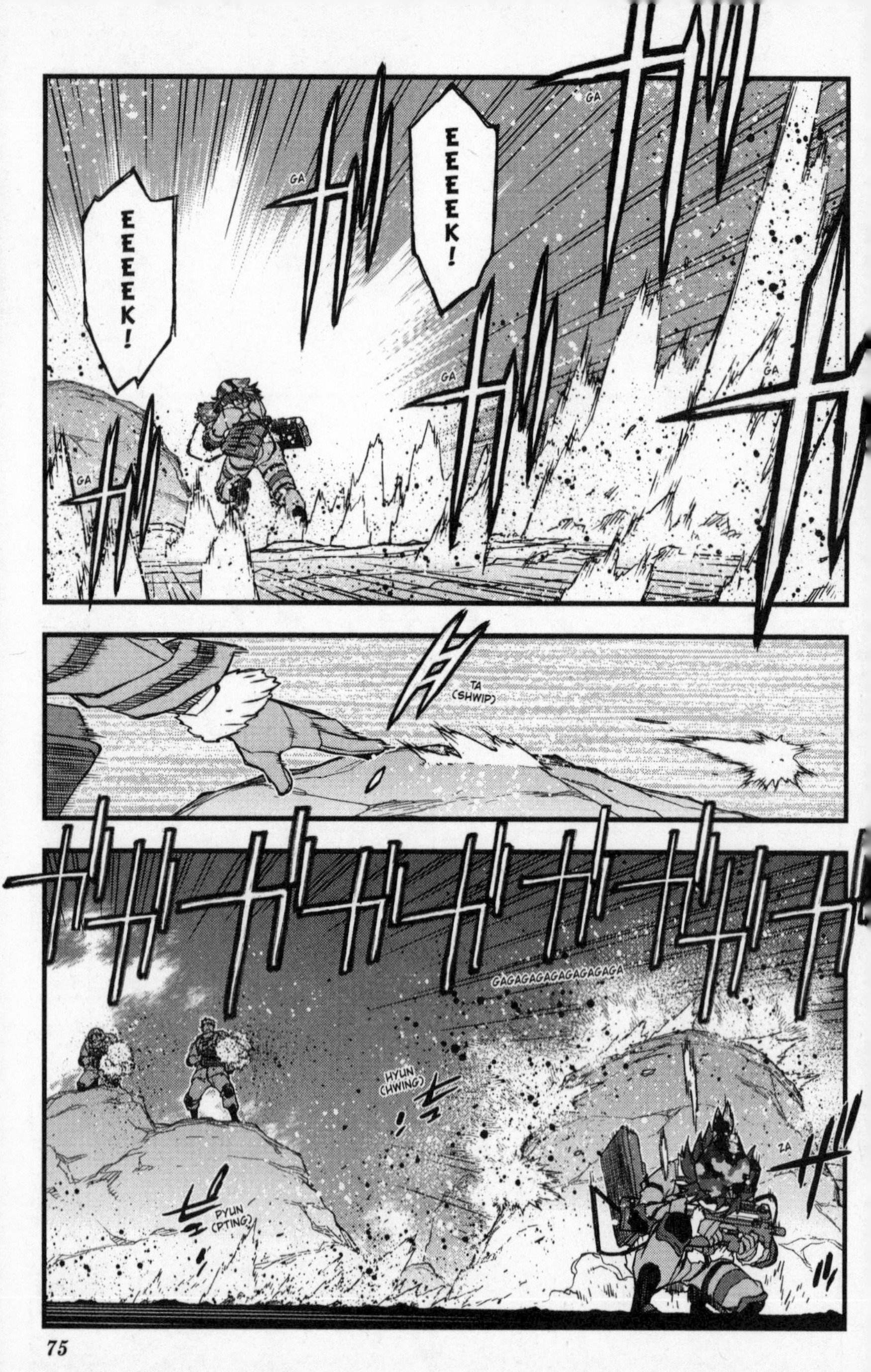
GA
EEEEK!
GA
EEEEK!
GA
GA
GA
TA (SHWIP)
GAGAGAGAGAGAGAGAGA
ZA
HYUN (HWING)
PYUN (PTING)

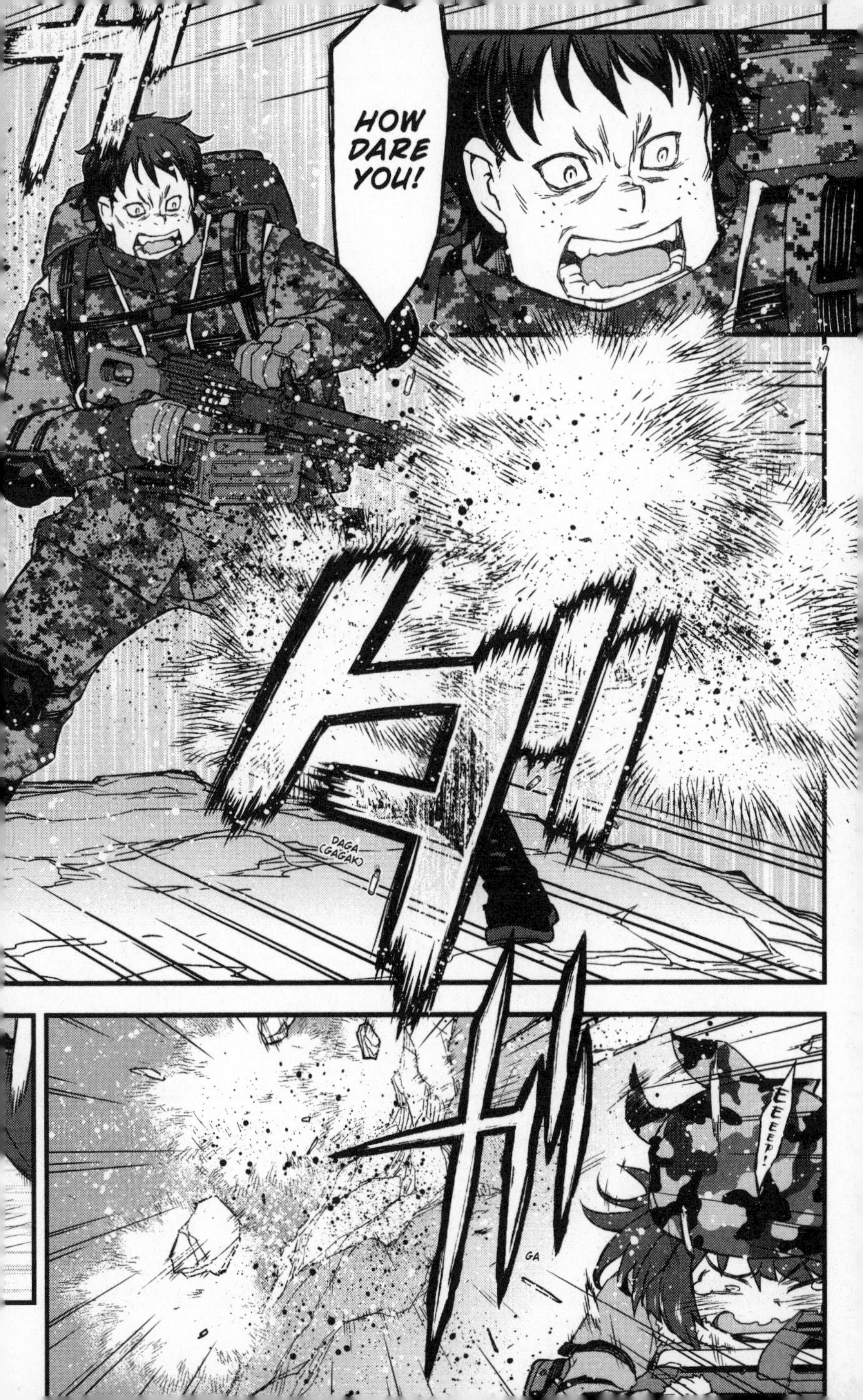
HOW DARE YOU!
DAGA (GAGAK)
EEEEEP!
GA

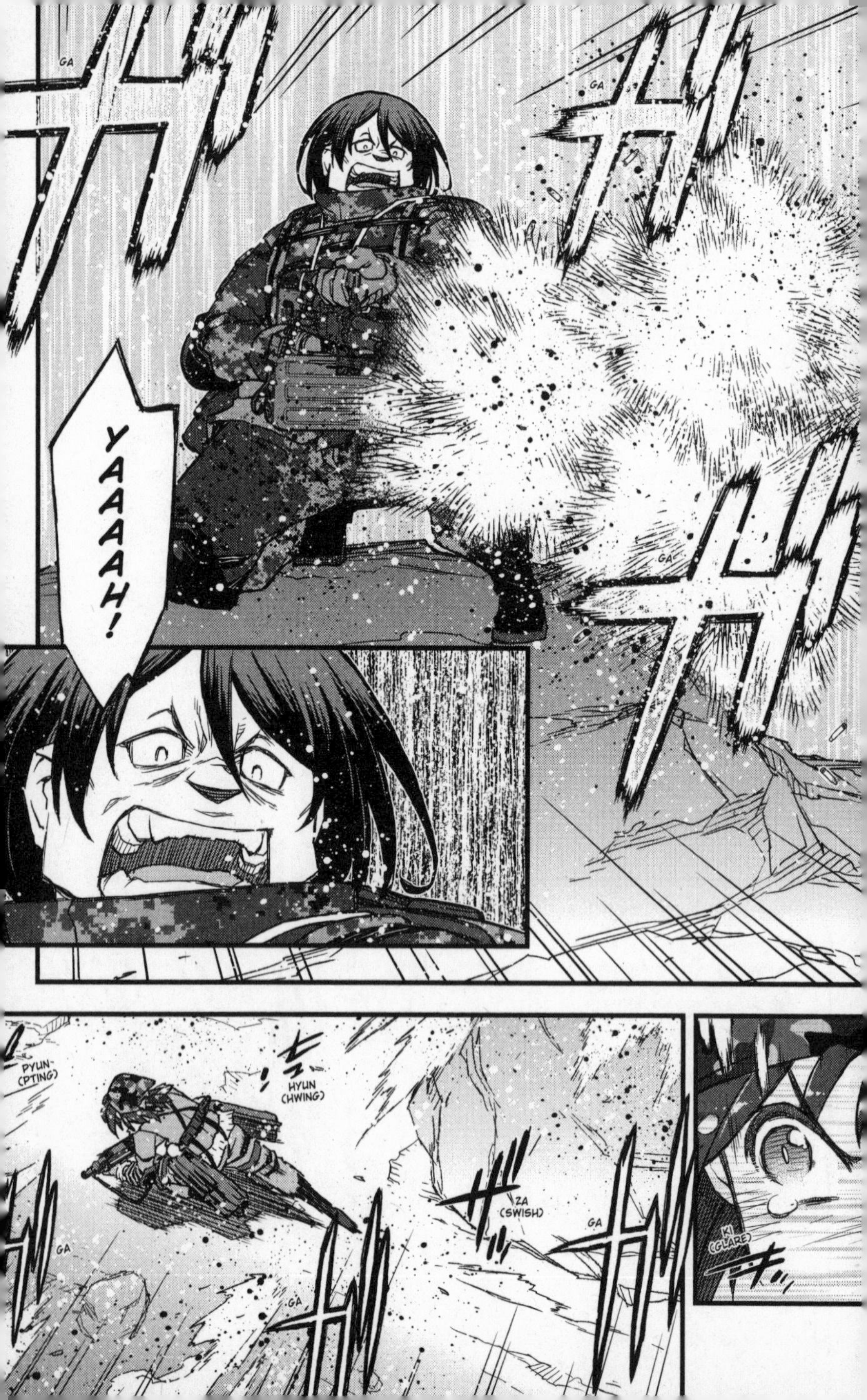
GA
GA
GA
YAAAAH!
KI (GLARE)
HYUN (HWING)
PYUN- (PTING)
GA
ZA (SWISH)
GA
GA

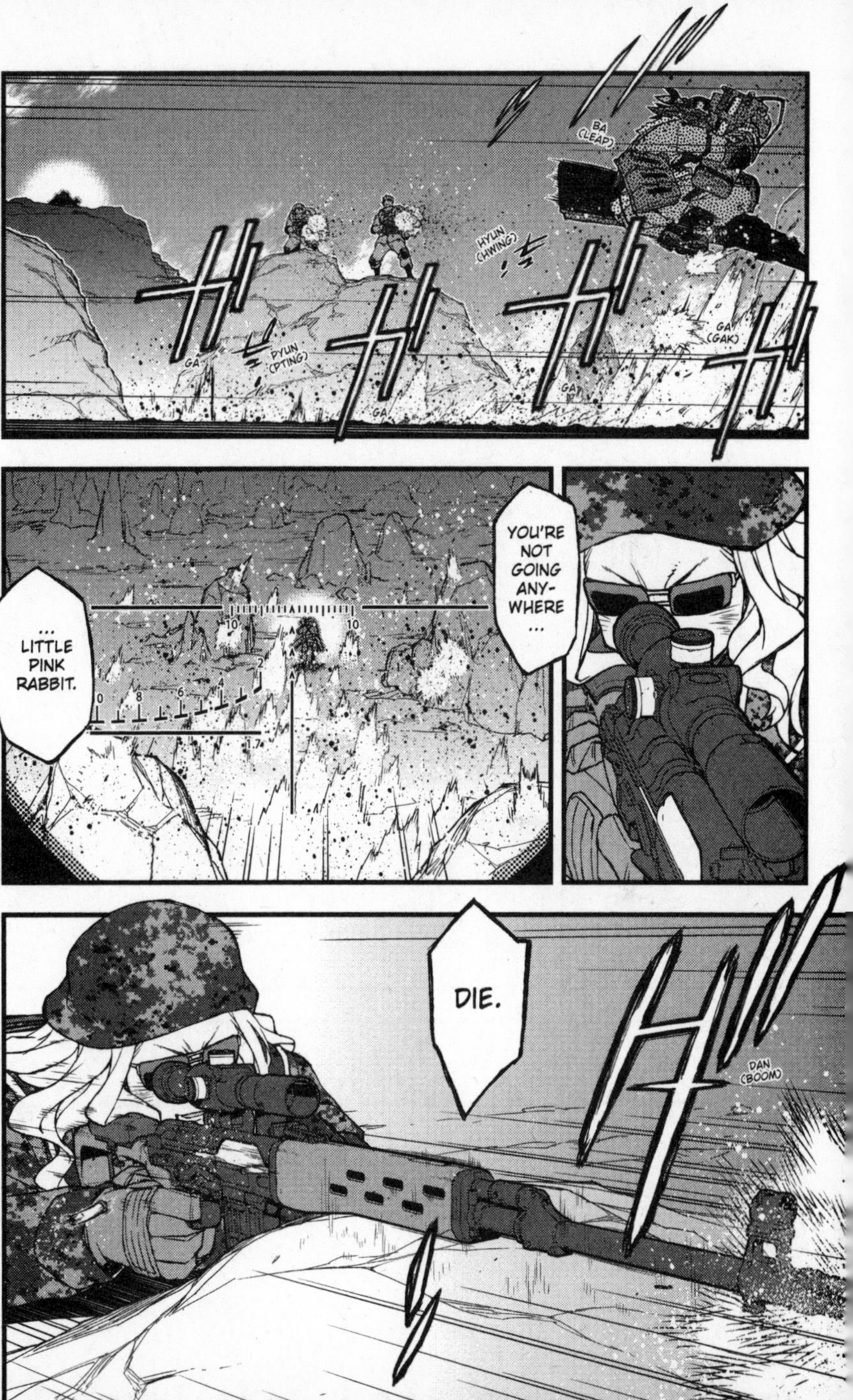

BA (LEAP)
HYUN (HWING)
GA (GAK)
PYUN (PTING)
GA
GA
GA
YOU'RE NOT GOING ANY-WHERE ...
... LITTLE PINK RABBIT.
DIE.
DAN (BOOM)

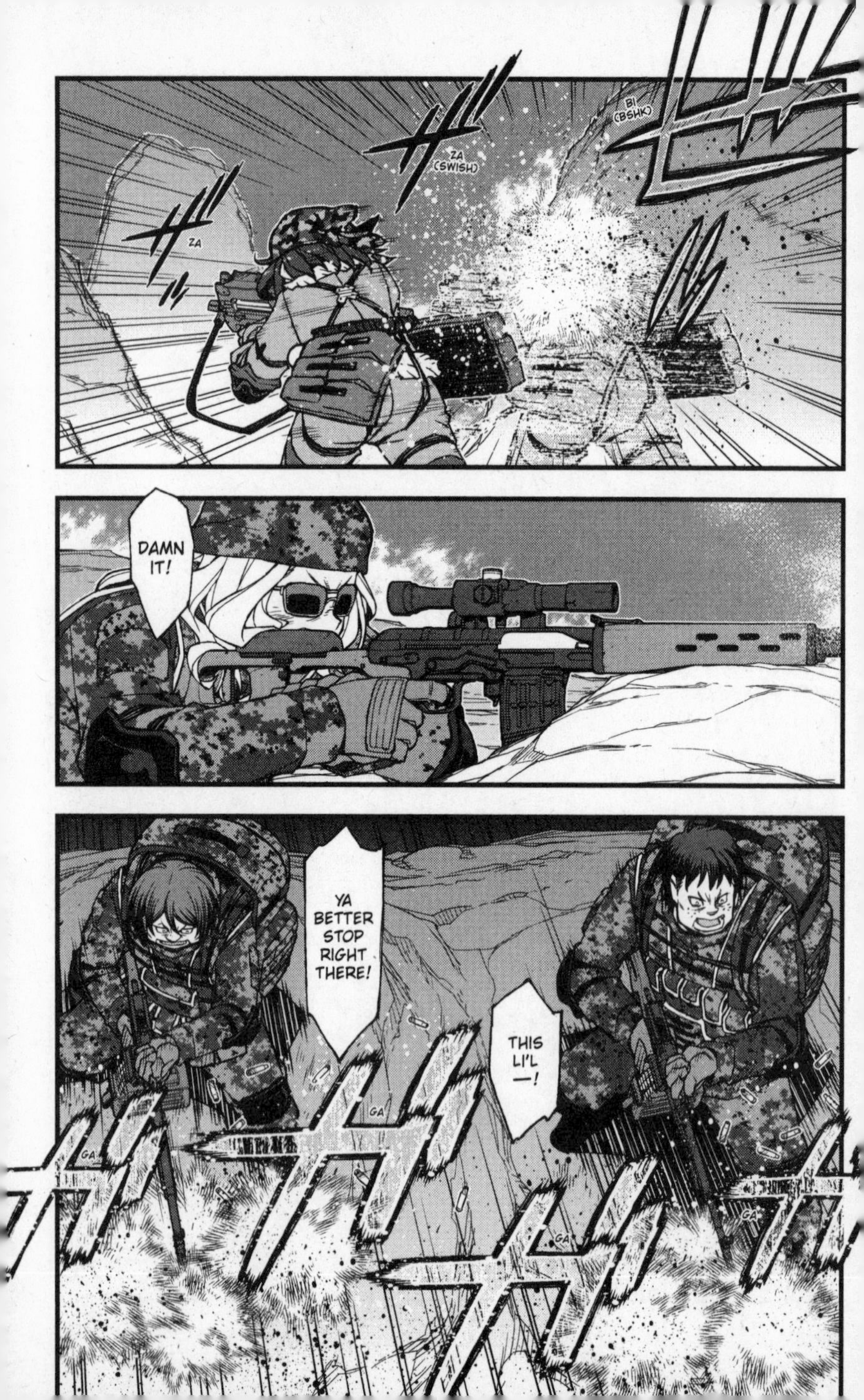
BI (BSHK)
ZA (SWISH)
ZA
DAMN IT!
YA BETTER STOP RIGHT THERE!
THIS LI'L —!
GA
GA
GA
GA

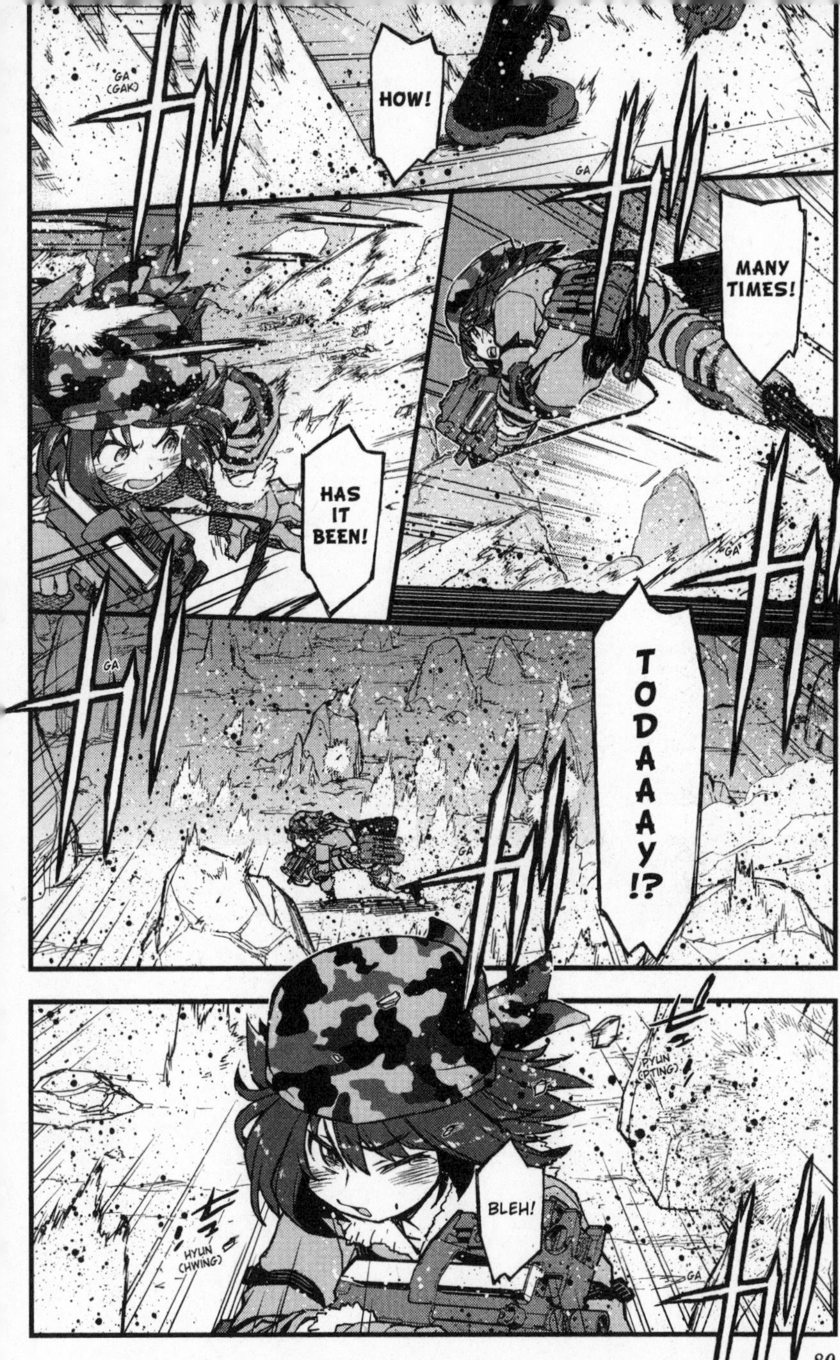
GA
HOW!
GA
(GAK)
MANY TIMES!
GA
HAS IT BEEN!
TODAAAY!?
GA
GA
PYUN
(PTING)
BLEH!
HYUN
(CHWING)
GA

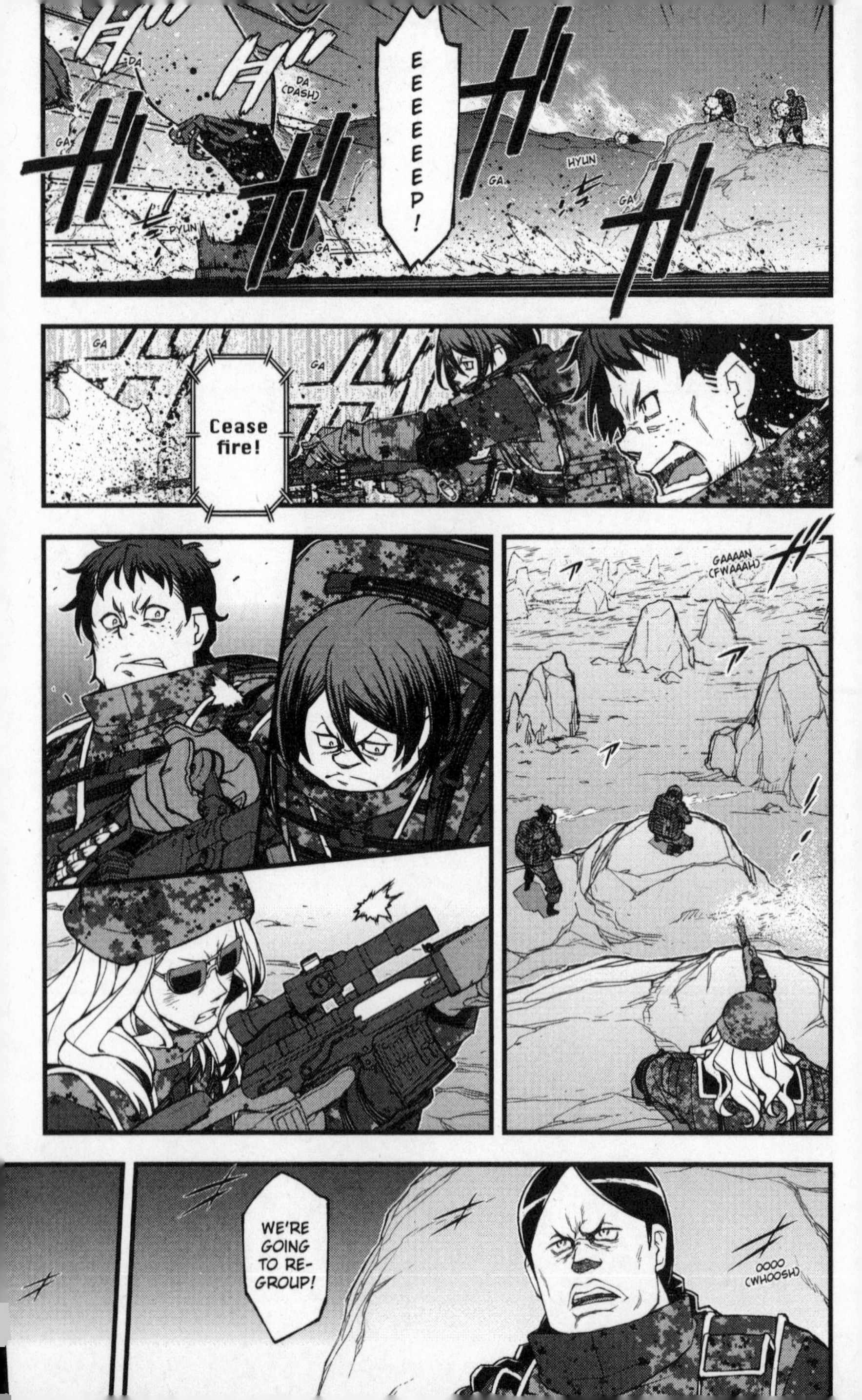
HYUN
GA
GA
EEEEEEEP!
DA (DASH)
DA
GA
PYUN
GA
GA
Cease fire!
GA
GAAAAN (FWAAAH)
OOOO (WHOOSH)
WE'RE GOING TO RE-GROUP!

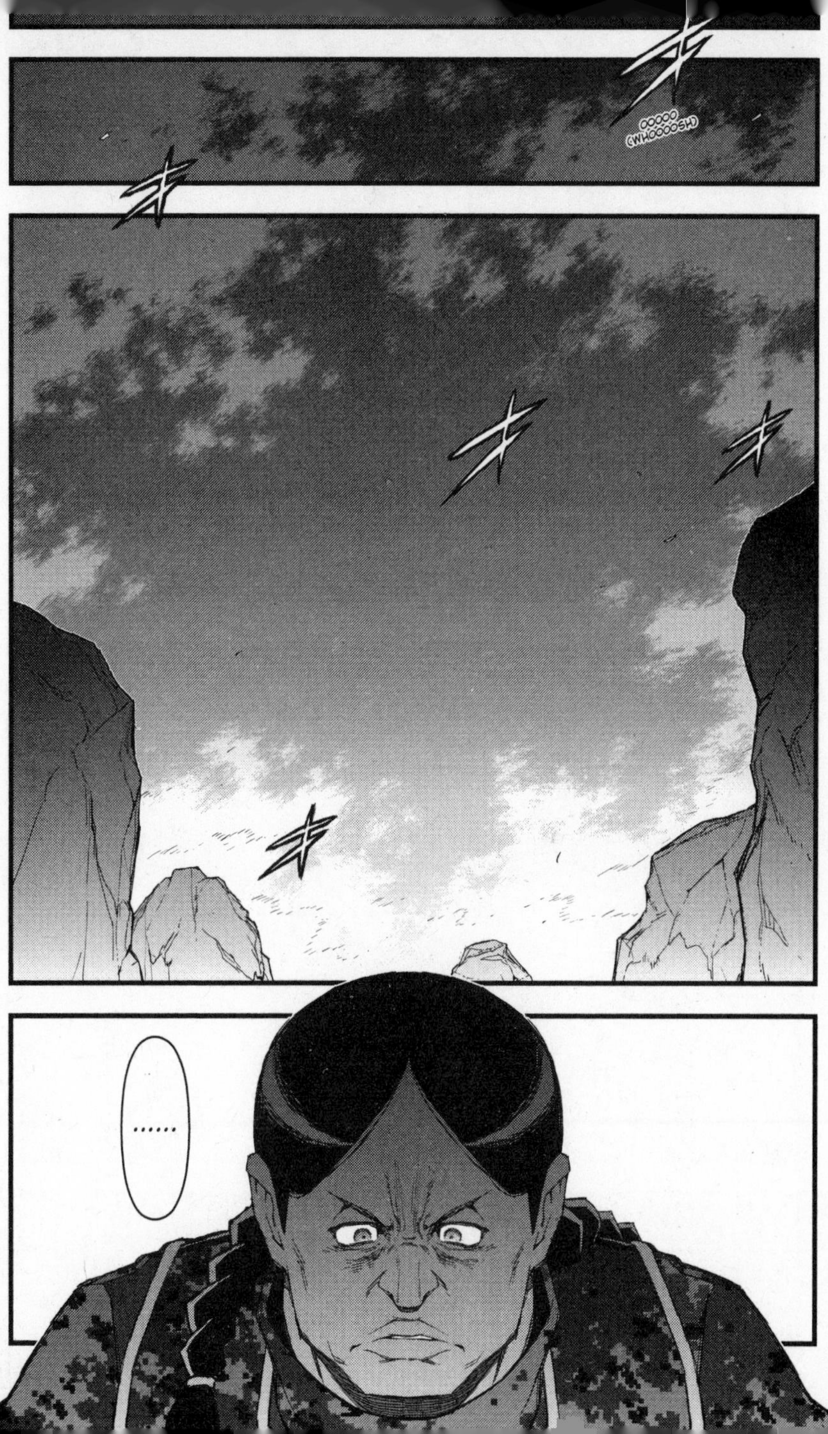
(WHOOOOOSH)
OOOOO
……

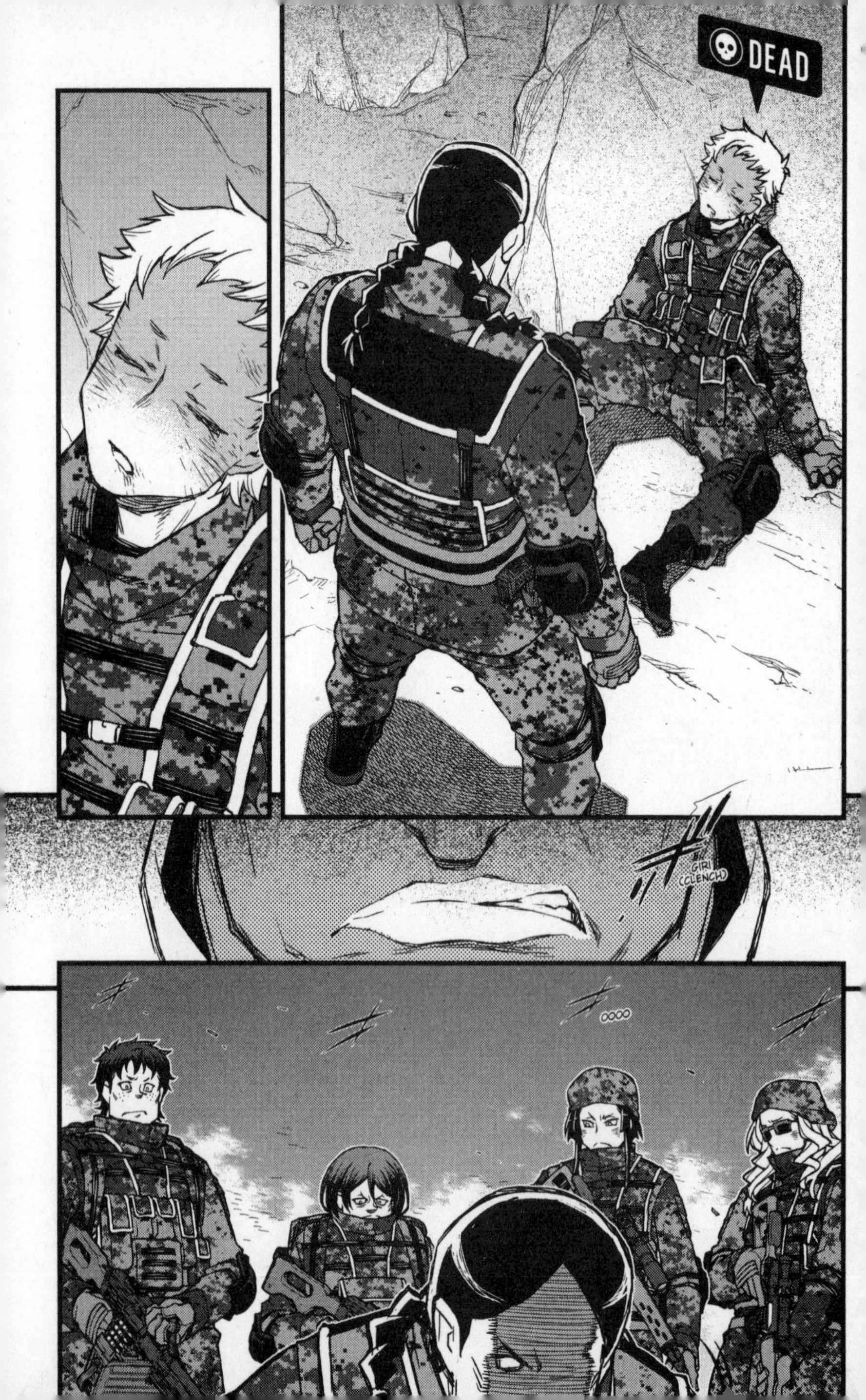
DEAD
GIRI (CLENCH)
....

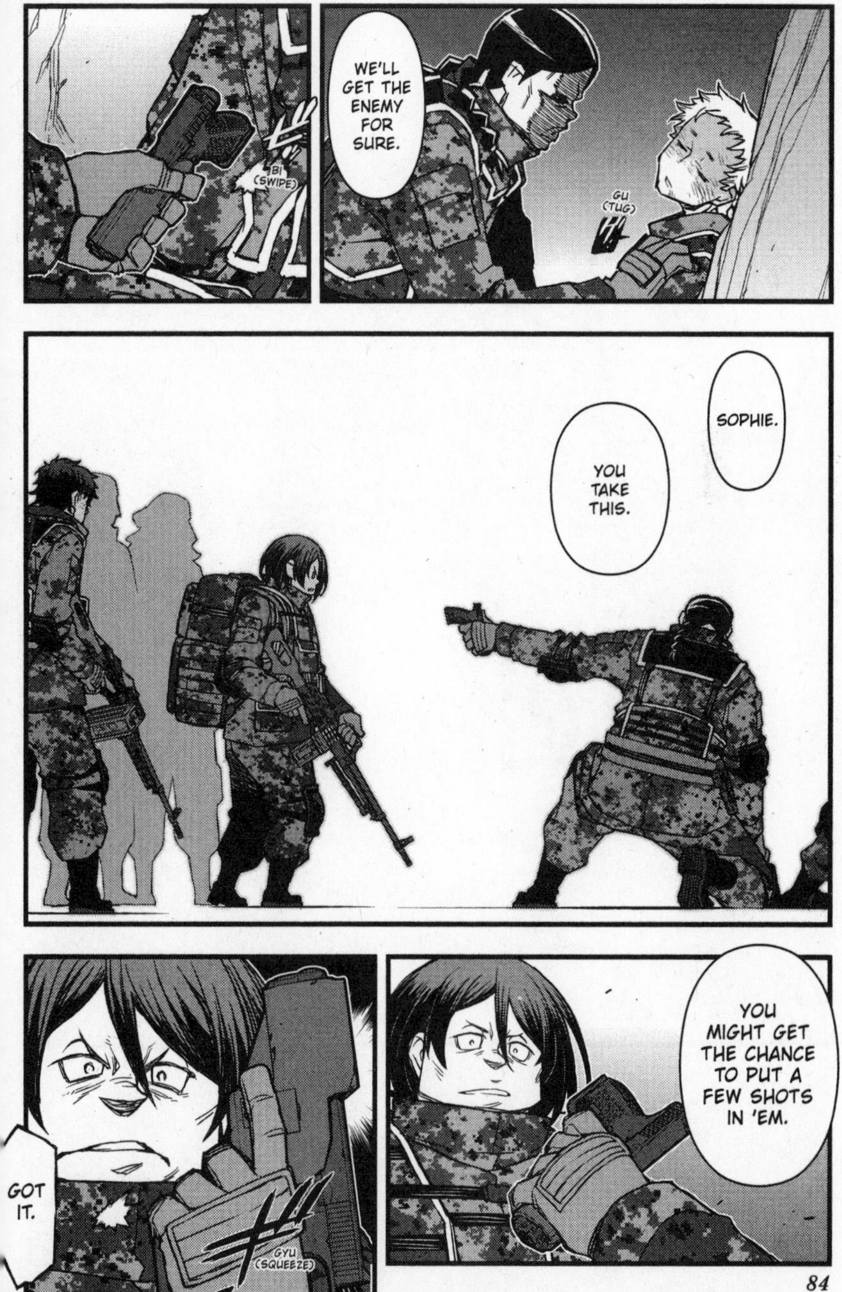
WE'LL GET THE ENEMY FOR SURE.
GU (TUG)
BI (SWIPE)
SOPHIE.
YOU TAKE THIS.
YOU MIGHT GET THE CHANCE TO PUT A FEW SHOTS IN 'EM.
GOT IT.
GYU (SQUEEZE)

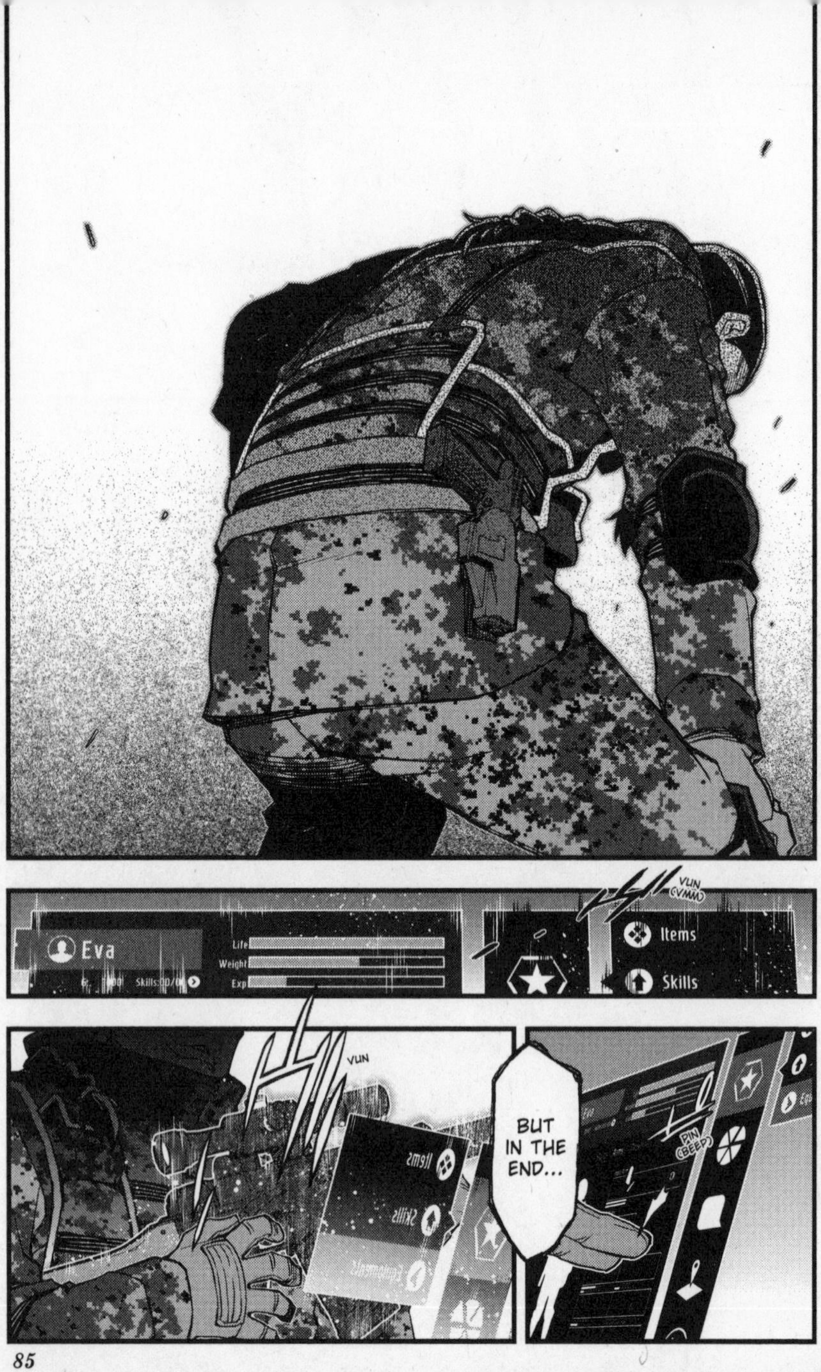
VUN (VMM)
Eva
Life
Weight
Exp
Items
Skills
BUT IN THE END...
PIN (BEEP)
VUN

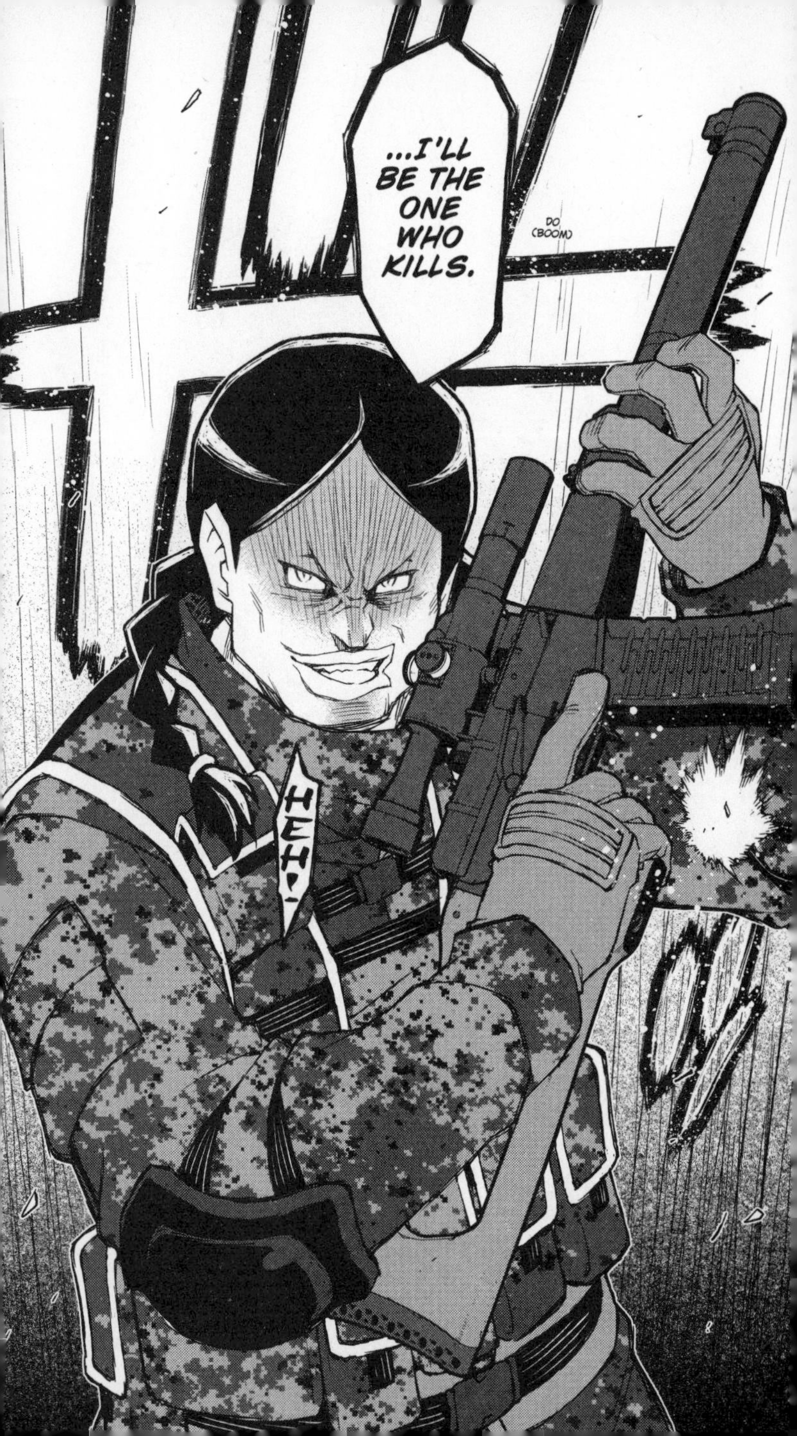
...I'LL BE THE ONE WHO KILLS.
DO (BOOM)
HEH!

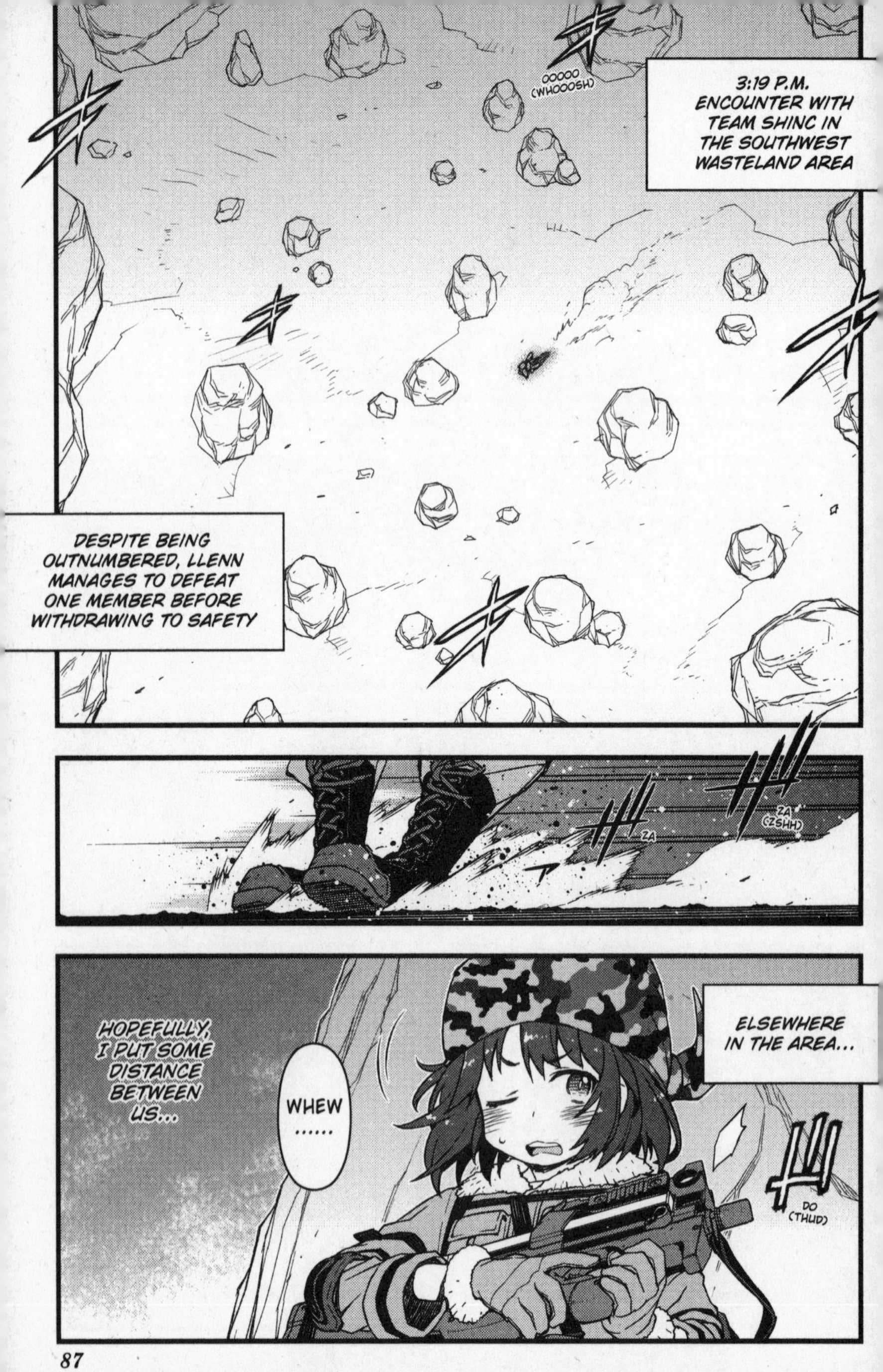
3:19 P.M. ENCOUNTER WITH TEAM SHINC IN THE SOUTHWEST WASTELAND AREA
OOOOO (WHOOOSH)
DESPITE BEING OUTNUMBERED, LLENN MANAGES TO DEFEAT ONE MEMBER BEFORE WITHDRAWING TO SAFETY
ZA (ZSHH)
ZA
ELSEWHERE IN THE AREA...
DO (THUD)
WHEW ......
HOPEFULLY, I PUT SOME DISTANCE BETWEEN US...

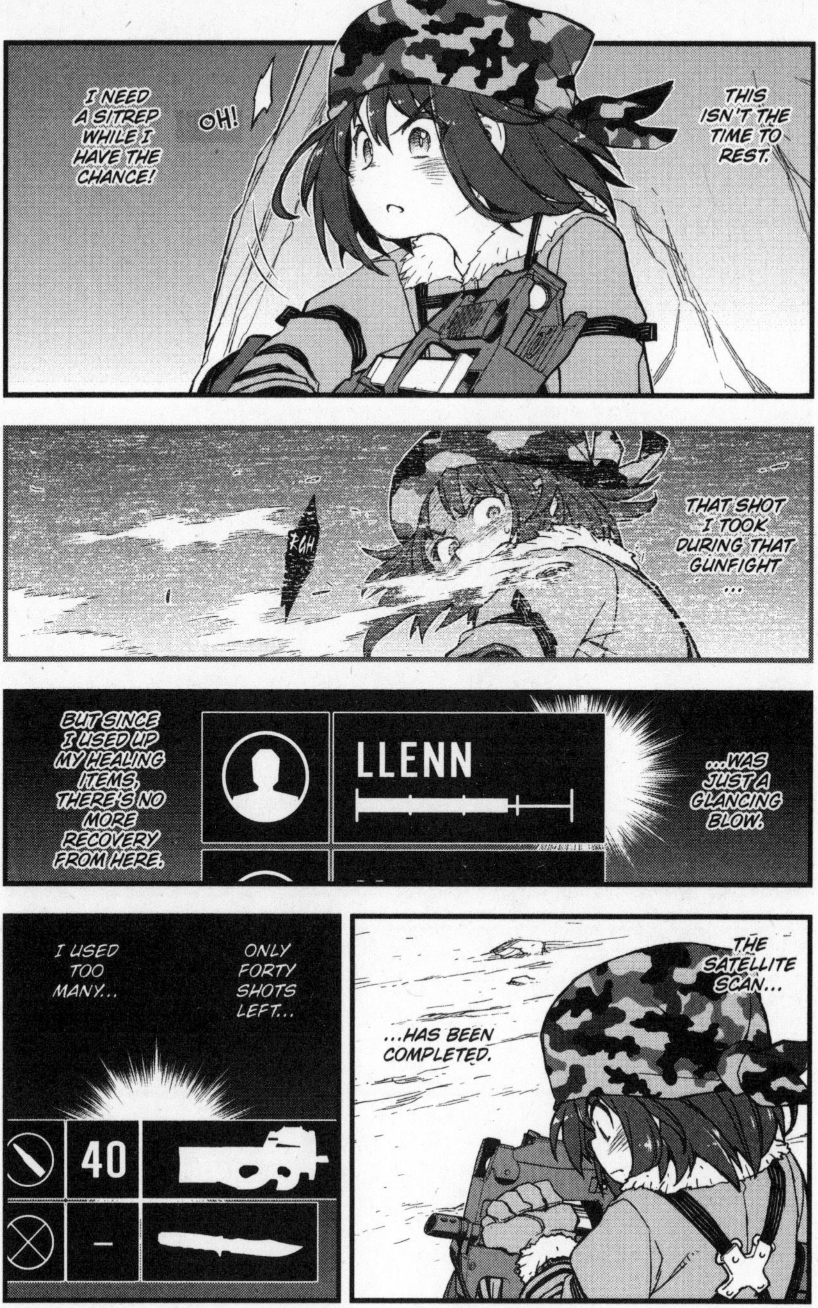
THIS ISN'T THE TIME TO REST.
OH!
I NEED A SITREP WHILE I HAVE THE CHANCE!
THAT SHOT I TOOK DURING THAT GUNFIGHT ...
RGH
...WAS JUST A GLANCING BLOW.
LLENN
BUT SINCE I USED UP MY HEALING ITEMS, THERE'S NO MORE RECOVERY FROM HERE.
THE SATELLITE SCAN...
...HAS BEEN COMPLETED.
ONLY FORTY SHOTS LEFT...
I USED TOO MANY...
40
–

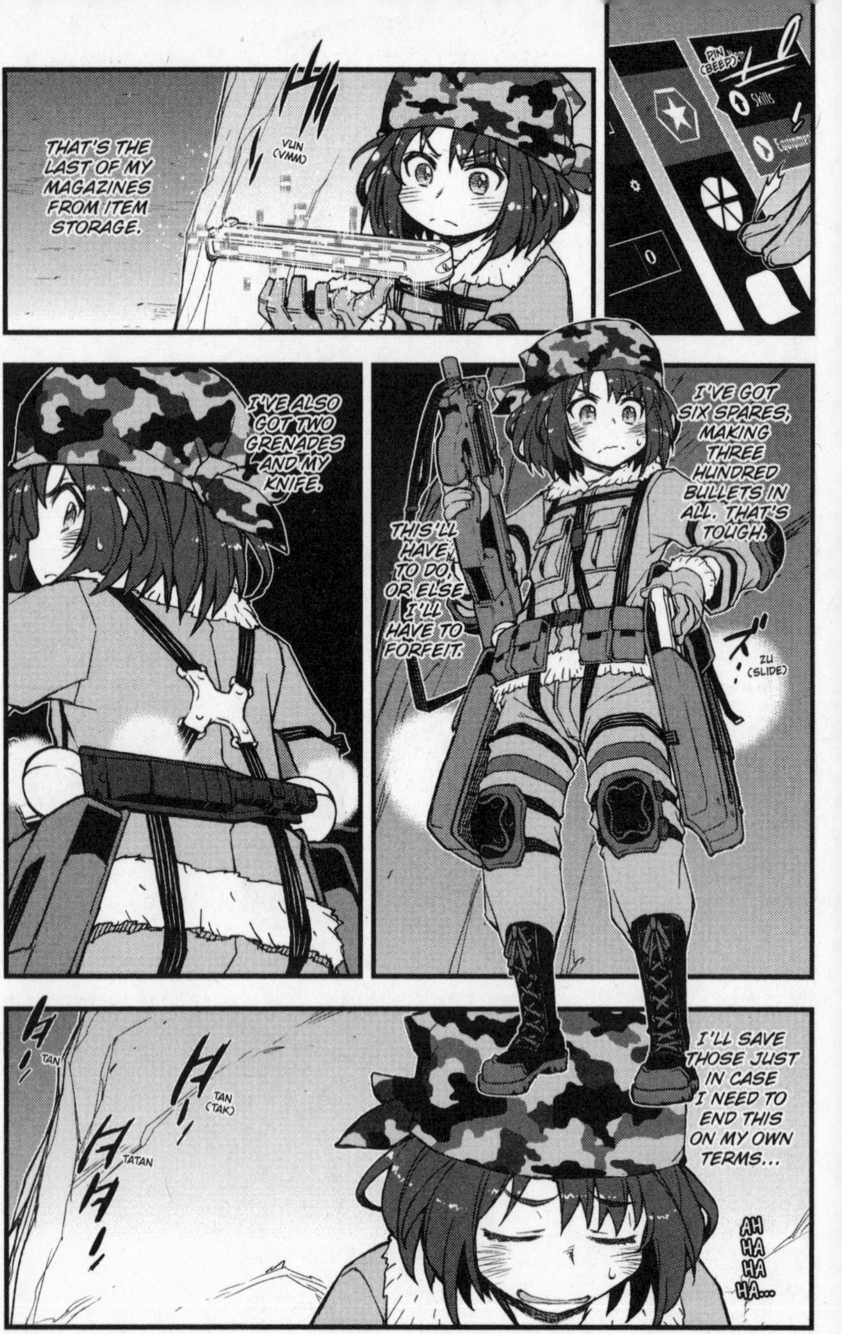
PIN (BEEP)
Skills
0
VUN (VMM)
THAT'S THE LAST OF MY MAGAZINES FROM ITEM STORAGE.
I'VE GOT SIX SPARES, MAKING THREE HUNDRED BULLETS IN ALL. THAT'S TOUGH.
THIS'LL HAVE TO DO, OR ELSE I'LL HAVE TO FORFEIT.
ZU (SLIDE)
I'VE ALSO GOT TWO GRENADES AND MY KNIFE.
I'LL SAVE THOSE JUST IN CASE I NEED TO END THIS ON MY OWN TERMS...
AH HA HA HA HA...
TAN (TAK)
TATAN
TAN

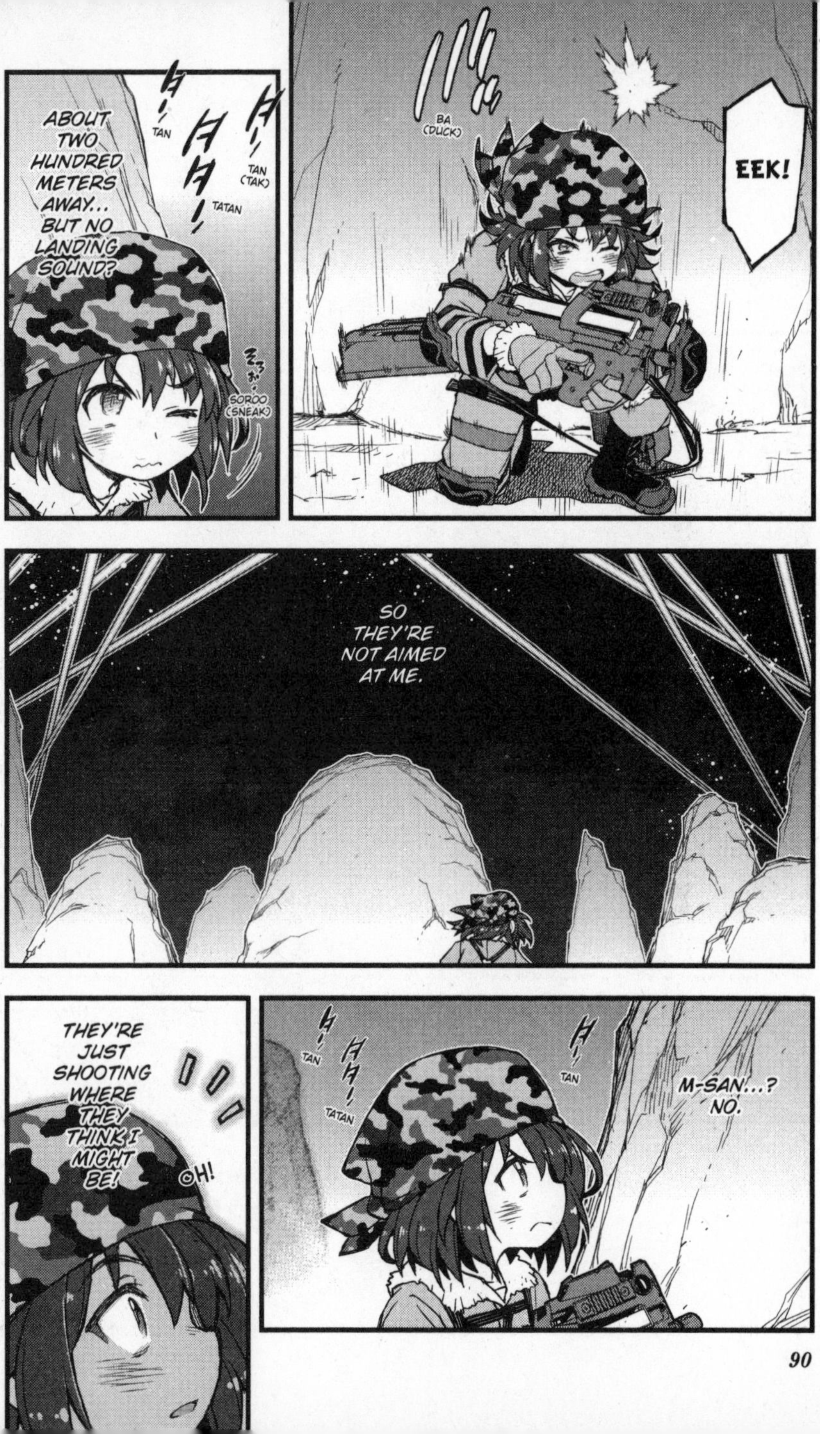
BA (DUCK)
EEK!
TAN
TAN (TAK)
TATAN
ABOUT TWO HUNDRED METERS AWAY... BUT NO LANDING SOUND?
SOROO (SNEAK)
SO THEY'RE NOT AIMED AT ME.
TAN
M-SAN...? NO.
TAN
TATAN
THEY'RE JUST SHOOTING WHERE THEY THINK I MIGHT BE!
OH!

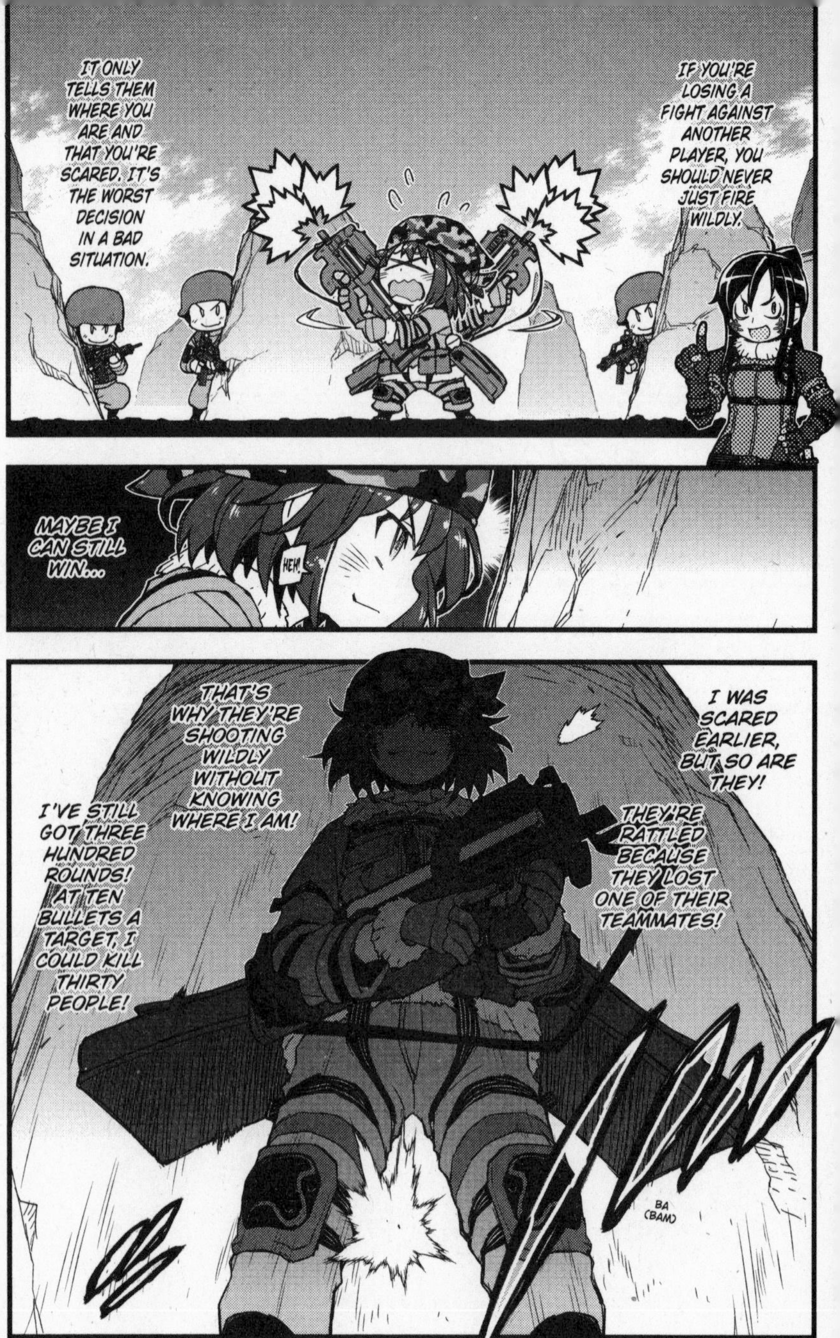
IF YOU'RE LOSING A FIGHT AGAINST ANOTHER PLAYER, YOU SHOULD NEVER JUST FIRE WILDLY.
IT ONLY TELLS THEM WHERE YOU ARE AND THAT YOU'RE SCARED. IT'S THE WORST DECISION IN A BAD SITUATION.
HEH!
MAYBE I CAN STILL WIN...
I WAS SCARED EARLIER, BUT SO ARE THEY!
THEY'RE RATTLED BECAUSE THEY LOST ONE OF THEIR TEAMMATES!
THAT'S WHY THEY'RE SHOOTING WILDLY WITHOUT KNOWING WHERE I AM!
I'VE STILL GOT THREE HUNDRED ROUNDS! AT TEN BULLETS A TARGET, I COULD KILL THIRTY PEOPLE!
BA (BAM)

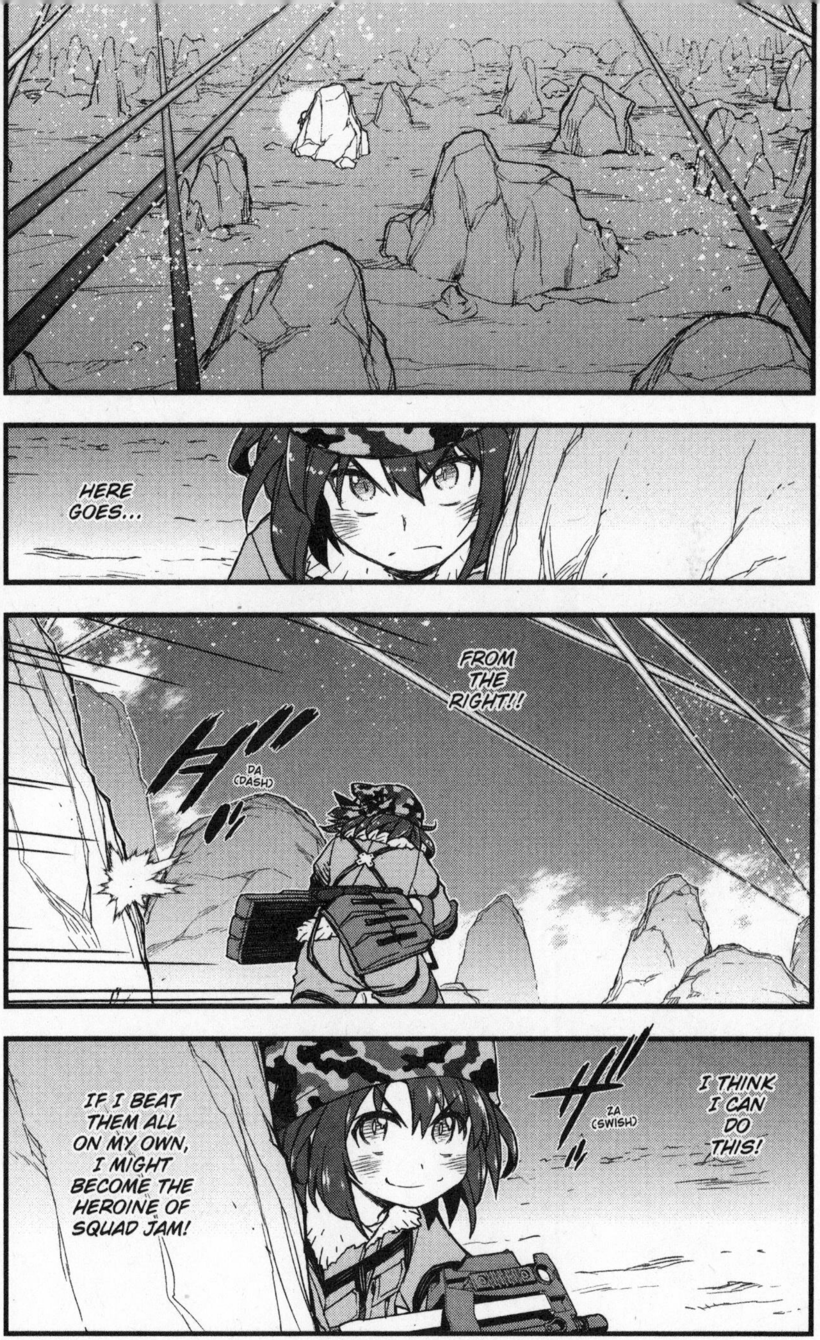
HERE GOES...
FROM THE RIGHT!!
DA (DASH)
I THINK I CAN DO THIS!
ZA (SWISH)
IF I BEAT THEM ALL ON MY OWN, I MIGHT BECOME THE HEROINE OF SQUAD JAM!

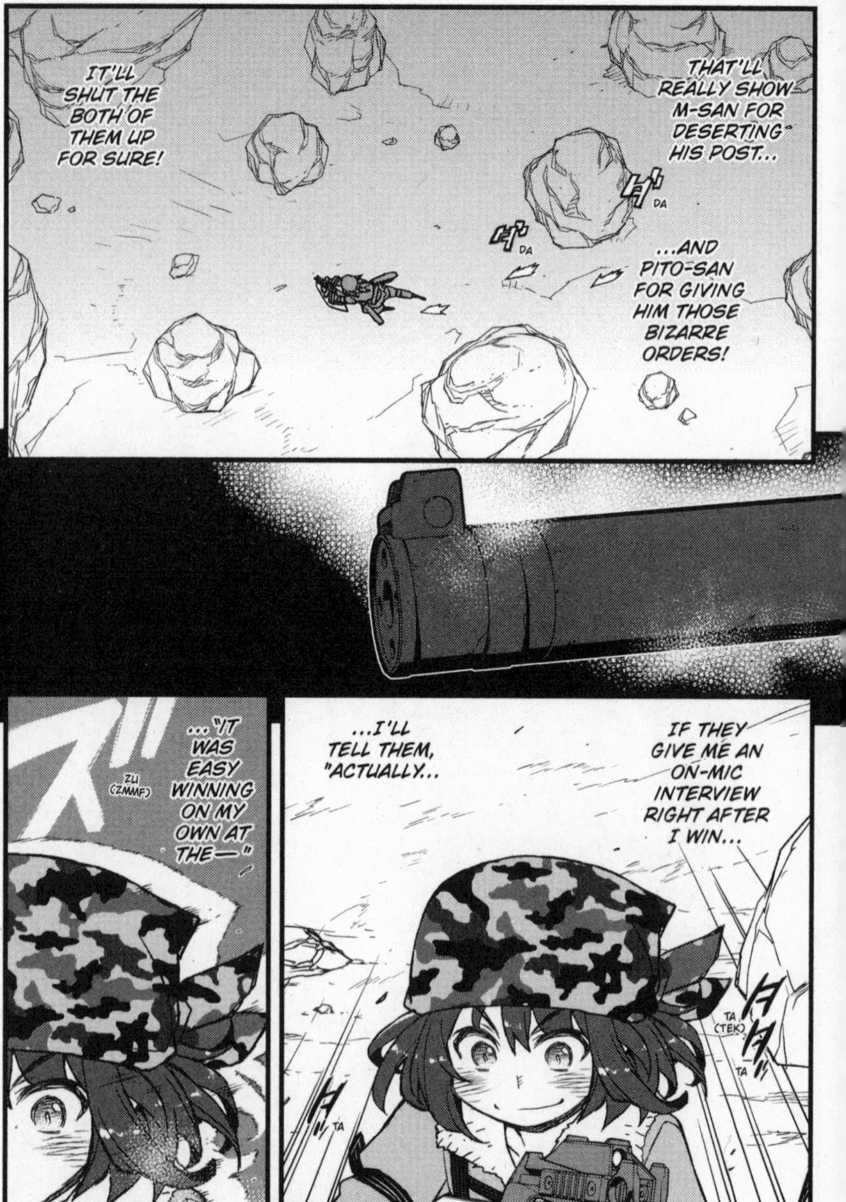
THAT'LL REALLY SHOW M-SAN FOR DESERTING HIS POST...
DA
DA
...AND PITO-SAN FOR GIVING HIM THOSE BIZARRE ORDERS!
IT'LL SHUT THE BOTH OF THEM UP FOR SURE!
IF THEY GIVE ME AN ON-MIC INTERVIEW RIGHT AFTER I WIN...
...I'LL TELL THEM, "ACTUALLY...
TA (TEK)
TA
TA
..."IT WAS EASY WINNING ON MY OWN AT THE—"
ZU (ZMMF)

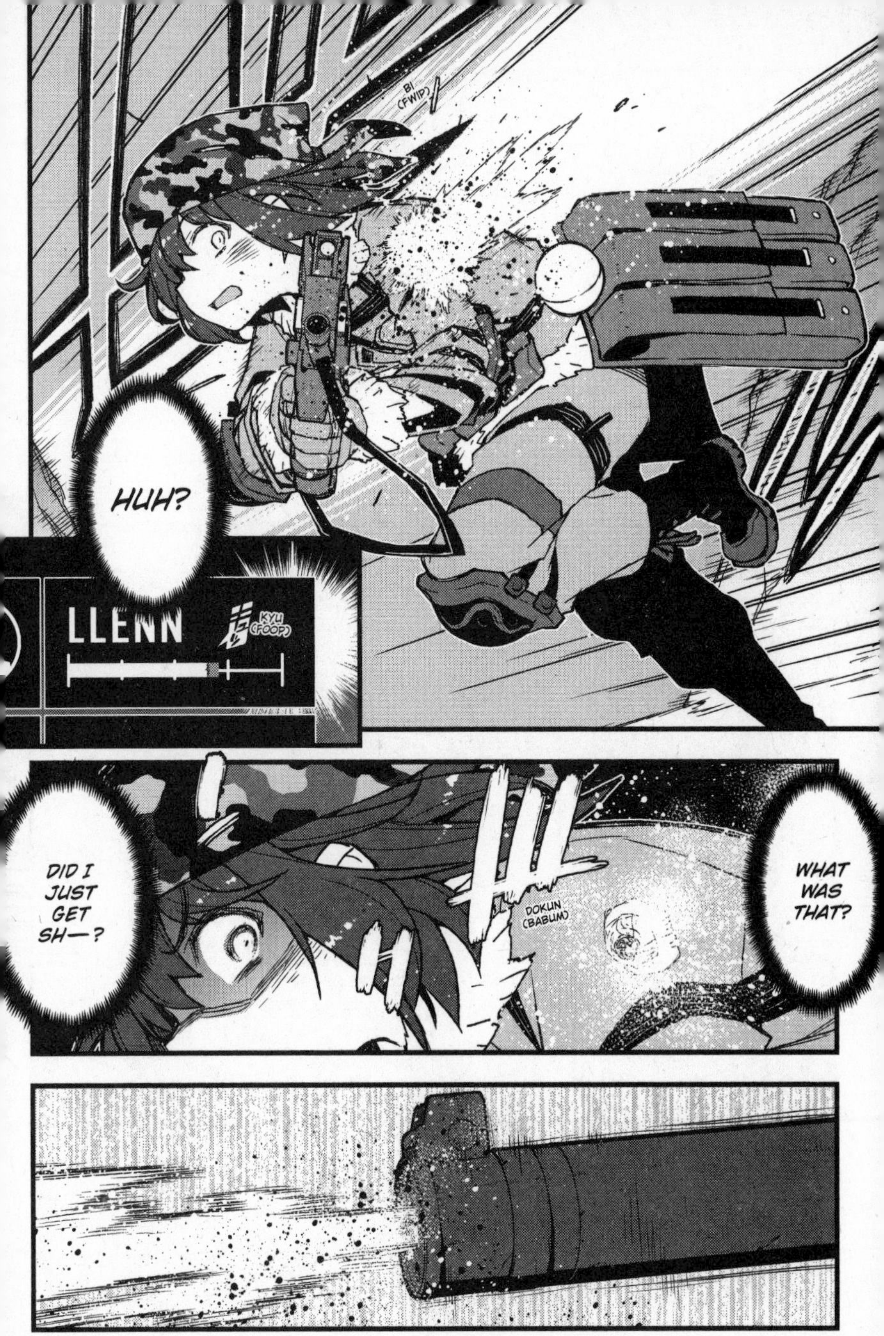
BI
(FWIP)
HUH?
LLENN
KYU
(FOOP)
WHAT WAS THAT?
DOKUN
(BABUM)
DID I JUST GET SH—?

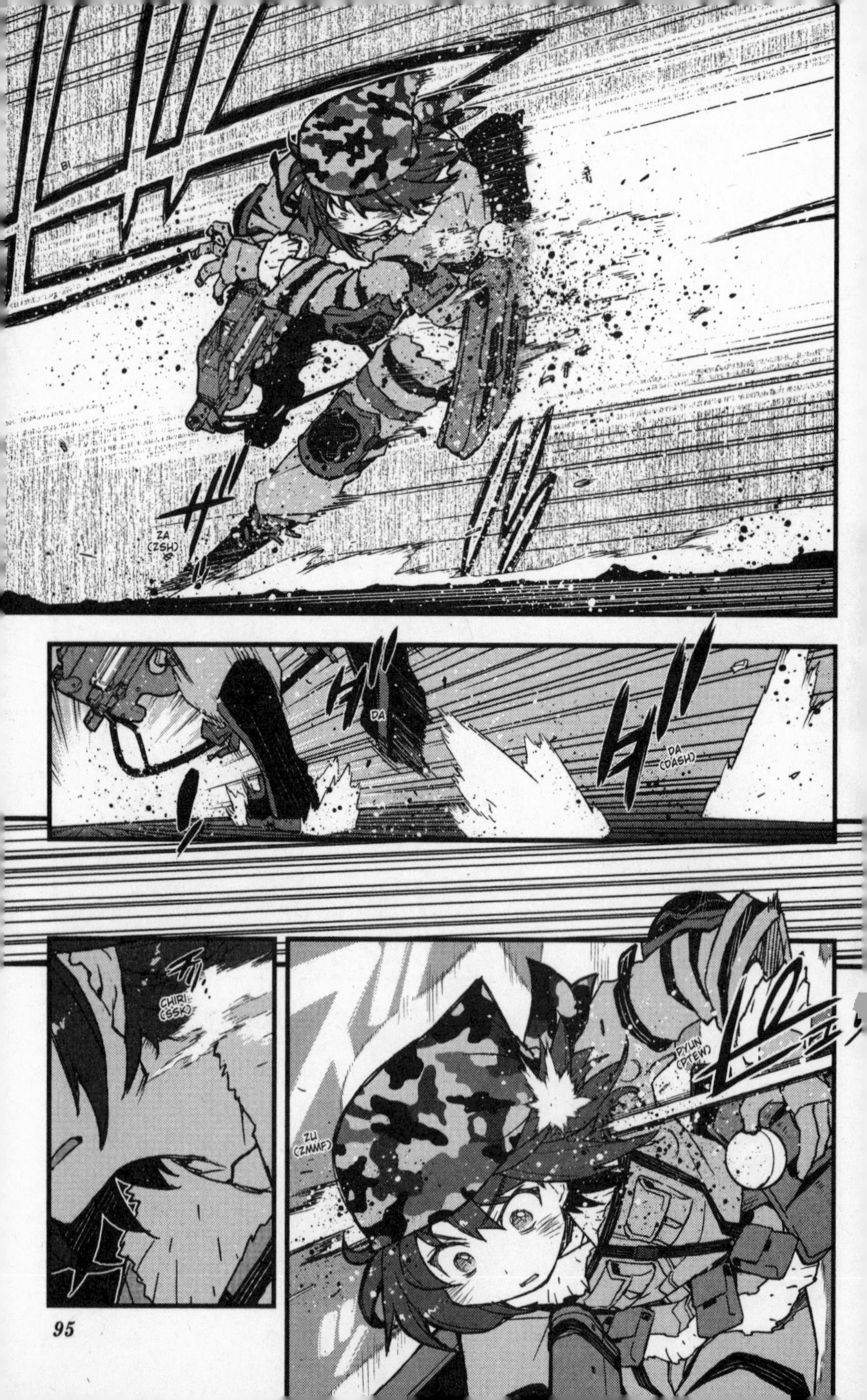
BI
ZA (ZSH)
DA (DASH)
DA
PYUN (PTEW)
ZU (ZMMF)
CHIRI (SSK)

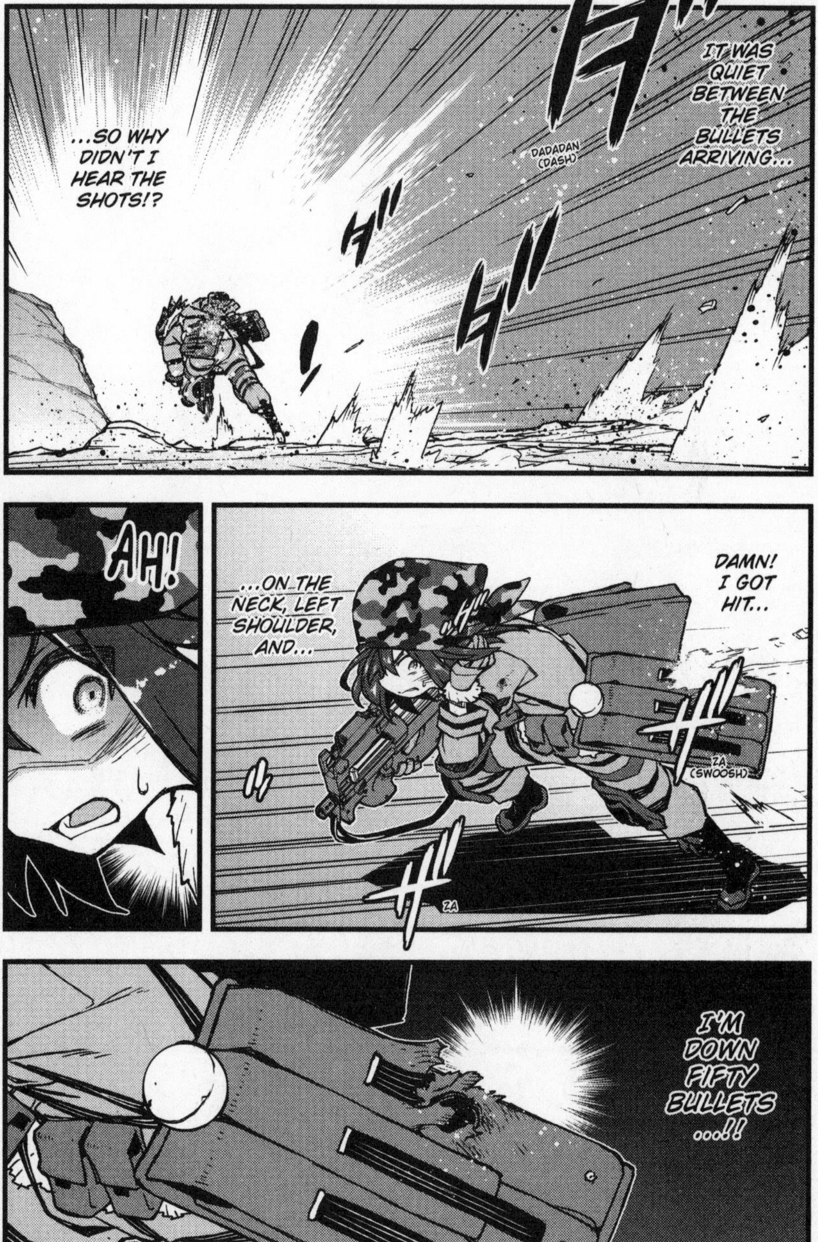
IT WAS QUIET BETWEEN THE BULLETS ARRIVING...
DADADAN (DASH)
...SO WHY DIDN'T I HEAR THE SHOTS!?
DAMN! I GOT HIT...
...ON THE NECK, LEFT SHOULDER, AND...
ZA (SWOOSH)
ZA
AH!
I'M DOWN FIFTY BULLETS ...!!

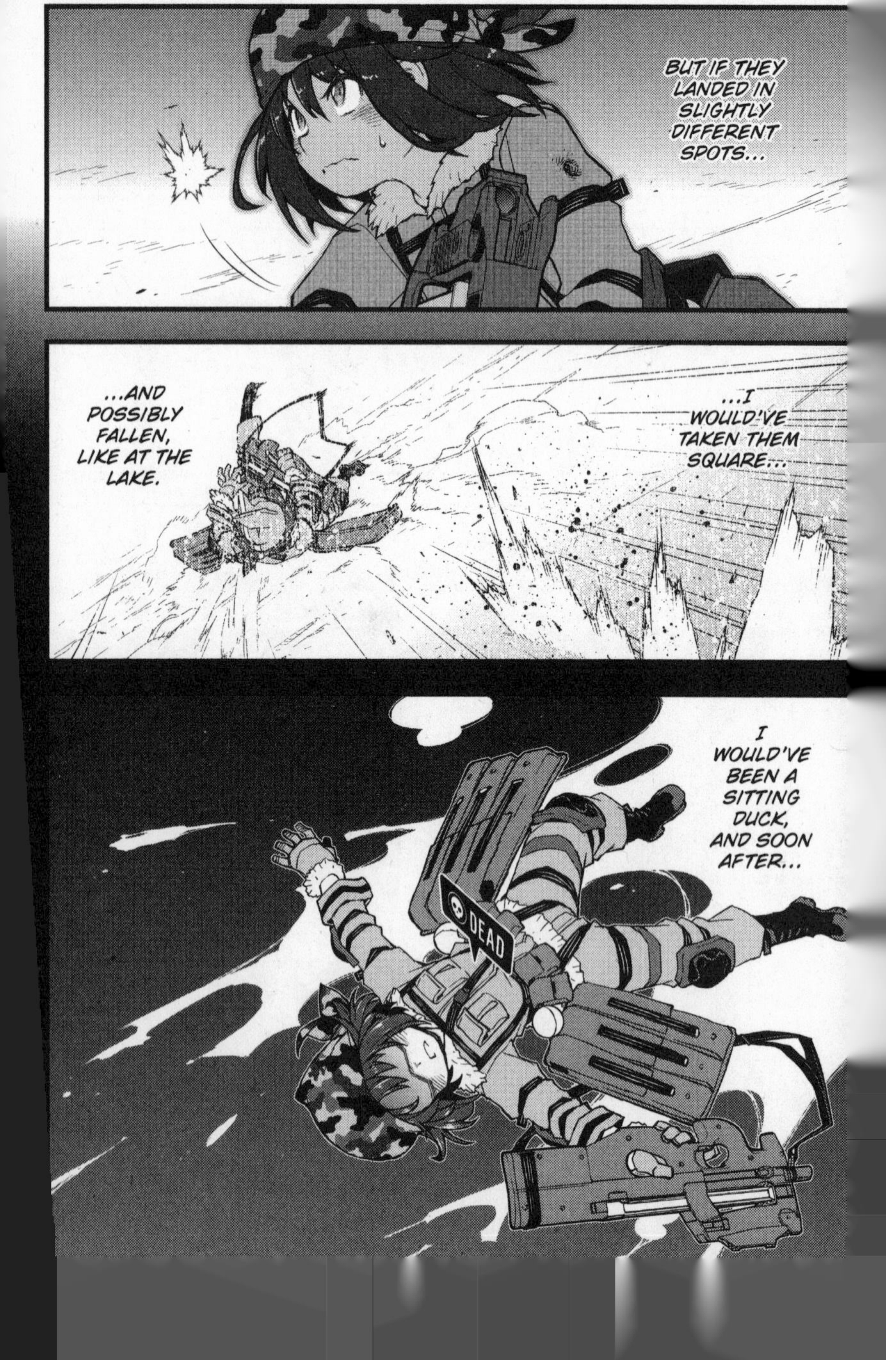
BUT IF THEY LANDED IN SLIGHTLY DIFFERENT SPOTS...
...I WOULD'VE TAKEN THEM SQUARE...
...AND POSSIBLY FALLEN, LIKE AT THE LAKE.
I WOULD'VE BEEN A SITTING DUCK, AND SOON AFTER...
DEAD

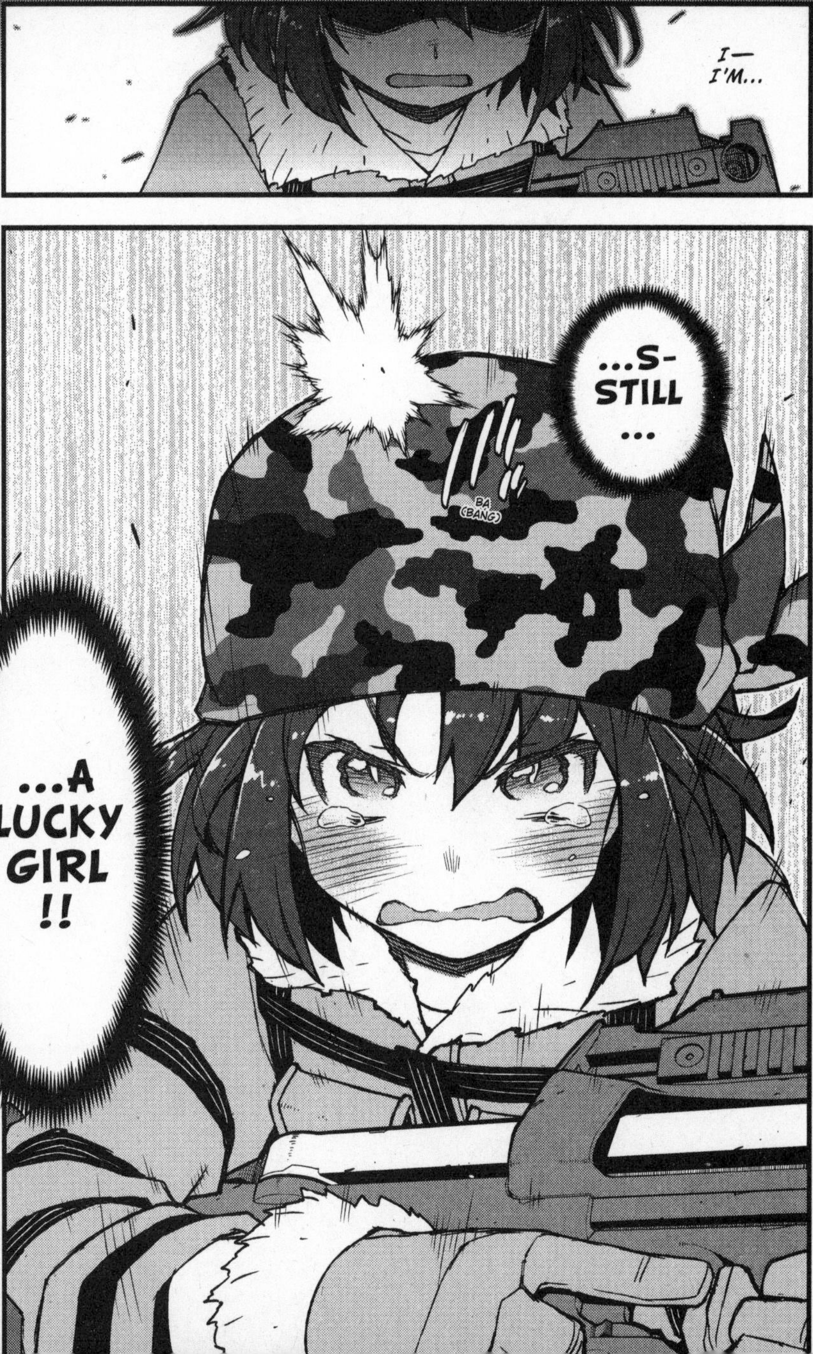
I—
I'M...
...S-
STILL
...
BA
(BANG)
...A
LUCKY
GIRL
!!

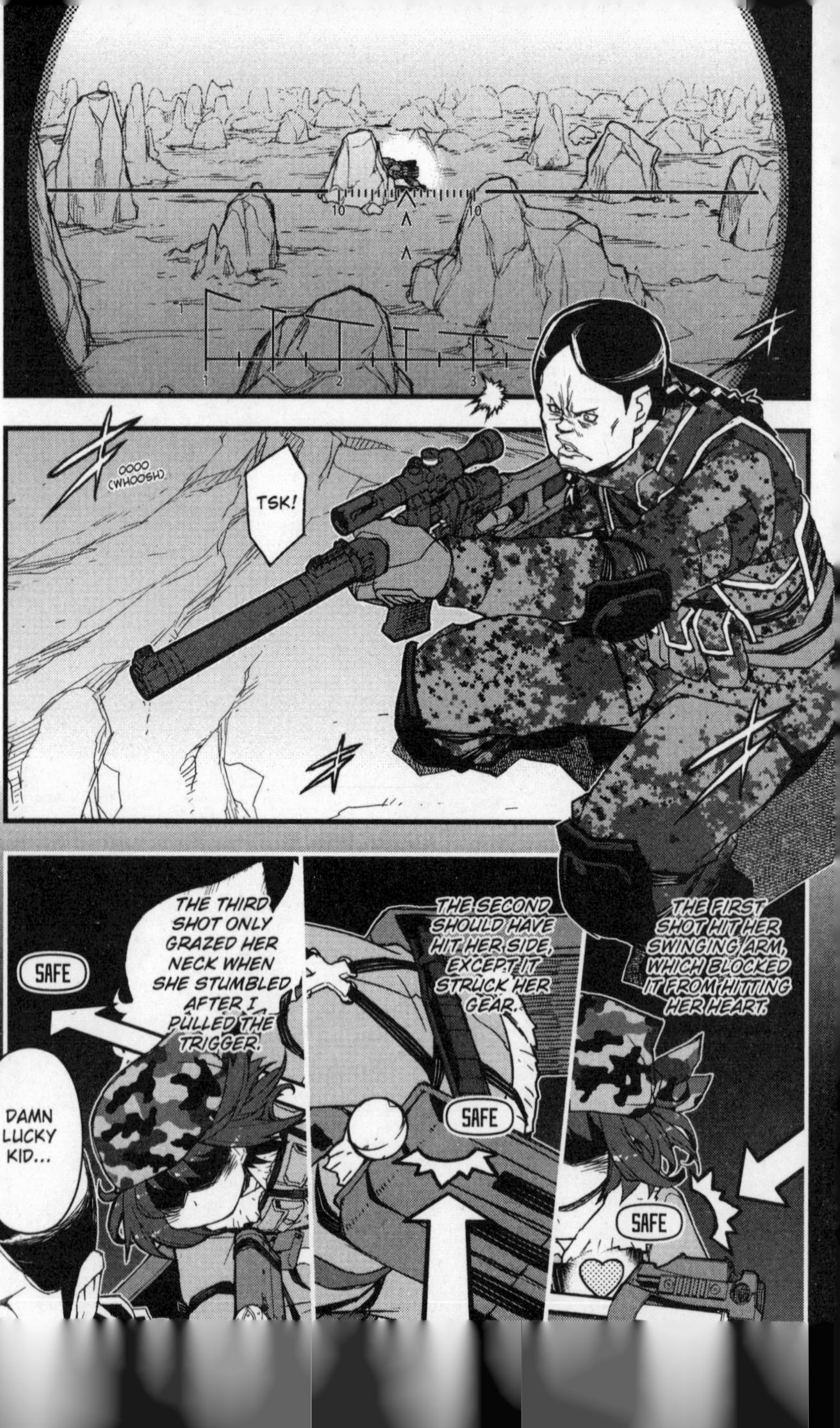
OOOO (WHOOSH)
TSK!
THE FIRST SHOT HIT HER SWINGING ARM, WHICH BLOCKED IT FROM HITTING HER HEART.
SAFE
THE SECOND SHOULD HAVE HIT HER SIDE, EXCEPT IT STRUCK HER GEAR.
SAFE
THE THIRD SHOT ONLY GRAZED HER NECK WHEN SHE STUMBLED AFTER I PULLED THE TRIGGER.
SAFE
DAMN LUCKY KID...

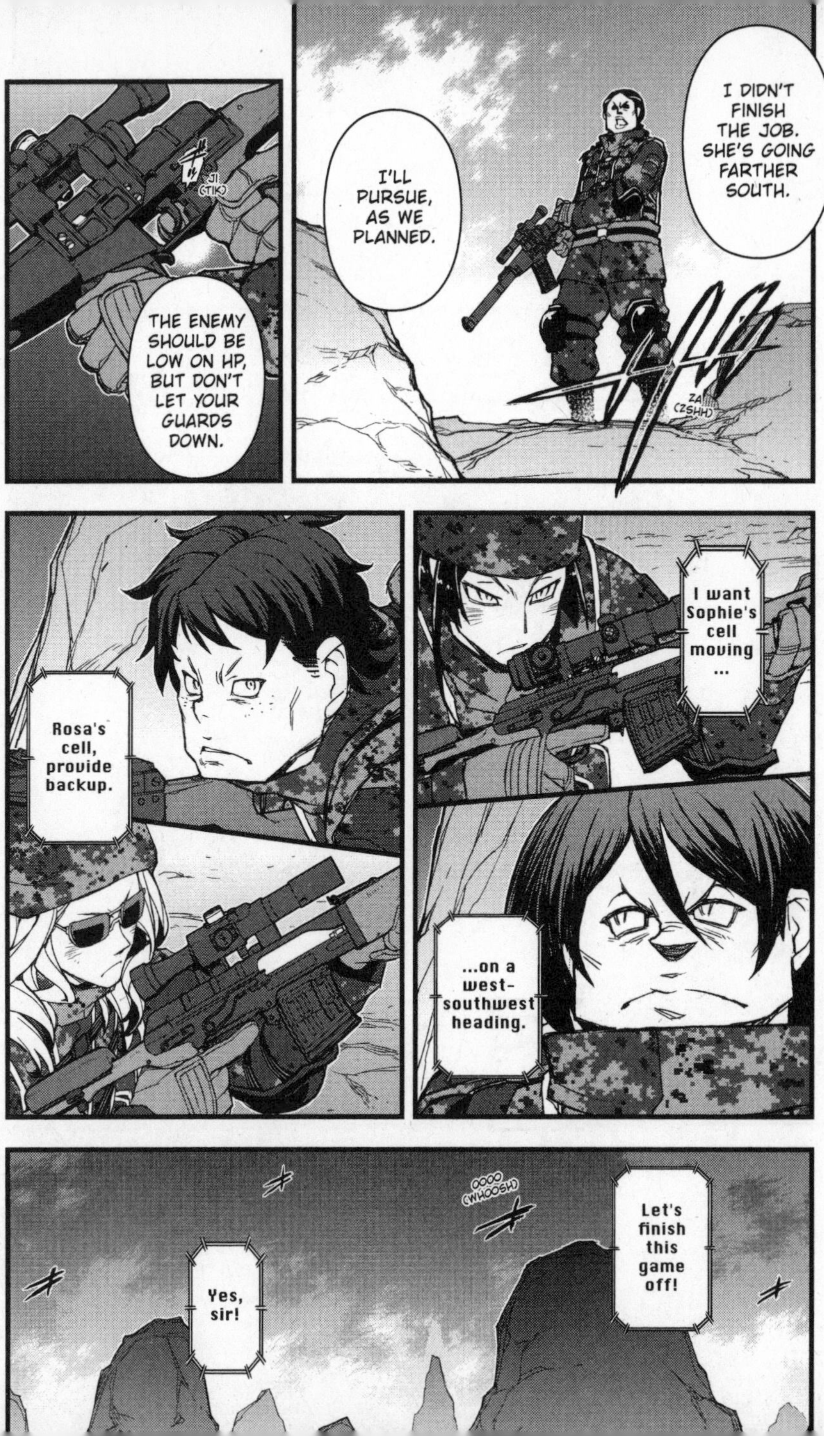
I DIDN'T FINISH THE JOB. SHE'S GOING FARTHER SOUTH.
I'LL PURSUE, AS WE PLANNED.
ZA (ZSHH)
JI (TIK)
THE ENEMY SHOULD BE LOW ON HP, BUT DON'T LET YOUR GUARDS DOWN.
I want Sophie's cell moving ...
...on a west-southwest heading.
Rosa's cell, provide backup.
OOOO (WHOOSH)
Let's finish this game off!
Yes, sir!

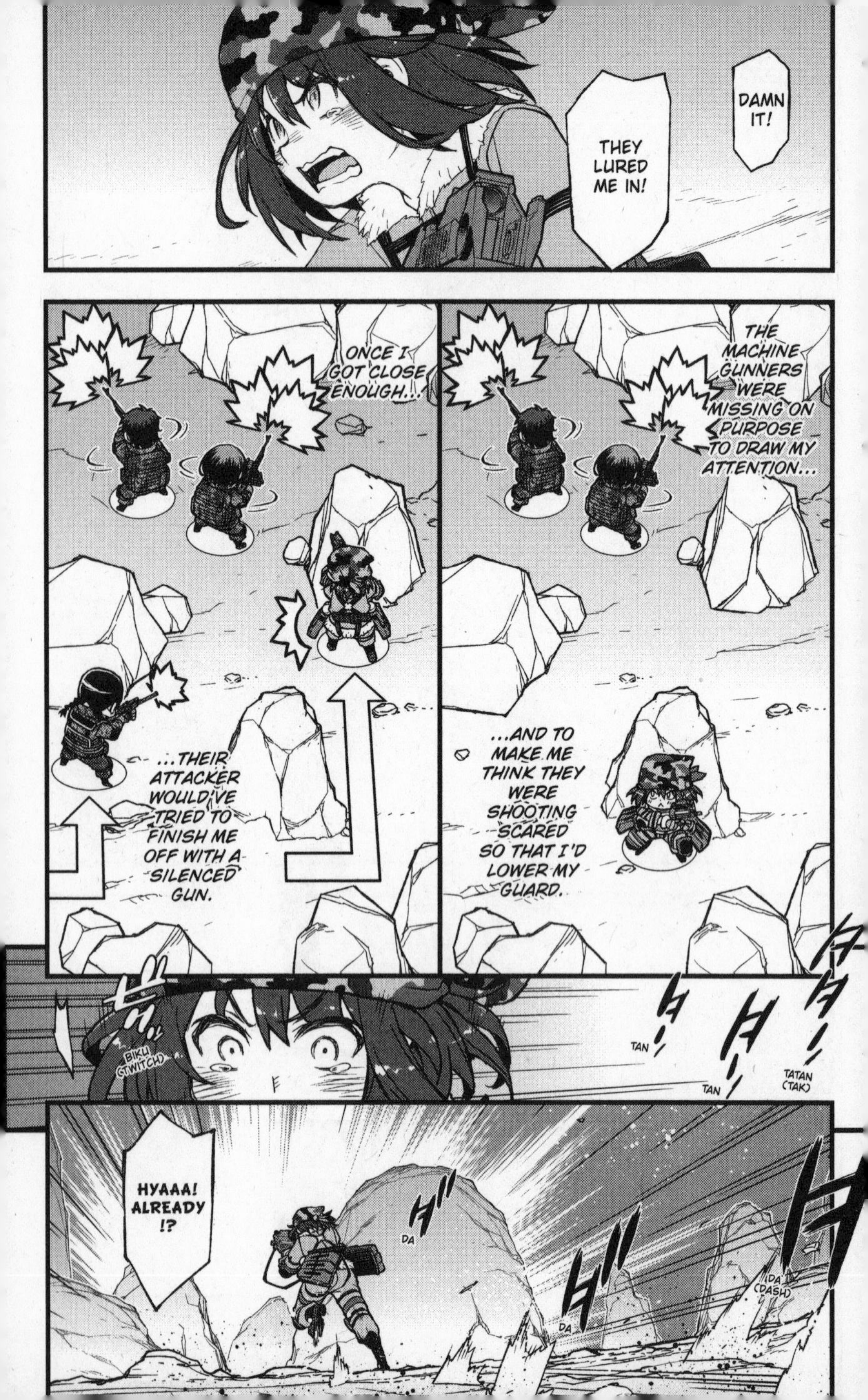
DAMN IT!
THEY LURED ME IN!
THE MACHINE GUNNERS WERE MISSING ON PURPOSE TO DRAW MY ATTENTION...
...AND TO MAKE ME THINK THEY WERE SHOOTING SCARED SO THAT I'D LOWER MY GUARD.
ONCE I GOT CLOSE ENOUGH...
...THEIR ATTACKER WOULD'VE TRIED TO FINISH ME OFF WITH A SILENCED GUN.
TATAN (TAK)
TAN
TAN
BIKU (TWITCH)
DA (DASH)
DA
DA
HYAAA! ALREADY !?

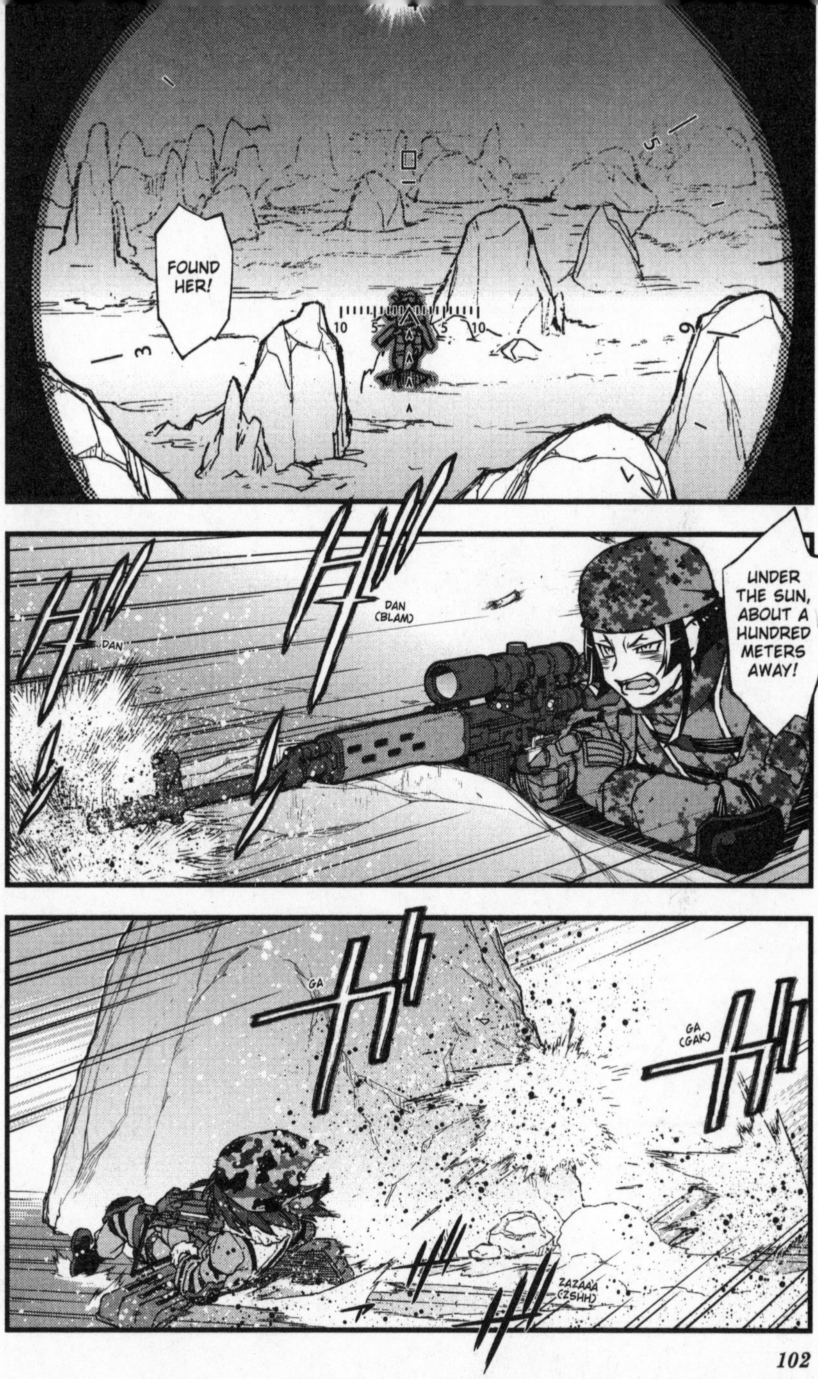
FOUND HER!
UNDER THE SUN, ABOUT A HUNDRED METERS AWAY!
DAN (BLAM)
DAN
GA (GAK)
GA
ZAZAAA (ZSHH)

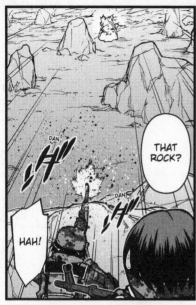

DAN

HAH!

THAT ROCK?

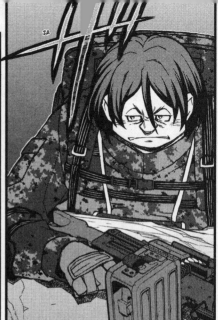

ZA

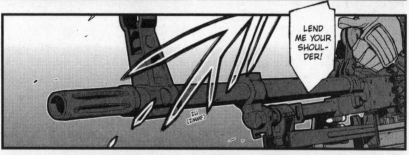

LEND ME YOUR SHOUL-DER!

ZU (ZMMF)

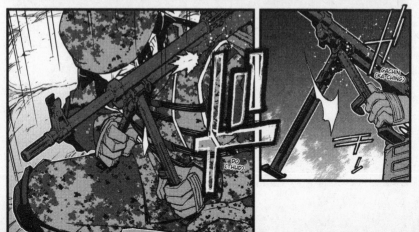

DO (THUD)

GACHIN (KA-CHING)

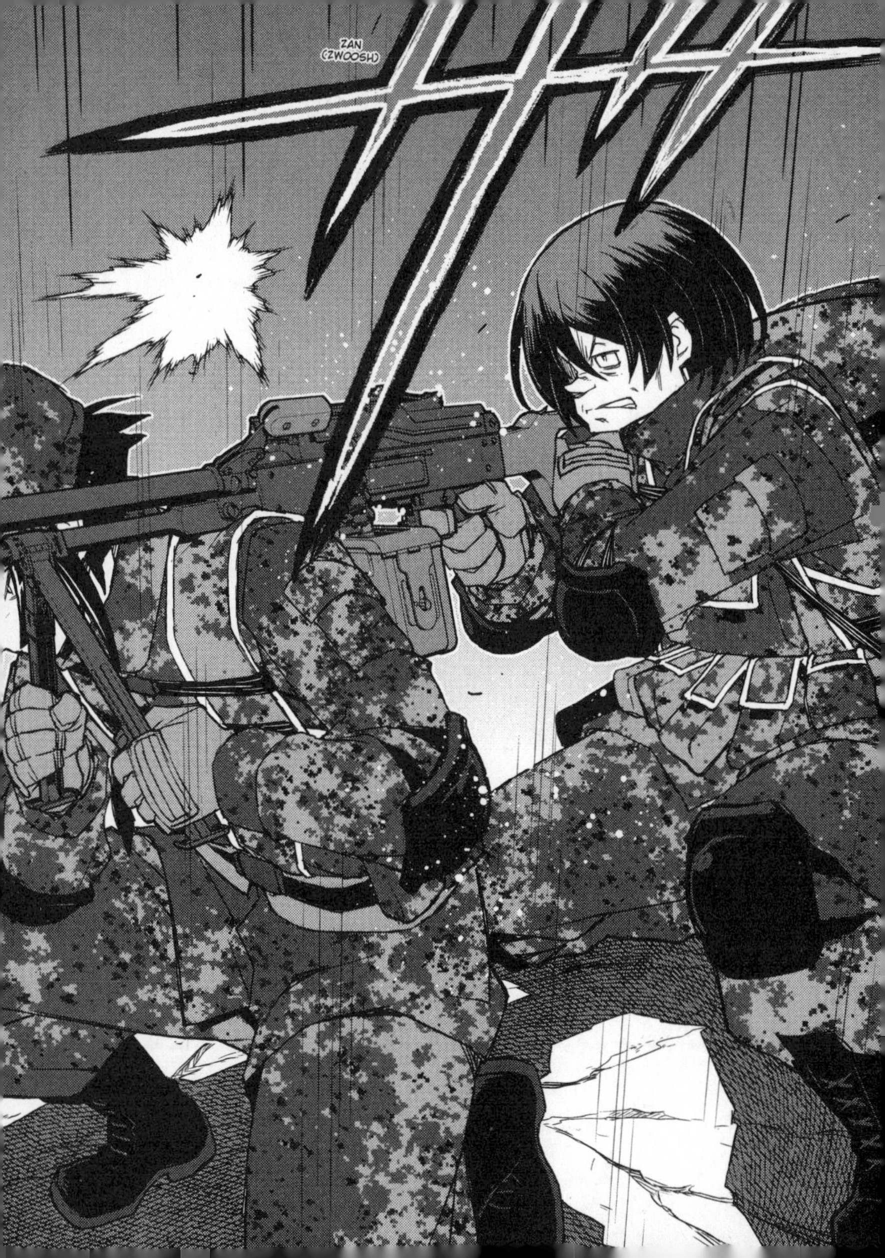
ZAN
(ZWOOSH)

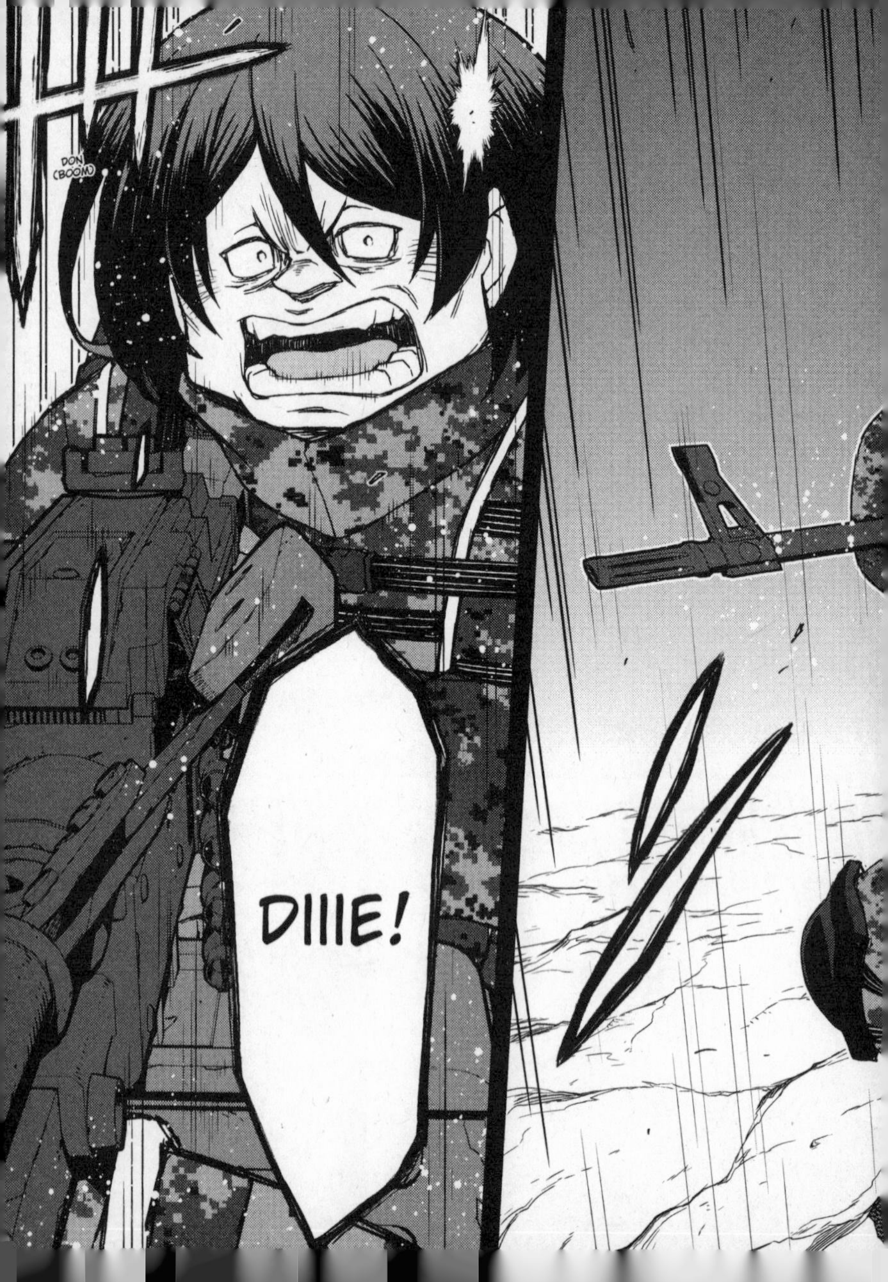
DON (BOOM)
DIIIE!

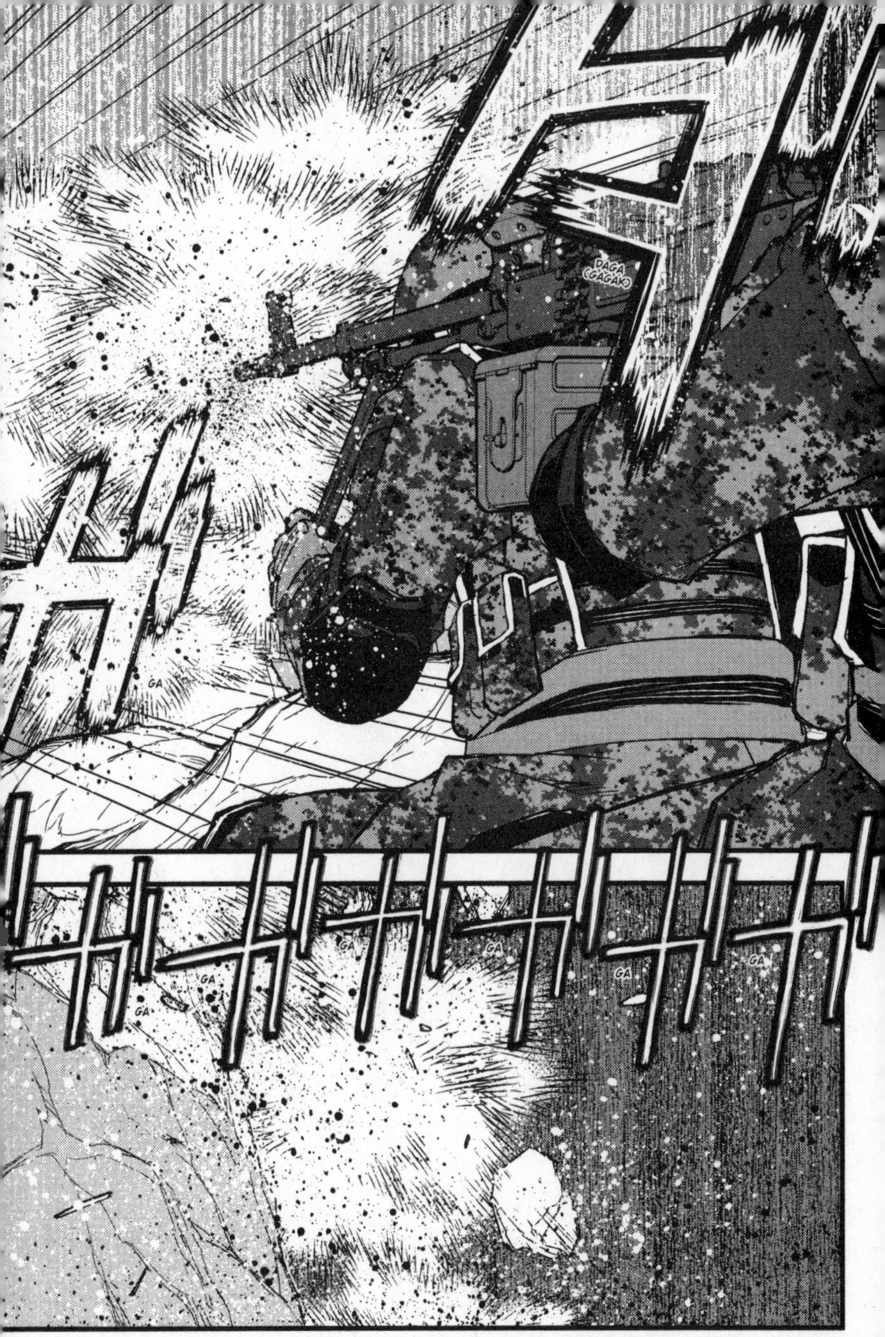
DAGA
(GAGAK)
GA
GA
GA
GA
GA
GA
GA

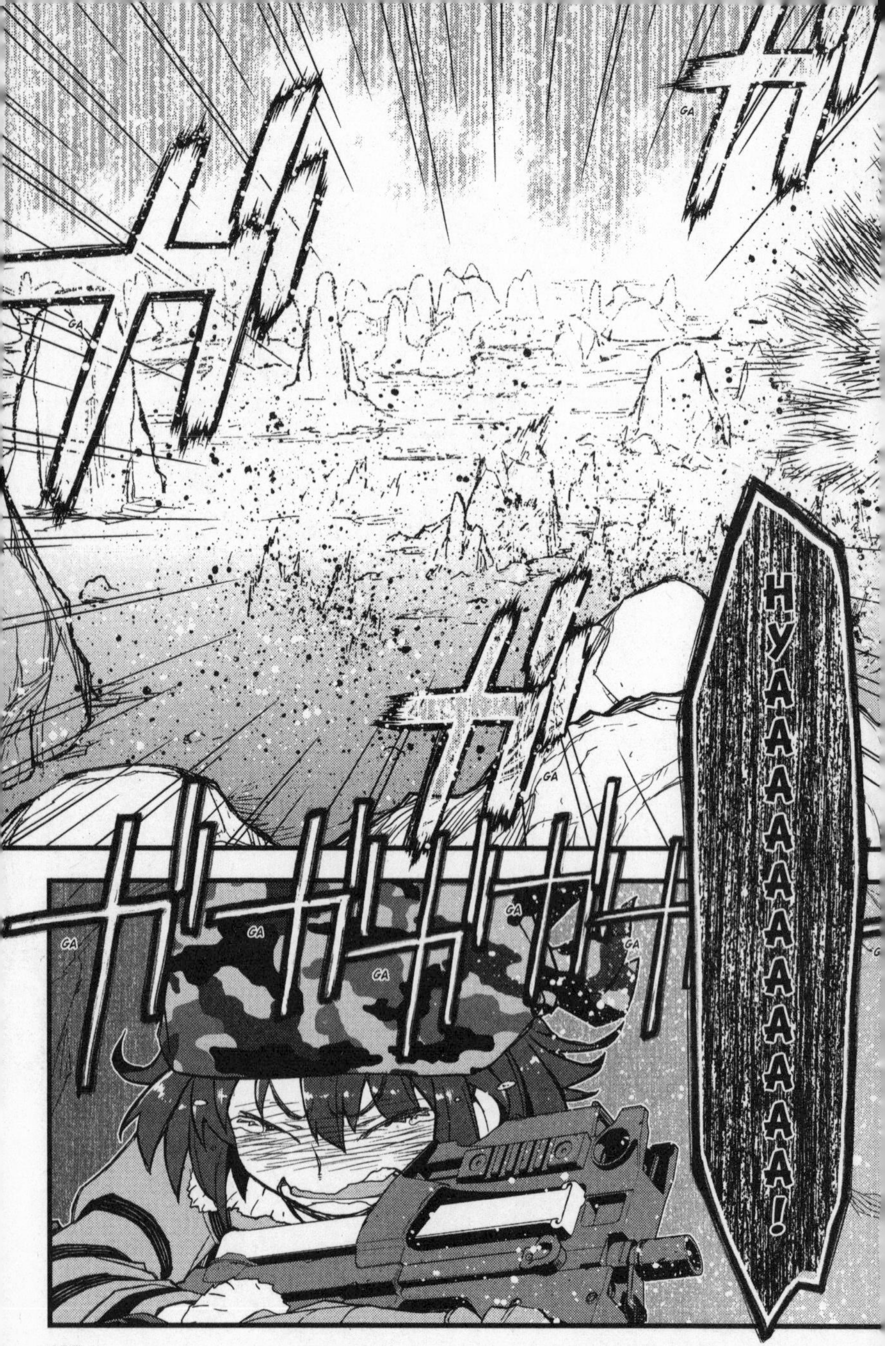
GA
GA
GA
HYAAAAAAAAAAAAAA!
GA
GA
GA
GA
GA

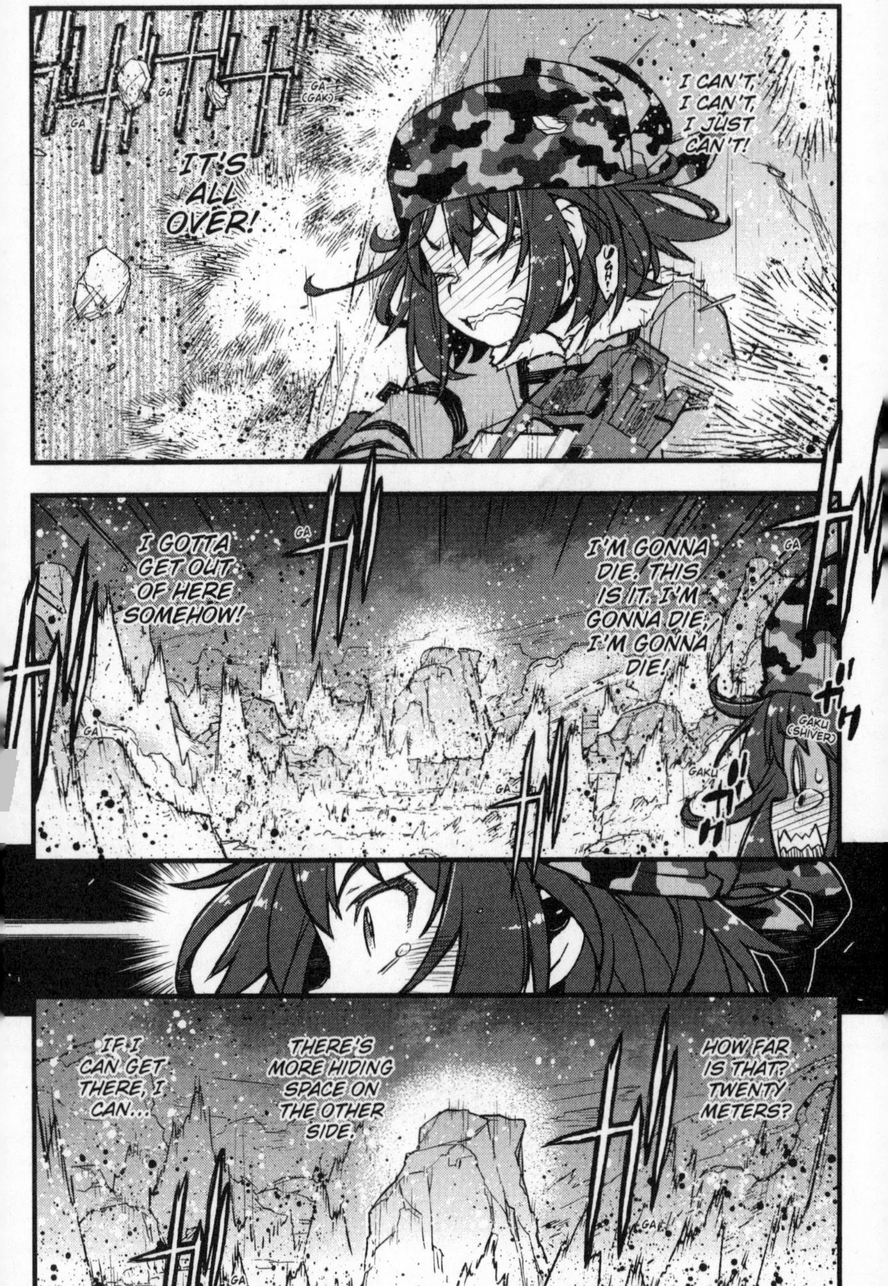
I CAN'T, I CAN'T, I JUST CAN'T!
GA (GAK)
UGH!
IT'S ALL OVER!
GA
GA
GA
GAKU (SHIVER)
GAKU
I'M GONNA DIE. THIS IS IT. I'M GONNA DIE, I'M GONNA DIE!
GA
GA
I GOTTA GET OUT OF HERE SOMEHOW!
GA
HOW FAR IS THAT? TWENTY METERS?
THERE'S MORE HIDING SPACE ON THE OTHER SIDE.
IF I CAN GET THERE, I CAN...
GA
GA

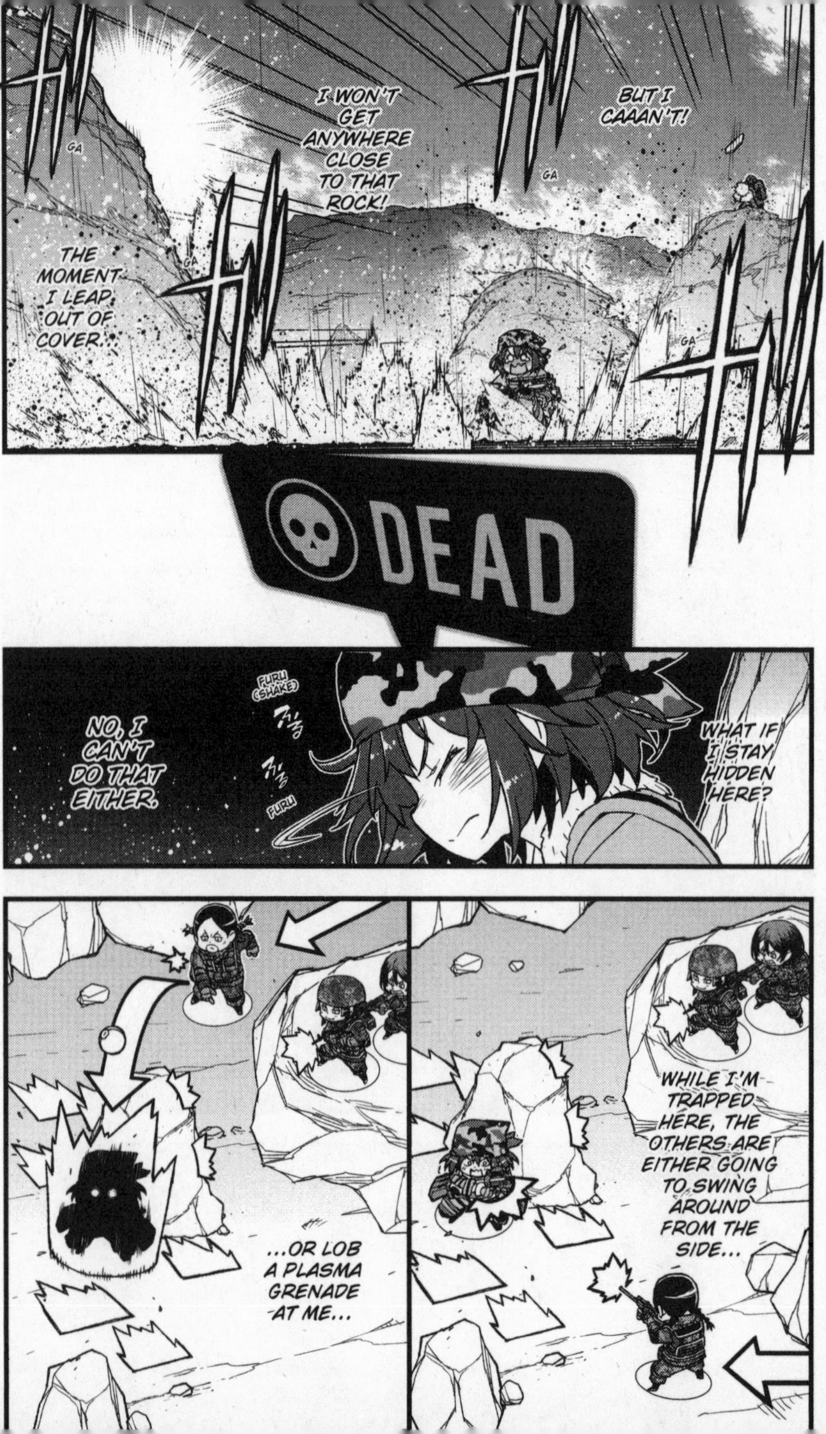

BUT I CAAAN'T!
GA
I WON'T GET ANYWHERE CLOSE TO THAT ROCK!
GA
GA
THE MOMENT I LEAP OUT OF COVER...
GA
DEAD
WHAT IF I STAY HIDDEN HERE?
FURU (SHAKE)
FURU
NO, I CAN'T DO THAT EITHER.
WHILE I'M TRAPPED HERE, THE OTHERS ARE EITHER GOING TO SWING AROUND FROM THE SIDE...
...OR LOB A PLASMA GRENADE AT ME...

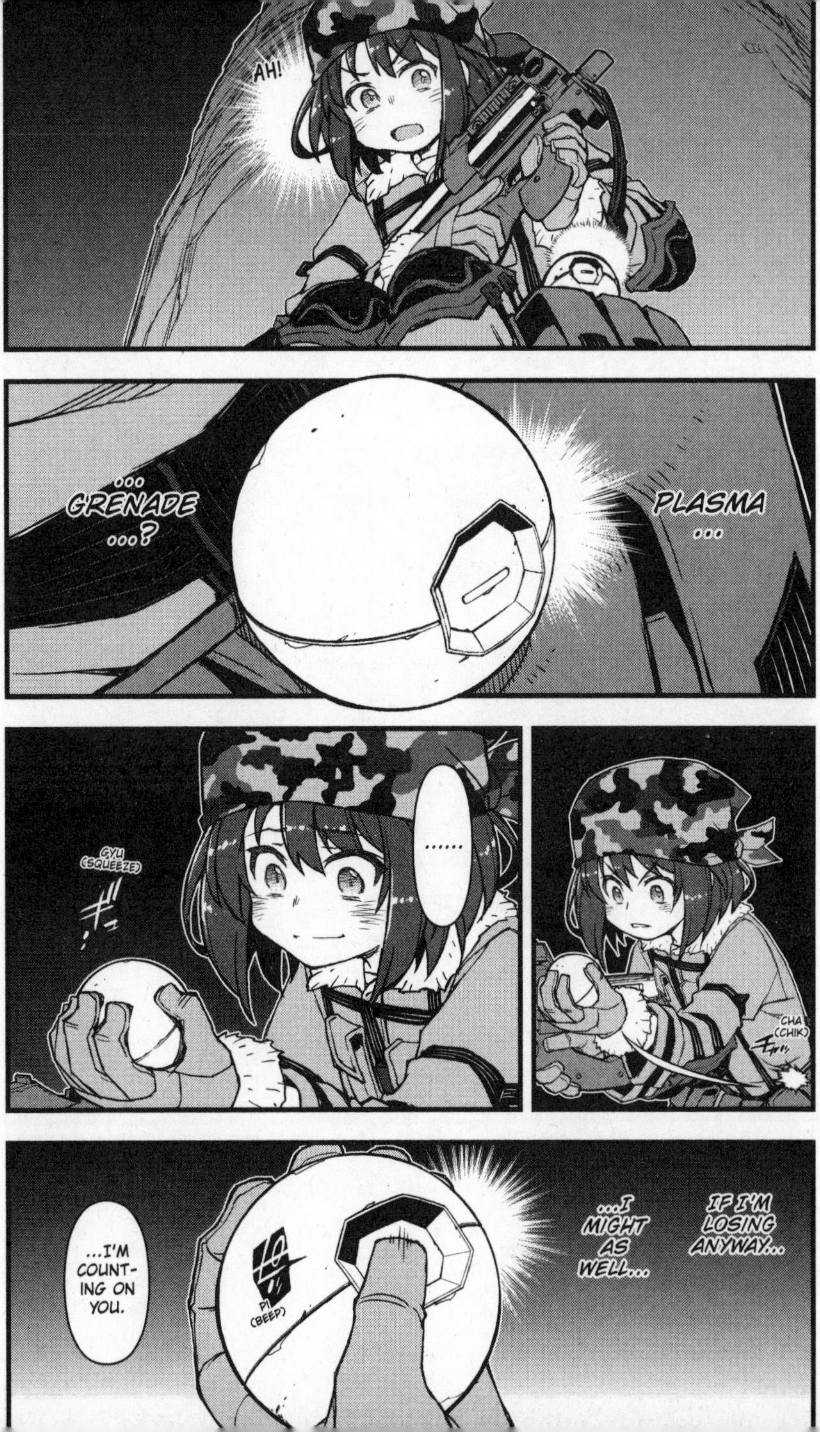
AH!
PLASMA ...
...GRENADE ...?
CHA (CHIK)
......
GYU (SQUEEZE)
IF I'M LOSING ANYWAY...
...I MIGHT AS WELL...
PI (BEEP)
...I'M COUNTING ON YOU.

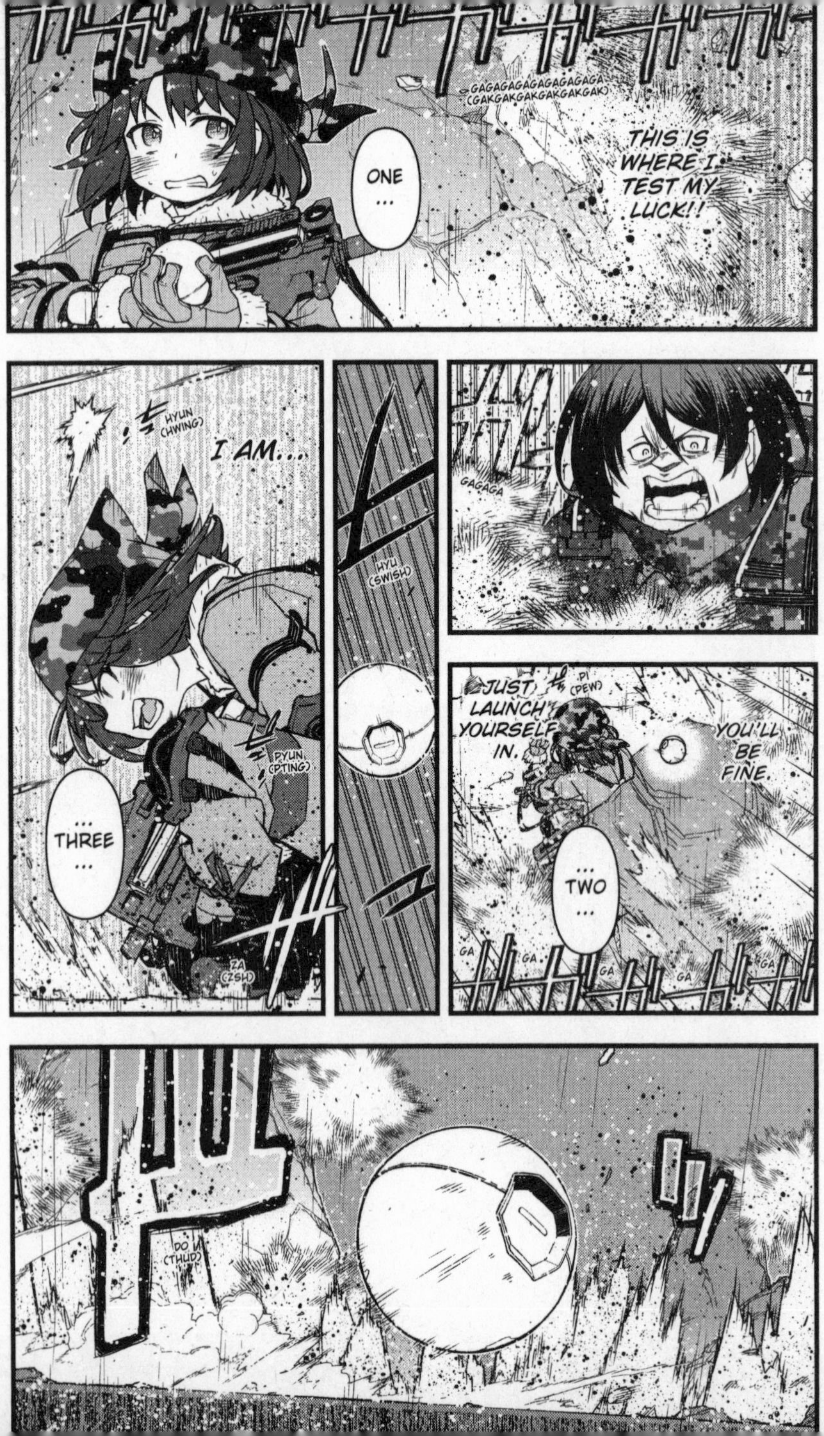
GAGAGAGAGAGAGAGAGA (GAKGAKGAKGAKGAKGAK)
THIS IS WHERE I TEST MY LUCK!!
ONE ...
GAGAGA
PI (PEW)
YOU'LL BE FINE.
JUST LAUNCH YOURSELF IN.
... TWO ...
GA
GA
GA
GA
GA
HYU (SWISH)
HYUN (HWING)
I AM...
PYUN (PTING)
... THREE ...
ZA (ZSH)
DO (THUD)

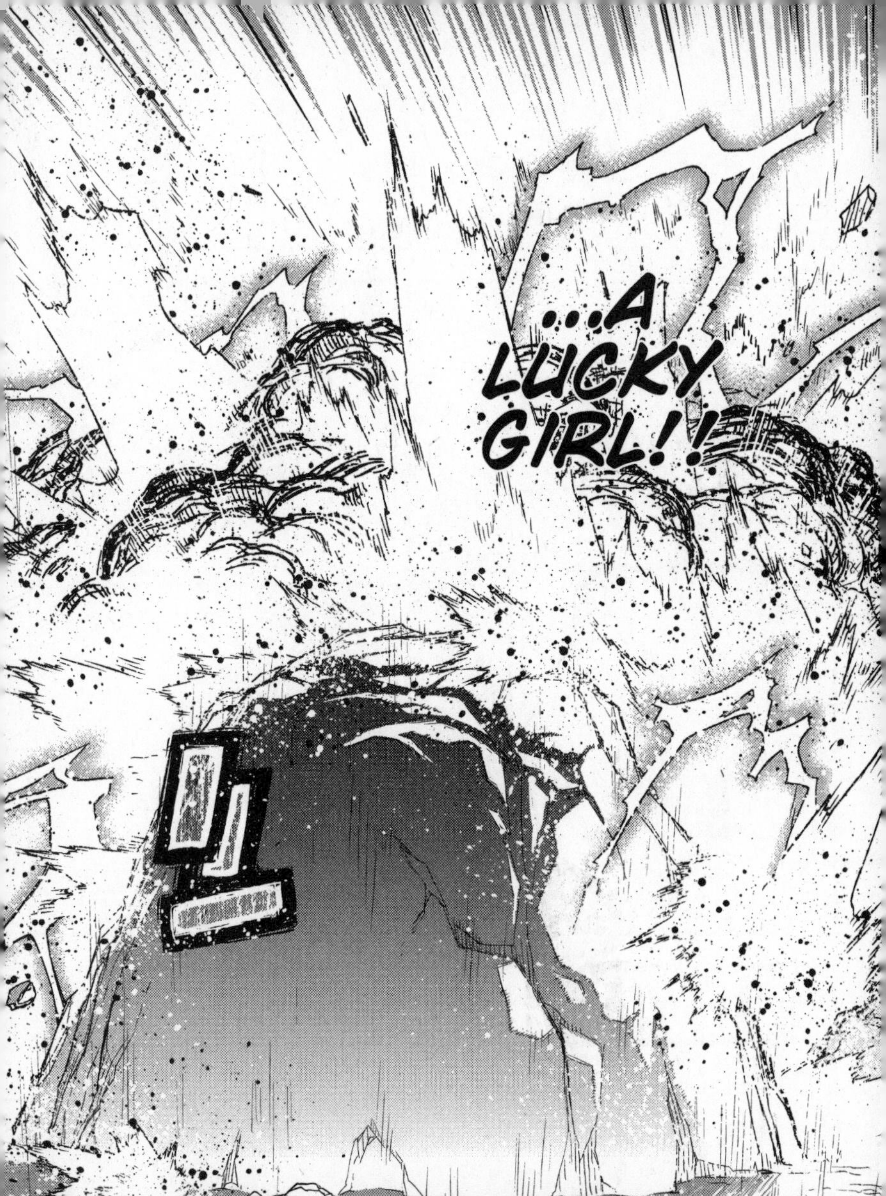
...A LUCKY GIRL!!

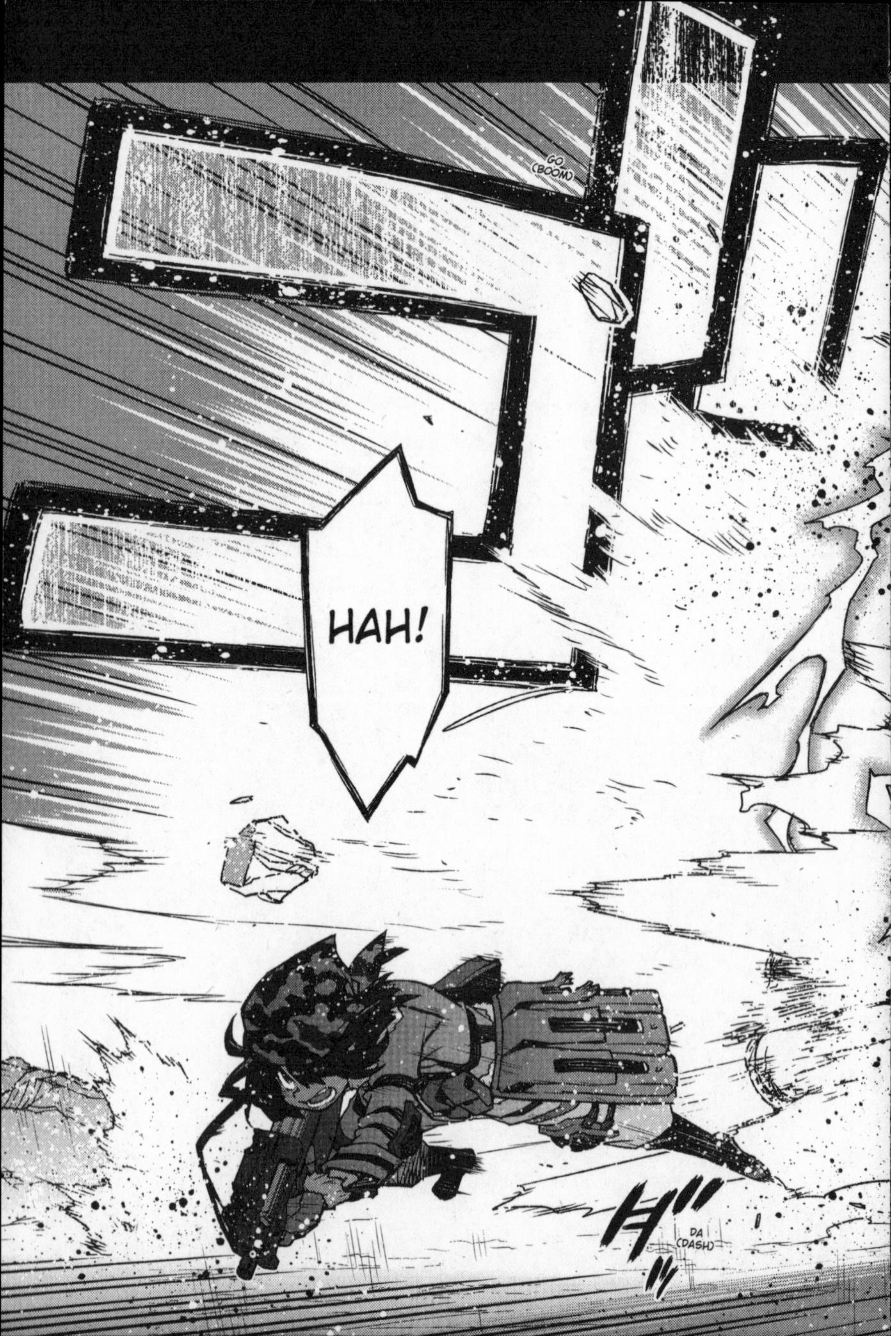
GO
(BOOM)
HAH!
DA
(DASH)

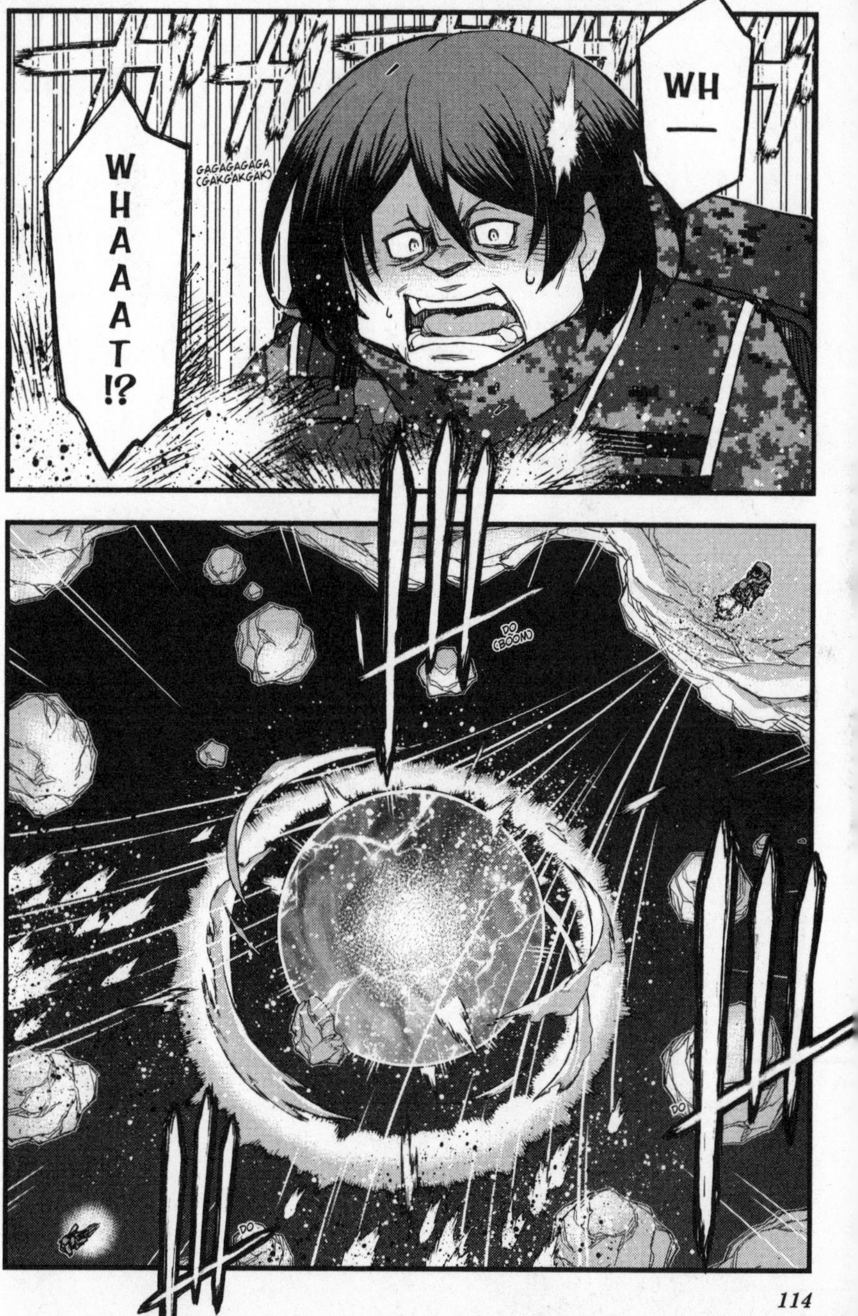
WH—
GAGAGAGAGA (GAKGAKGAK)
WHAAAAT!?
DO (BOOM)
DO
DO

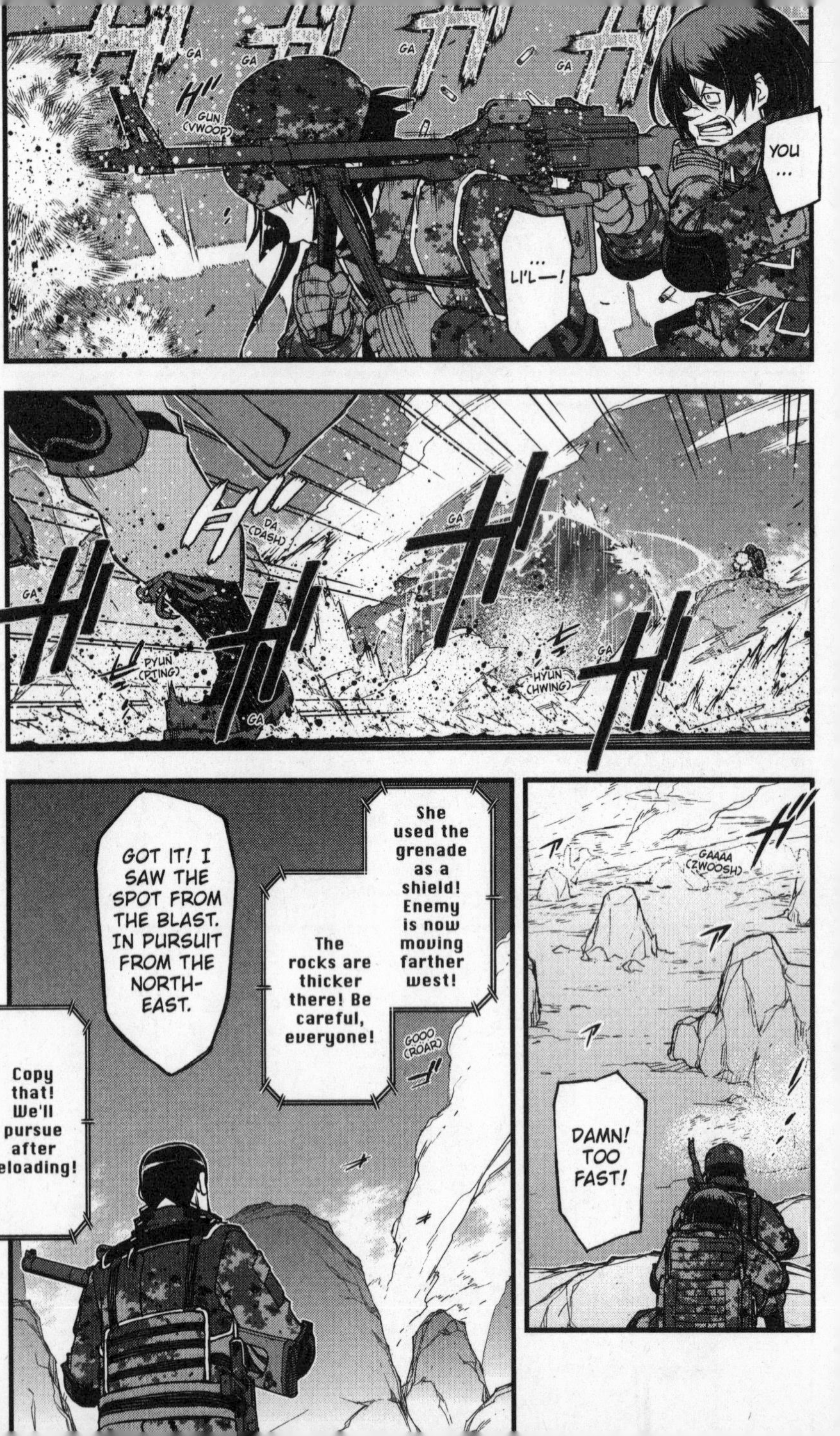
GA
YOU ...
GA
GA
GA
GUN (VWOOP)
... LI'L—!
GA
DA (DASH)
GA
HYUN (CHWING)
PYUN (PTING)
GA
GAAAA (ZWOOSH)
DAMN! TOO FAST!
She used the grenade as a shield! Enemy is now moving farther west!
The rocks are thicker there! Be careful, everyone!
GOT IT! I SAW THE SPOT FROM THE BLAST. IN PURSUIT FROM THE NORTH-EAST.
GOOO (ROAR)
Copy that! We'll pursue after reloading!

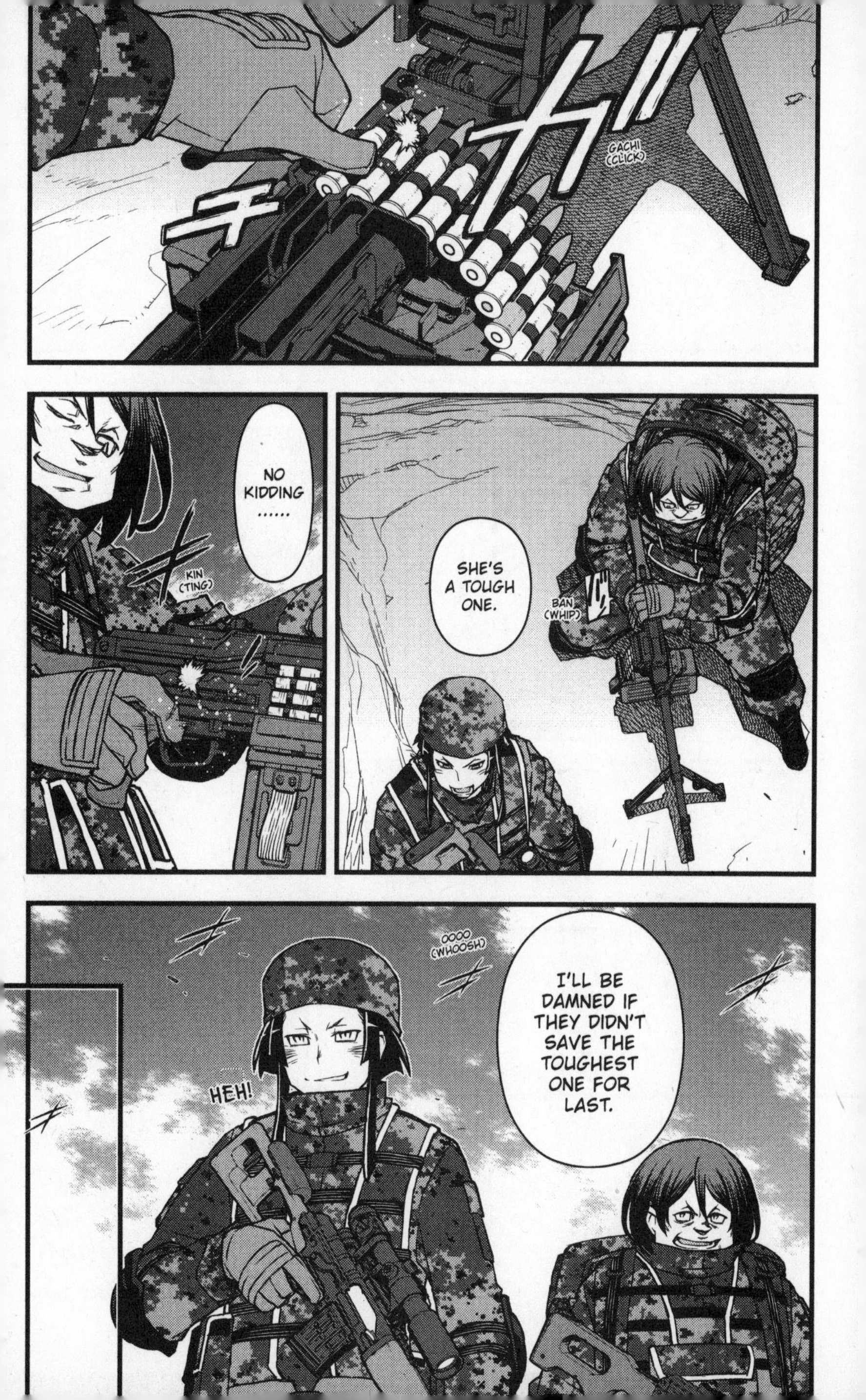
GACHI (CLICK)
SHE'S A TOUGH ONE.
BAN (WHIP)
NO KIDDING ......
KIN (TING)
I'LL BE DAMNED IF THEY DIDN'T SAVE THE TOUGHEST ONE FOR LAST.
OOOO (WHOOSH)
HEH!

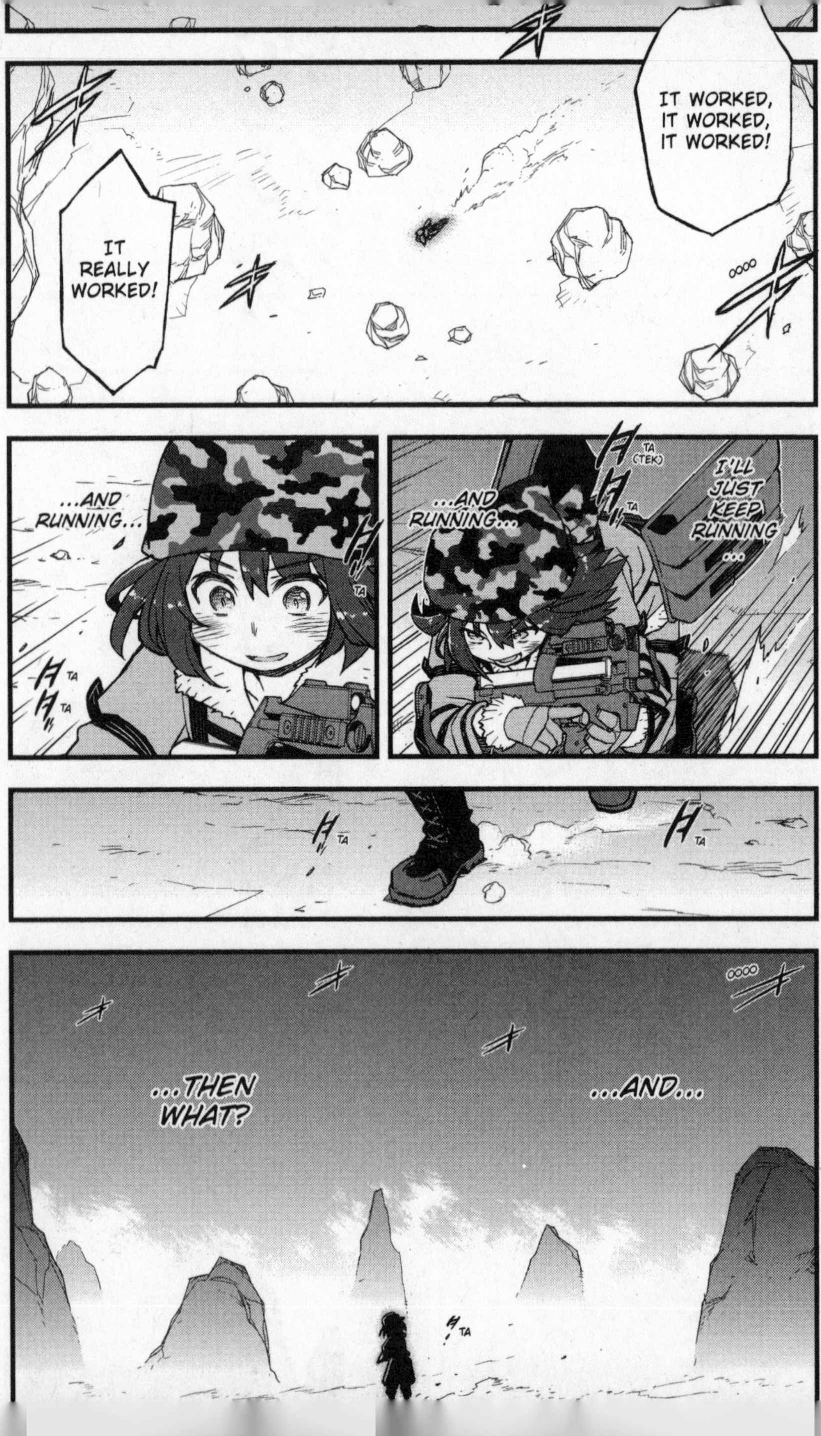
IT WORKED, IT WORKED, IT WORKED!
OOOO
IT REALLY WORKED!
TA (TEK)
I'LL JUST KEEP RUNNING...
TA
...AND RUNNING...
...AND RUNNING...
TA
TA
TA
TA
TA
OOOO
...AND...
...THEN WHAT?
TA

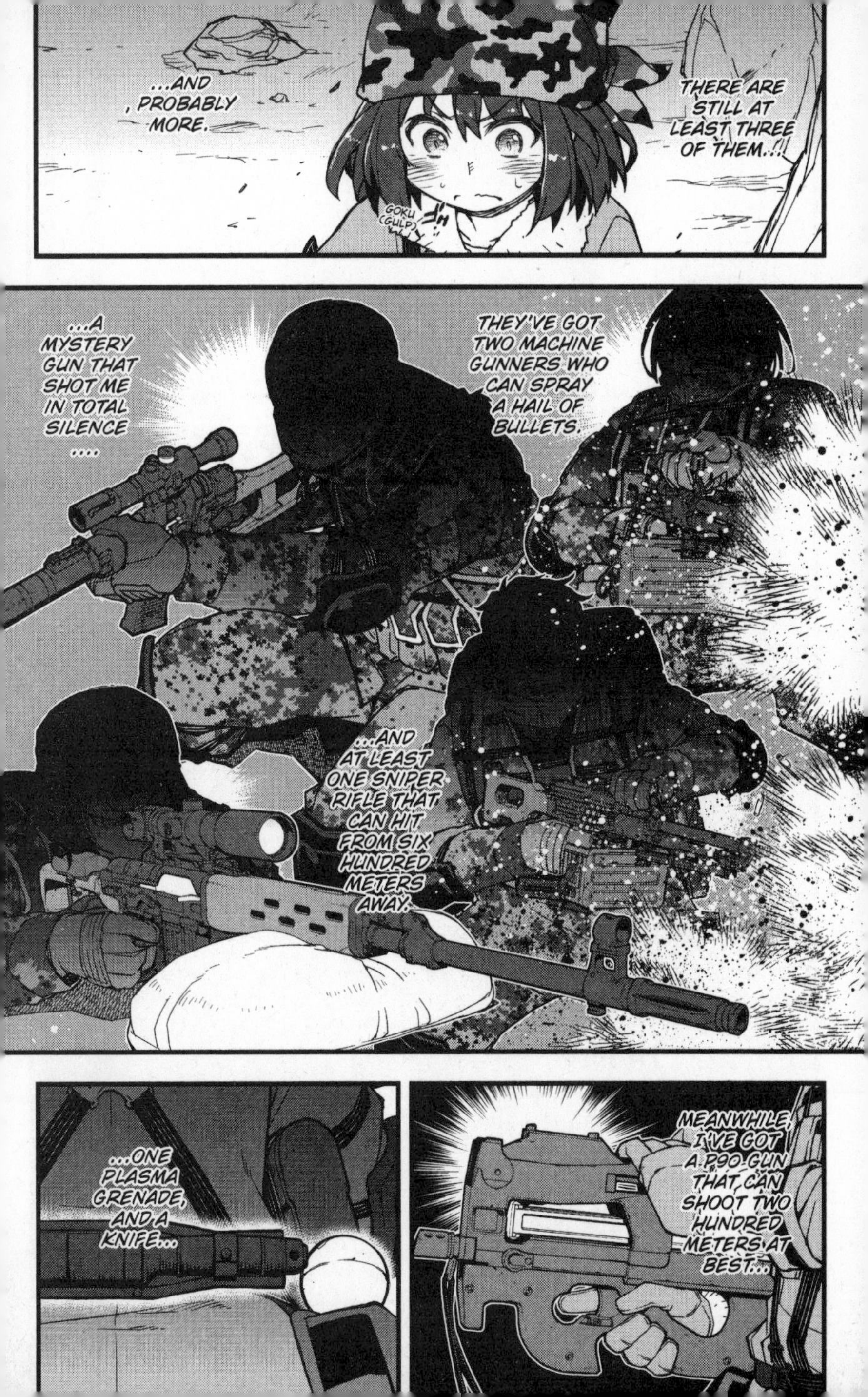
THERE ARE STILL AT LEAST THREE OF THEM...!!
...AND, PROBABLY MORE.
GOKU (GULP)
THEY'VE GOT TWO MACHINE GUNNERS WHO CAN SPRAY A HAIL OF BULLETS.
...A MYSTERY GUN THAT SHOT ME IN TOTAL SILENCE....
...AND AT LEAST ONE SNIPER RIFLE THAT CAN HIT FROM SIX HUNDRED METERS AWAY.
MEANWHILE, I'VE GOT A P90 GUN THAT CAN SHOOT TWO HUNDRED METERS AT BEST...
...ONE PLASMA GRENADE, AND A KNIFE...

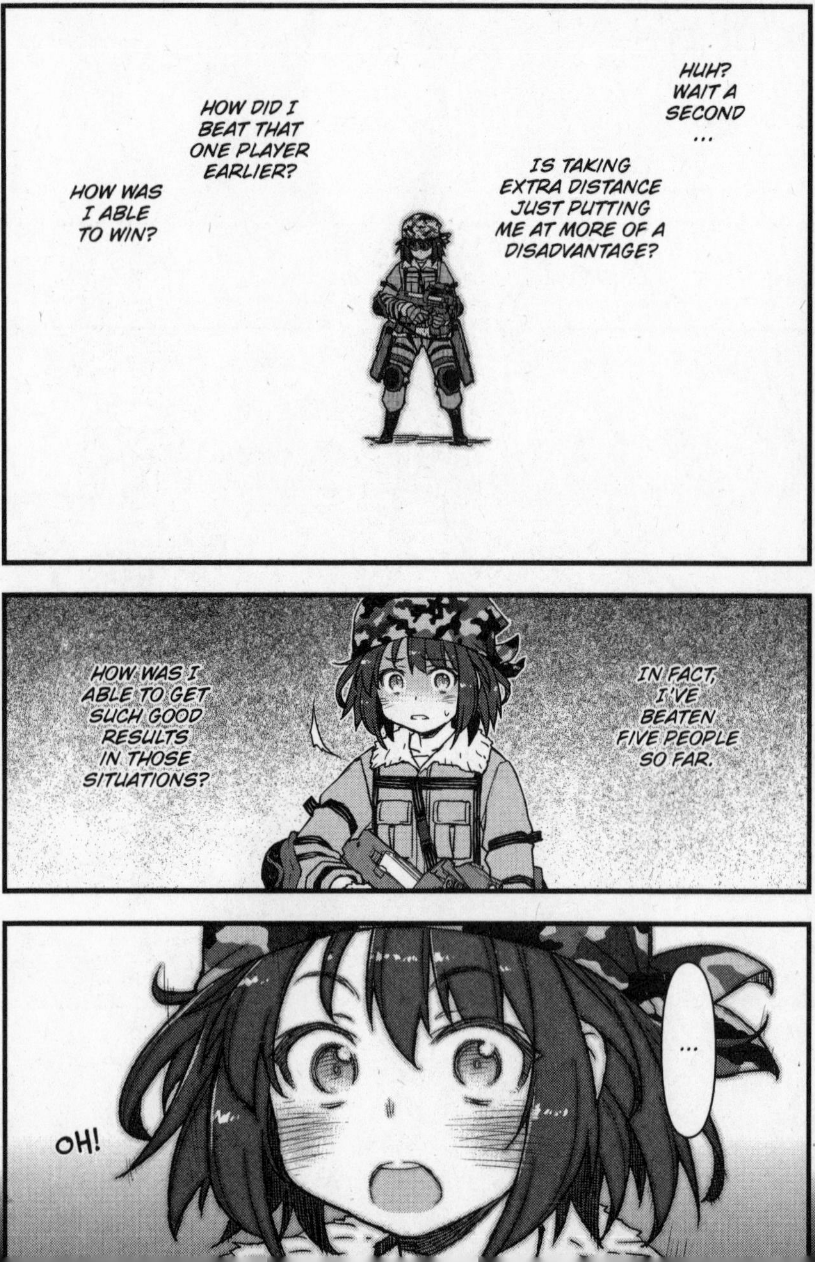
HUH? WAIT A SECOND ...
IS TAKING EXTRA DISTANCE JUST PUTTING ME AT MORE OF A DISADVANTAGE?
HOW DID I BEAT THAT ONE PLAYER EARLIER?
HOW WAS I ABLE TO WIN?
IN FACT, I'VE BEATEN FIVE PEOPLE SO FAR.
HOW WAS I ABLE TO GET SUCH GOOD RESULTS IN THOSE SITUATIONS?
...
OH!

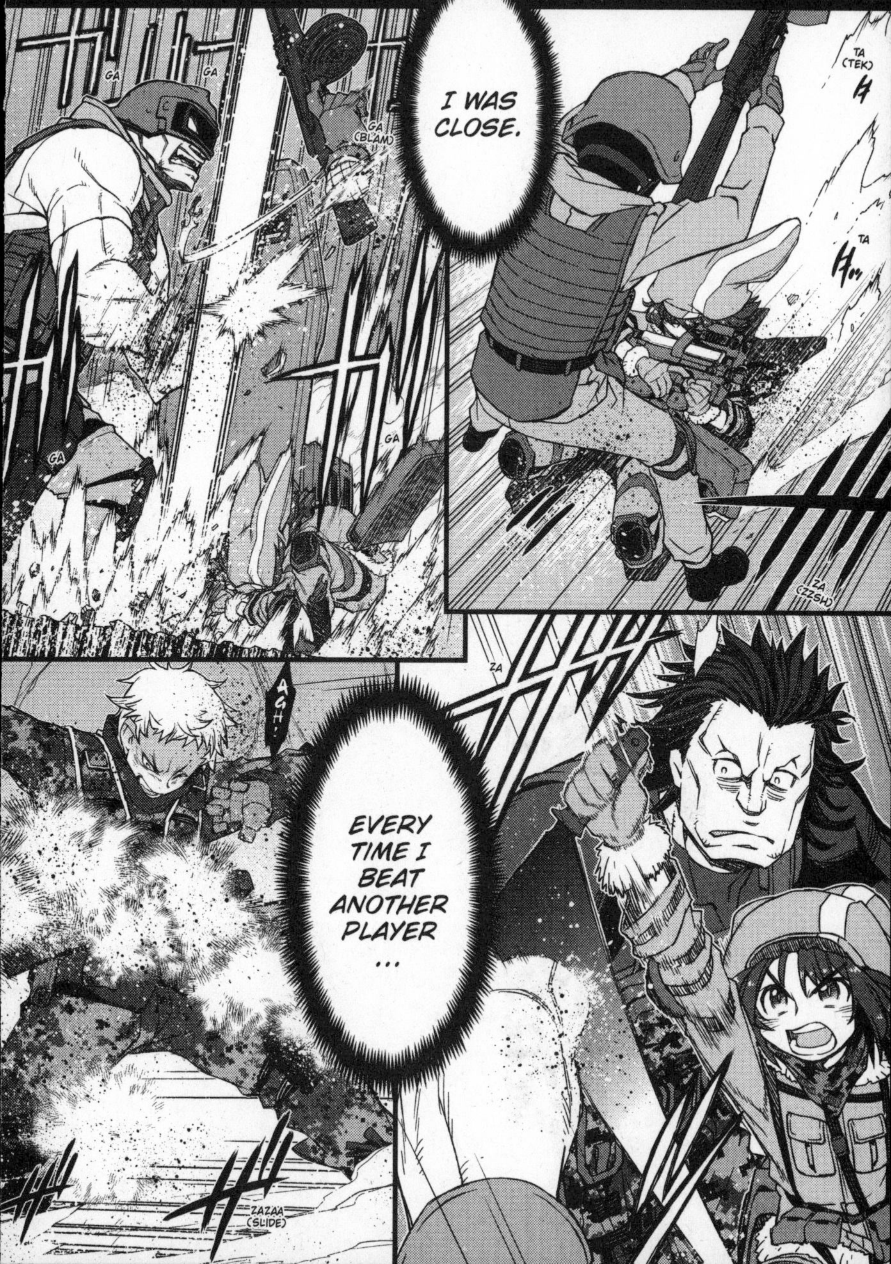
I WAS CLOSE.
TA (TEK)
TA
ZA (ZZSH)
GA
GA
GA (BLAM)
GA
GA
ZA
EVERY TIME I BEAT ANOTHER PLAYER ...
AGH!
ZAZAA (SLIDE)

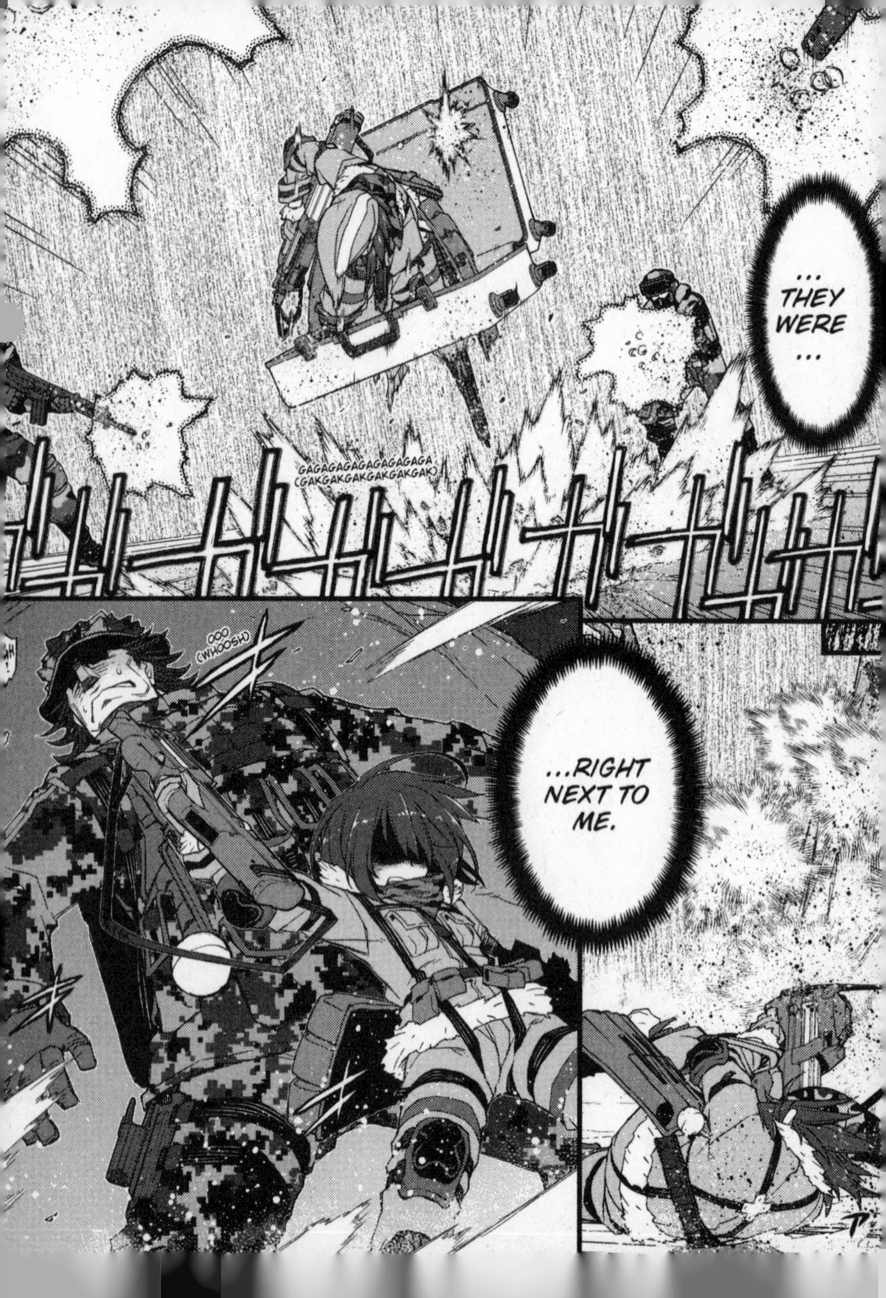

... THEY WERE ...
GAGAGAGAGAGAGAGAGA (GAKGAKGAKGAKGAKGAK)
...RIGHT NEXT TO ME.
OOO (WHOOSH)

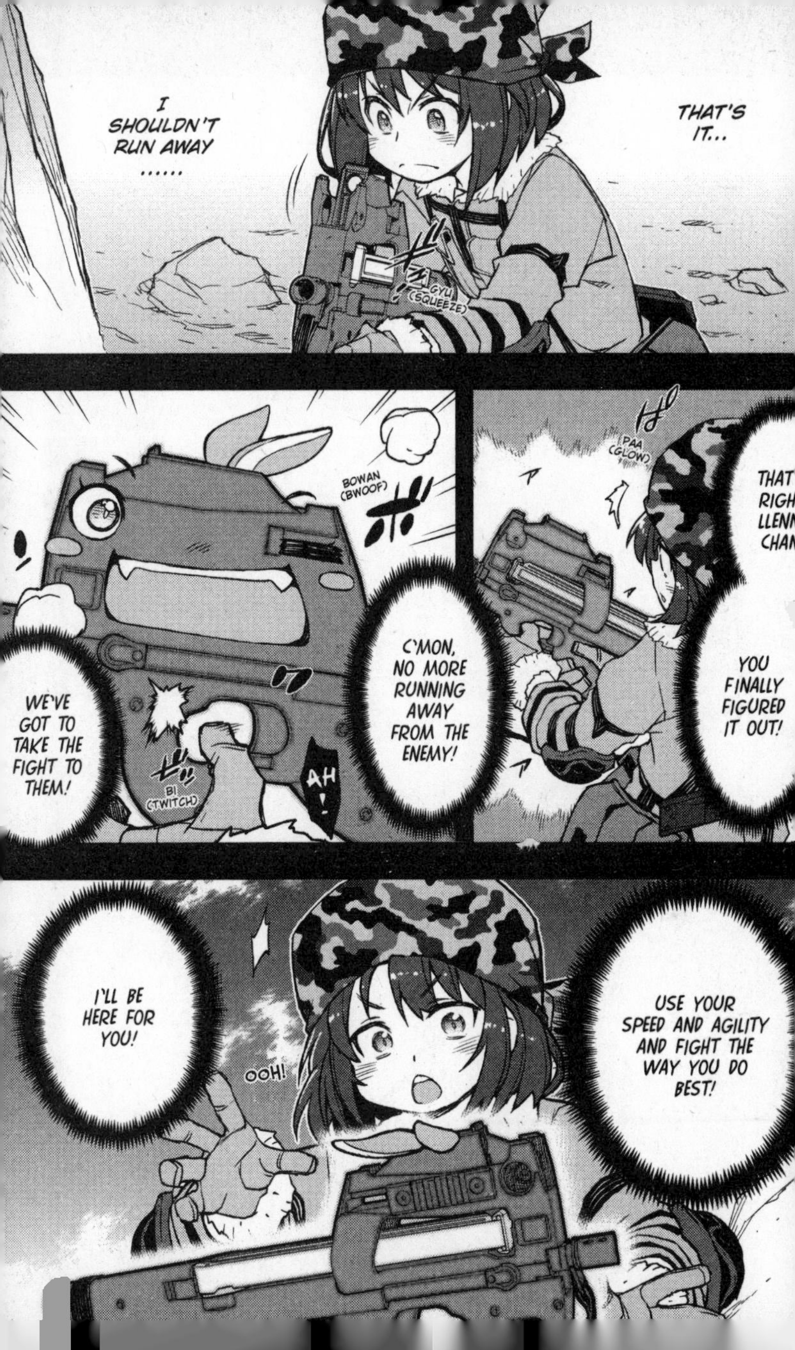
THAT'S IT...
I SHOULDN'T RUN AWAY ......
GYU (SQUEEZE)
PAA (GLOW)
THAT RIGH LLENN CHAN
YOU FINALLY FIGURED IT OUT!
BOWAN (BWOOF)
C'MON, NO MORE RUNNING AWAY FROM THE ENEMY!
AH!
BI (TWITCH)
WE'VE GOT TO TAKE THE FIGHT TO THEM!
USE YOUR SPEED AND AGILITY AND FIGHT THE WAY YOU DO BEST!
OOH!
I'LL BE HERE FOR YOU!

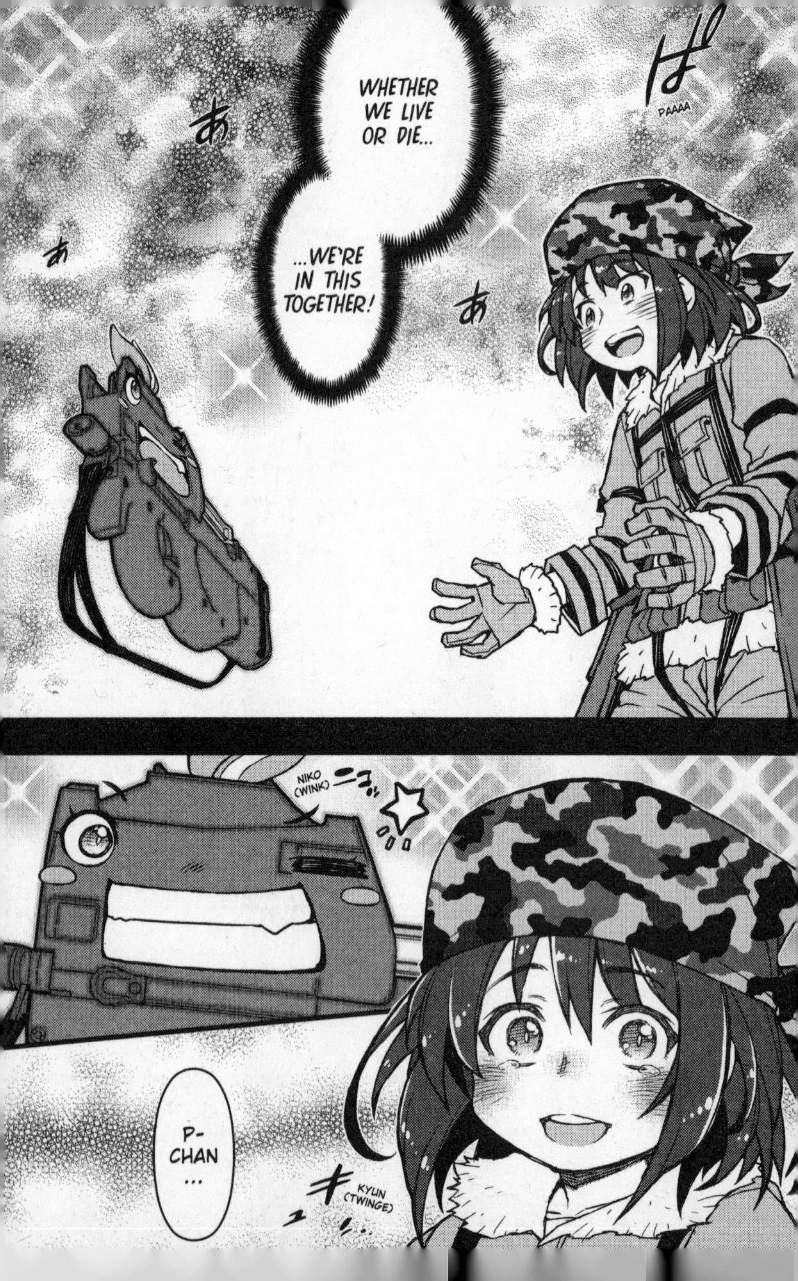
ぱ
PAAAA
WHETHER WE LIVE OR DIE...
...WE'RE IN THIS TOGETHER!
あ
あ
あ
ニコッ
NIKO (WINK)
P-CHAN...
キュ
KYUN (TWINGE)

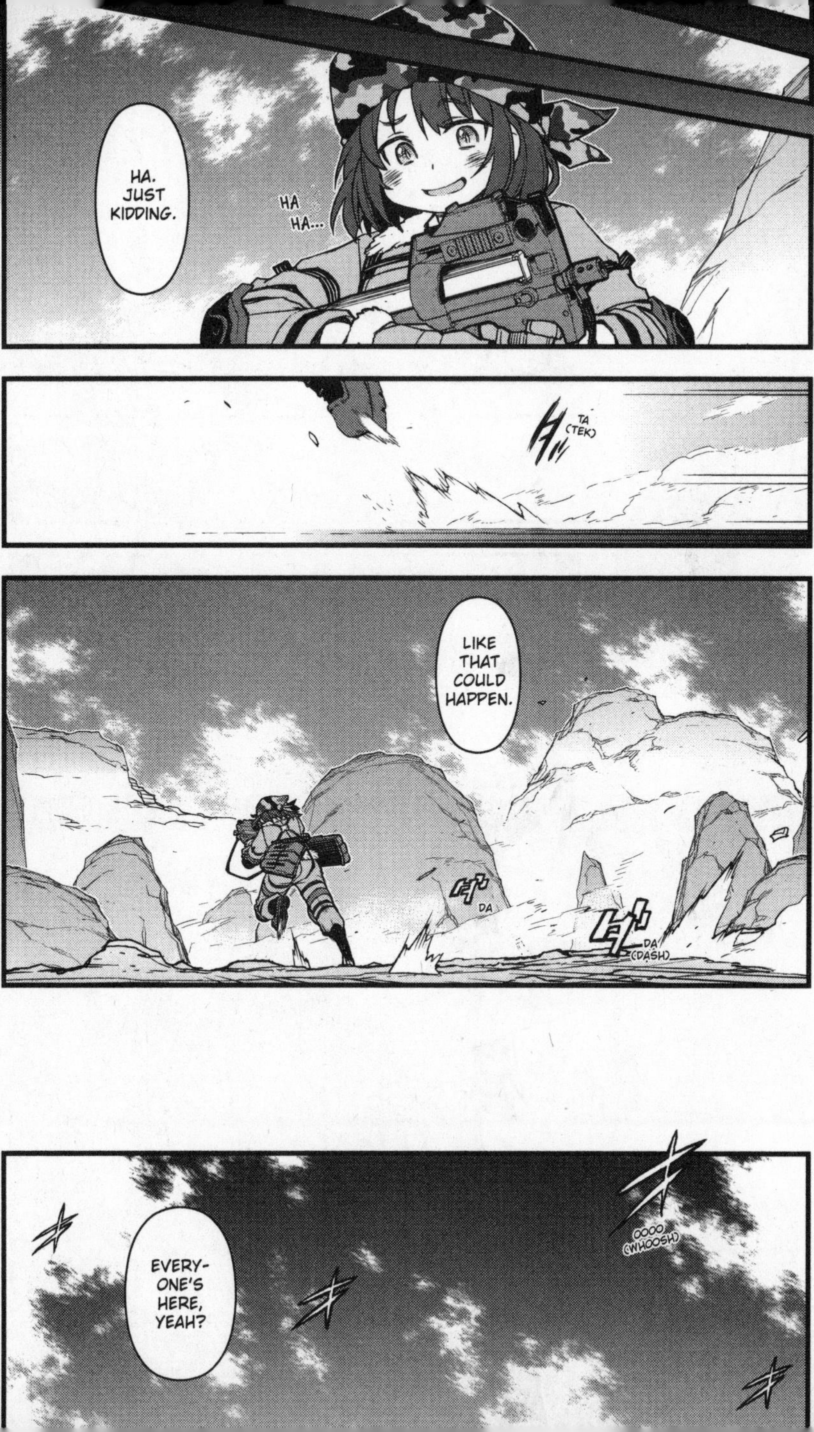
HA. JUST KIDDING.
HA HA...
TA (TEK)
LIKE THAT COULD HAPPEN.
DA
DA (DASH)
OOOO (WHOOSH)
EVERY-ONE'S HERE, YEAH?

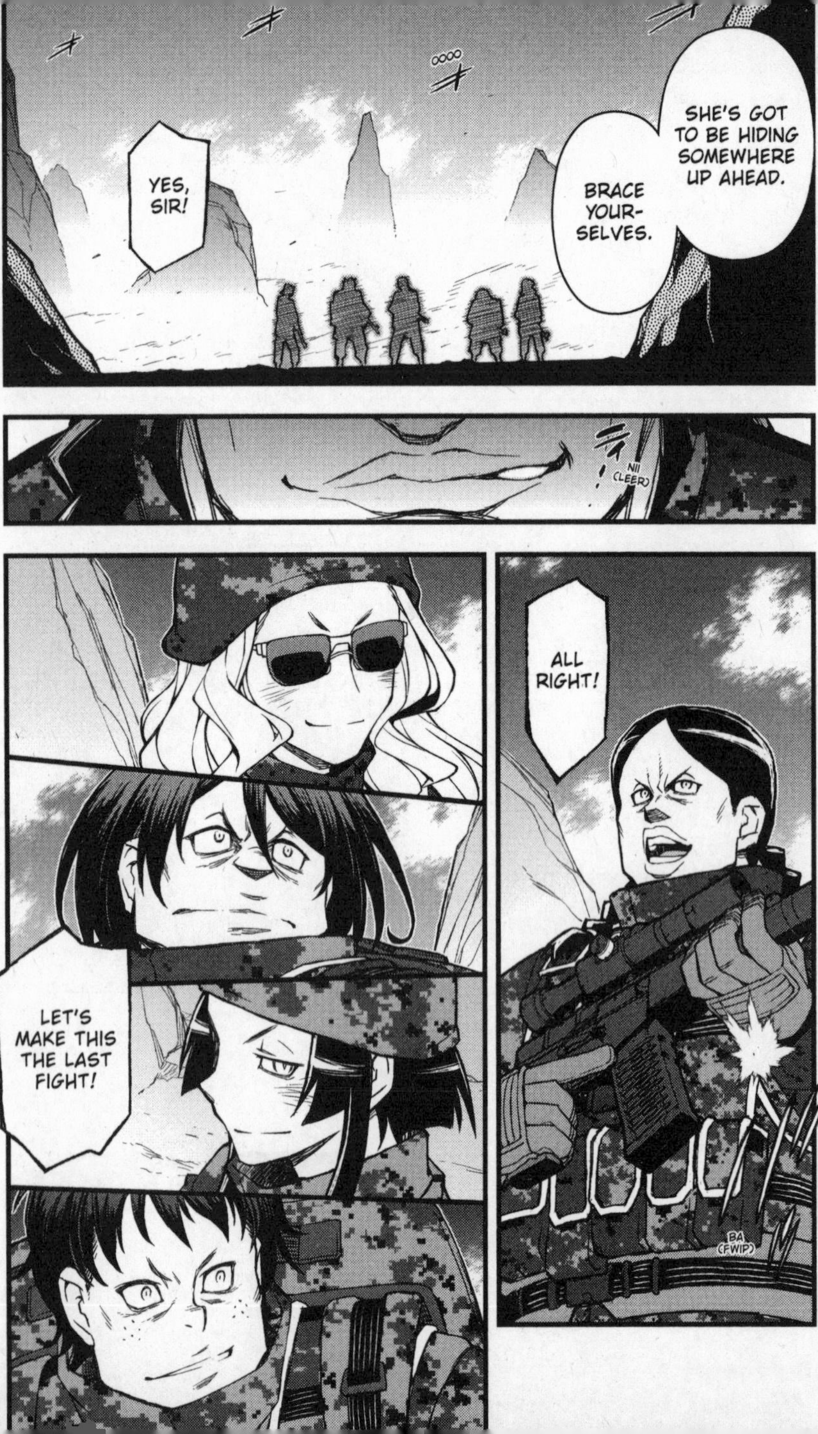
SHE'S GOT TO BE HIDING SOMEWHERE UP AHEAD.
BRACE YOUR-SELVES.
YES, SIR!
NII (LEER)
ALL RIGHT!
BA (FWIP)
LET'S MAKE THIS THE LAST FIGHT!

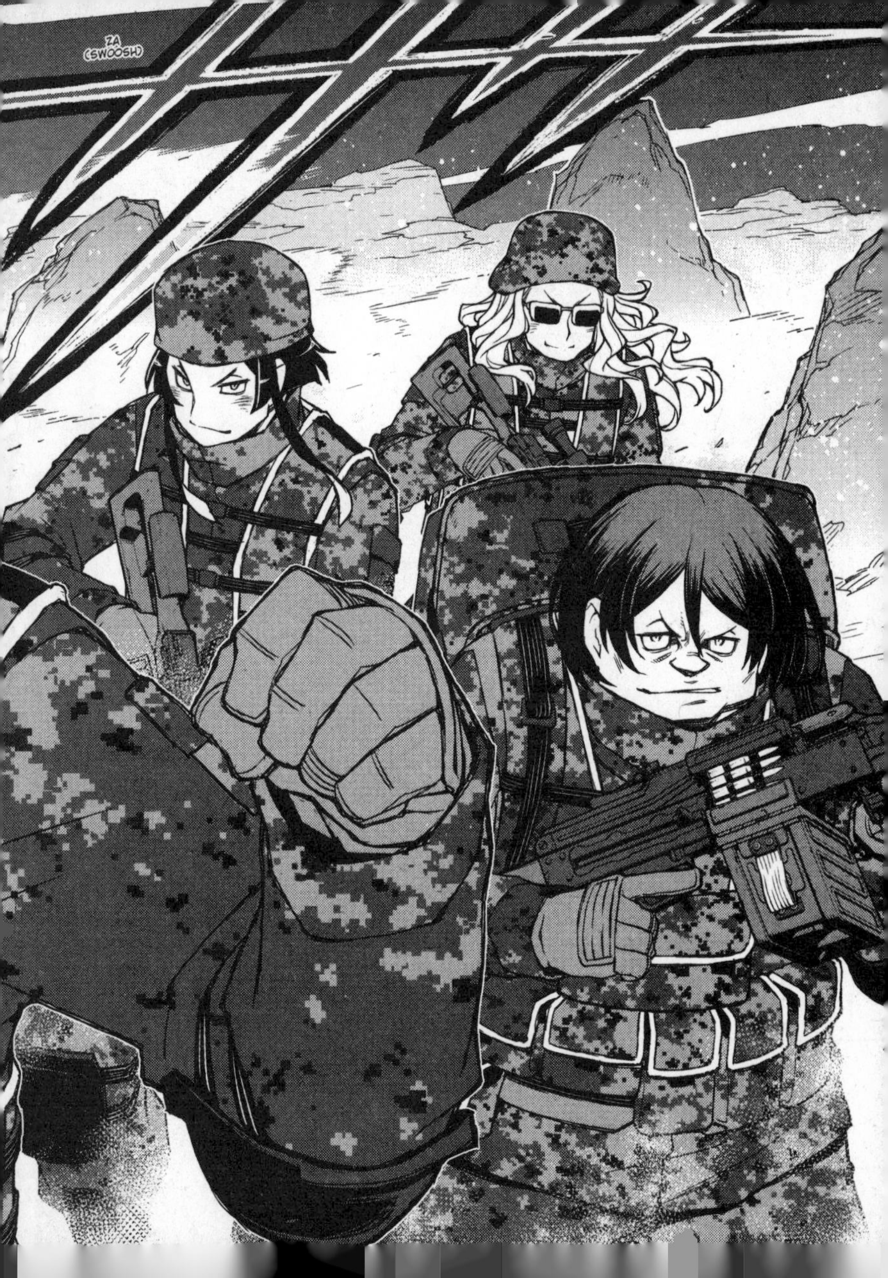
ZA
(SWOOSH)

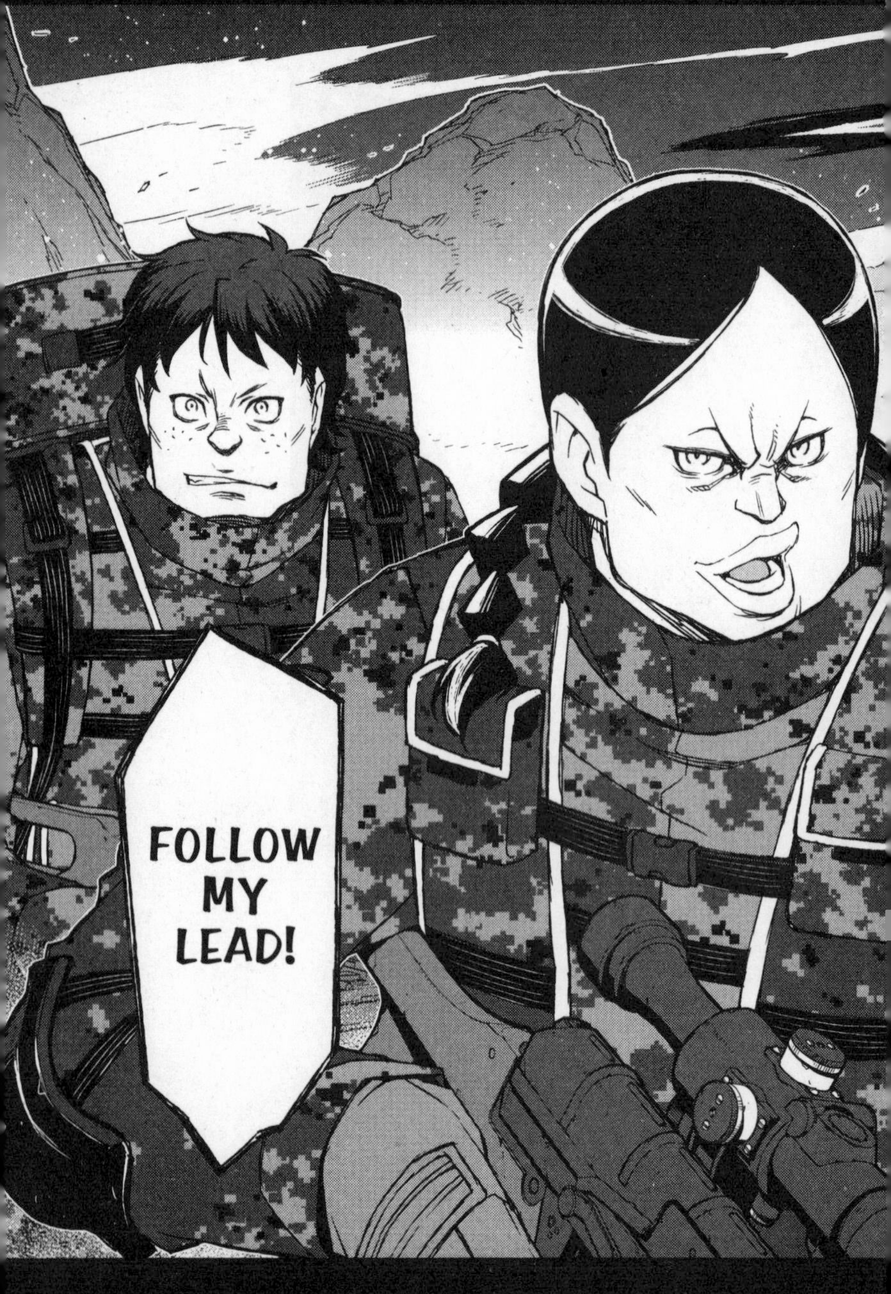
FOLLOW MY LEAD!

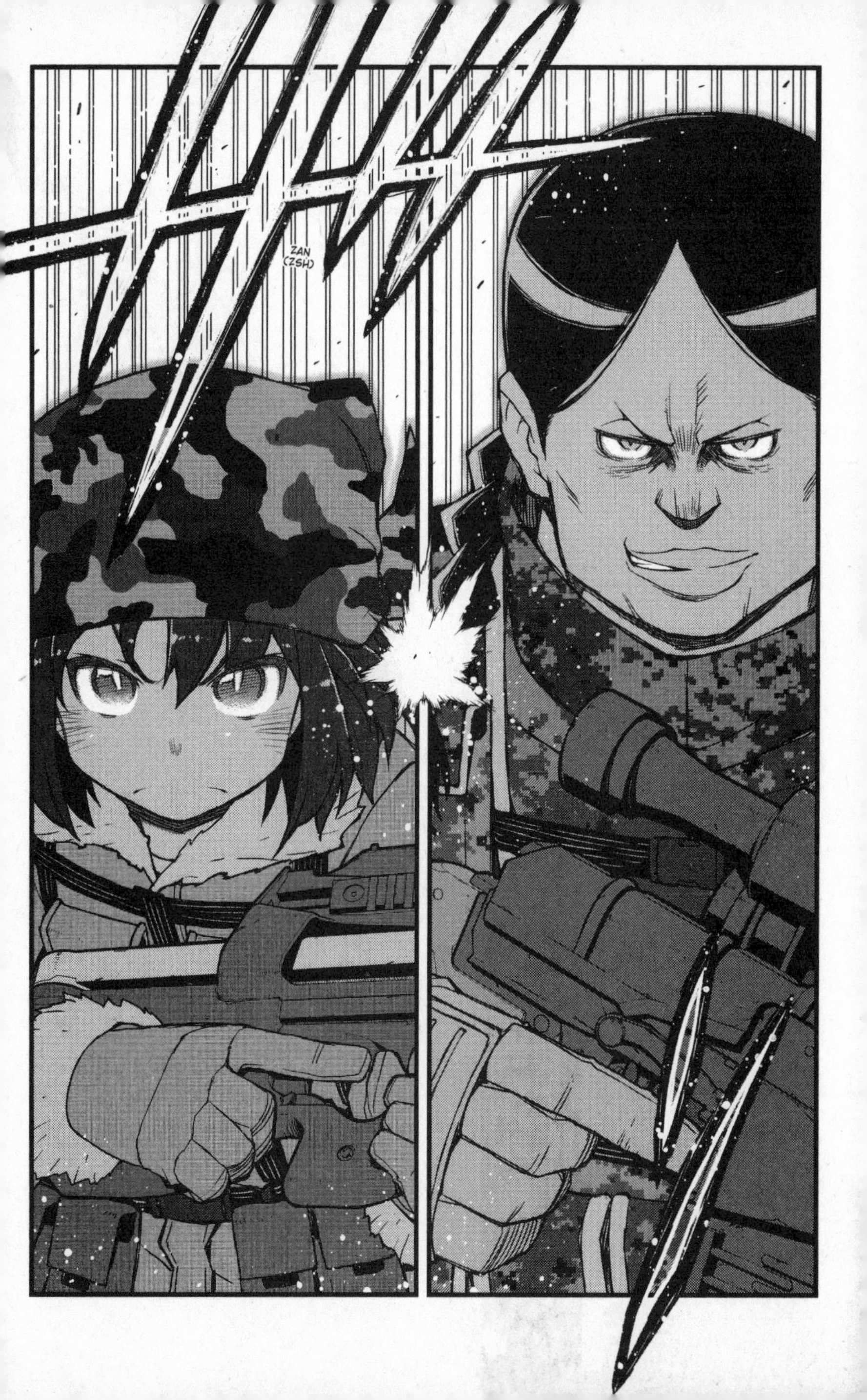
ZAN
(ZSH)

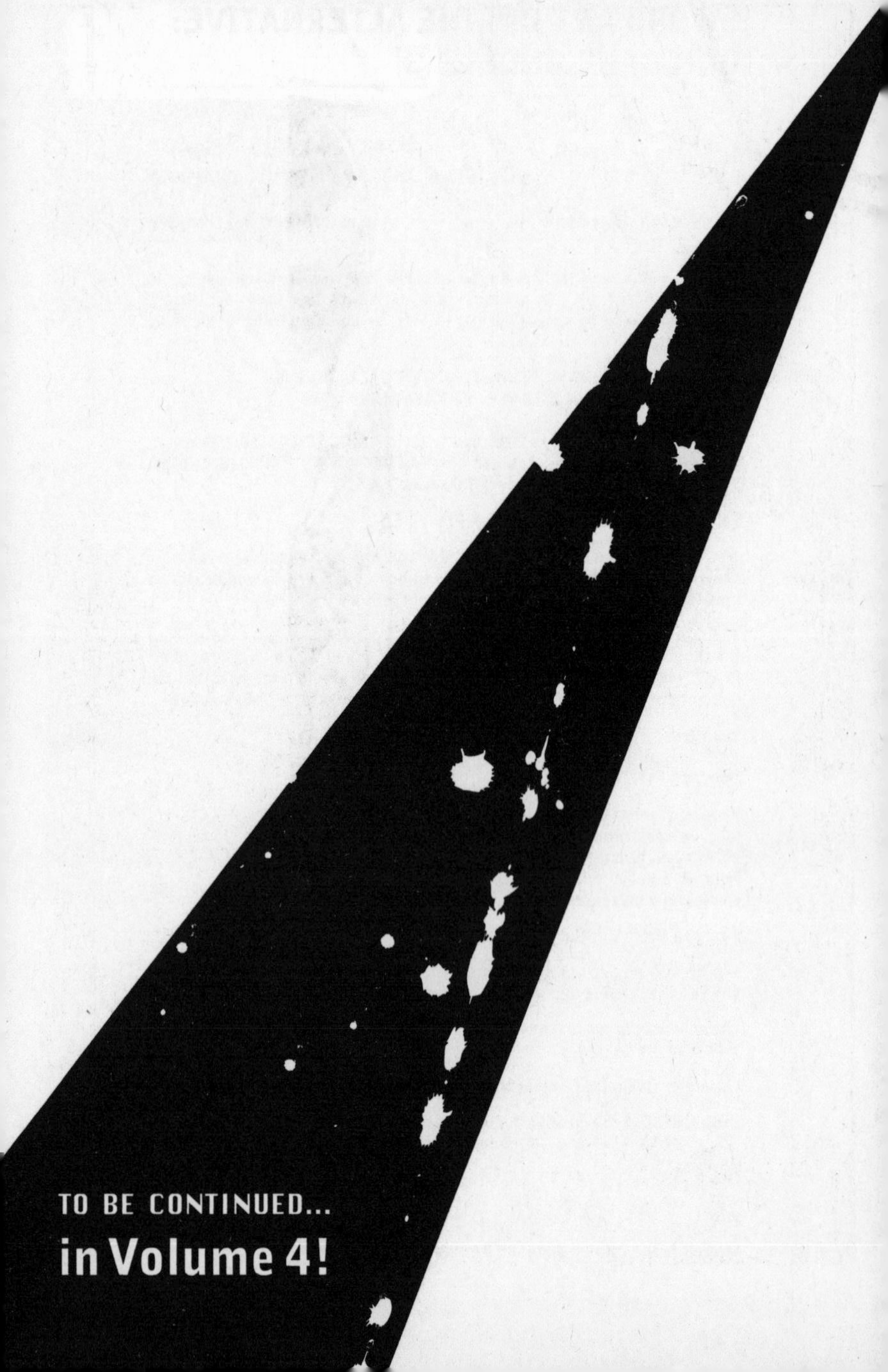
TO BE CONTINUED...
in Volume 4!

SWORD ART ONLINE GUN GALE ONLINE

SO-AFF-960

ART: TADADI TAMORI
STORY: KEIICHI SIGSAWA
ORIGINAL STORY: REKI KAWAHARA

Translation: Stephen Paul   Lettering: Barri Shrager

SWORD ART ONLINE ALTERNATIVE GUN GALE ONLINE
© KEIICHI SIGSAWA 2018 © REKI KAWAHARA 2018
© TADADI TAMORI 2018
First published in Japan in 2018 by KADOKAWA CORPORATION, Tokyo.
English translation rights arranged with KADOKAWA CORPORATION, Tokyo, through Tuttle-Mori Agency, Inc., Tokyo.

English translation © 2019 by Yen Press, LLC

Yen Press
1290 Avenue of the Americas
New York, NY 10104

Visit us at yenpress.com
facebook.com/yenpress
twitter.com/yenpress
yenpress.tumblr.com
instagram.com/yenpress

First Yen Press Edition: June 2019

Yen Press is an imprint of Yen Press, LLC.
The Yen Press name and logo are trademarks of Yen Press, LLC.

The publisher is not responsible for websites (or their content) that are not owned by the publisher.

Library of Congress Control Number: 2017954143

ISBNs: 978-1-9753-5765-8 (paperback)
        978-1-9753-8467-8 (ebook)

10 9 8 7 6 5 4 3 2 1

WOR

Printed in the United States of America